CULTURE, PLACE, AND NATURE
Studies in Anthropology and the Environment
K. Sivaramakrishnan, Series Editor

Centered in anthropology, the Culture, Place, and Nature series encompasses new interdisciplinary social science research on environmental issues, focusing on the intersection of culture, ecology, and politics in global, national, and local contexts. Contributors to the series view environmental knowledge and issues from the multiple and often conflicting perspectives of various cultural systems.

Sacred Cows and Chicken Manchurian

THE EVERYDAY POLITICS OF
EATING MEAT IN INDIA

James Staples

UNIVERSITY OF WASHINGTON PRESS

Seattle

Sacred Cows and Chicken Manchurian was made possible in part by a grant from the Samuel and Althea Stroum Endowed Book Fund.

Copyright © 2020 by the University of Washington Press

Composed in Warnock Pro, typeface designed by Robert Slimbach
All photographs are by the author.
Cover design and illustrations by Stacy Wakefield

24 23 22 21 20   5 4 3 2 1

Printed and bound in the United States of America

All rights reserved. No part of this publication may be reproduced or transmitted in any form or by any means, electronic or mechanical, including photocopy, recording, or any information storage or retrieval system, without permission in writing from the publisher.

UNIVERSITY OF WASHINGTON PRESS
uwapress.uw.edu

LIBRARY OF CONGRESS CATALOGING-IN-PUBLICATION DATA
Names: Staples, James, 1966– author.
Title: Sacred cows and chicken Manchurian : the everyday politics of eating meat in India / James Staples.
Description: Seattle : University of Washington Press, 2020. | Series: Culture, place, and nature | Includes bibliographical references and index.
Identifiers: LCCN 2020006817 (print) | LCCN 2020006818 (ebook) |
    ISBN 9780295747873 (hardcover) | ISBN 9780295747880 (paperback) |
    ISBN 9780295747897 (ebook)
Subjects: LCSH: Food habits—India. | Meat industry and trade—Social aspects—India. | Meat—Religious aspects—Hinduism.
Classification: LCC GT2853.I5 S73 2020 (print) | LCC GT2853.I5 (ebook) |
    DDC 394.1/20954—dc23
LC record available at https://lccn.loc.gov/2020006817
LC ebook record available at https://lccn.loc.gov/2020006818

The paper used in this publication is acid free and meets the minimum requirements of American National Standard for Information Sciences—Permanence of Paper for Printed Library Materials, ANSI Z39.48–1984.∞

In memory of M. Sambrajamma

CONTENTS

Foreword by K. Sivaramakrishnan ix

Acknowledgments xiii

Introduction: Sacred Cows and Chicken Manchurian 3

CHAPTER ONE
Differential Histories of Meat Eating in India 34

CHAPTER TWO
Everyday South Indian Foodways 53

CHAPTER THREE
From Cattle Shed to Dinner Plate 77

CHAPTER FOUR
Cattle Slaughter, Beef Eating, and Ambivalence 102

CHAPTER FIVE
Health, the Environment, and the Rise of the Chicken 119

CHAPTER SIX
From Caste to Class in Food 140

Conclusion: Taking on Sacred Cows 162

Glossary 181

Notes 187

References 201

Index 219

FOREWORD

In this age of global climate change, food—its sources, production, and consumption—is arguably more consequentially connected to the fate of the environment than ever before. Food also reveals extreme forms of preference: hunted game for wealthy consumers, exotic meats smuggled internationally, and the rising tide of veganism in many parts of the world. Food, especially in the form of meat, can expose fundamental social cleavages created by poverty and prejudice. Paying attention to these issues, James Staples focuses on the shifting practices, changing beliefs, and human dilemmas that always inform food cultures and, within them, the place afforded to meat.

The anthropology of food has always been a rewarding terrain on which to explore social change, as a distinguished body of scholarship has long demonstrated (Goody 1982; Mintz 1996). Often, however, what urban middle classes eat and how they do so have been the basis for studying food and culture at their various points of intersection (Ray and Srinivas 2012a; Conlon 1995). And such an approach has often served well a broader study of modernity in all its variations and dynamism as it takes shape somewhere far from Europe, in places such as colonial or postcolonial South Asia. In contrast, famine foods, native diets, and coarse grains consumption among the rural poor are topics that have delineated nonmodern modes of eating that have been marginalized along with their practitioners yet often valorized elsewhere in a romantic celebration of their stewardship of nature.

Staples turns away from such overdrawn contrasts, to the basic questions through which social change has been studied in South Asia over decades. He returns to the relationship between caste and class, and the ways in which religious pluralism exists uneasily alongside state-sponsored secularism. In doing so, he offers insight into these big questions gleaned from his ordinary village and urban interlocutors, from the quotidian vantage point of food, particularly meat, and how it may define identities, values, and livelihoods. By paying attention to how and when people eat meat, and also how the food is procured, prepared, and presented, he unites minute examination of everyday foodways with broader concern with the political economy of beef, the intense contestation over its production and sale, and the deep ambivalence many people feel when, as it has in the last two decades, cow slaughter becomes a flashpoint for renewed tension across communities.

Long in gestation, the project is timely in its fruition. Its timeliness lies in confronting hyperbolic, very urban, and very public conflict around beef and meat industries. It offers a nuanced and thoughtful examination of practices and deliberations through which beef and meat are pragmatically encountered, experienced, and consumed in everyday contexts, away from the glare of the media and heated political rhetoric in cities. With awareness earned through decades of research in the same region, Staples notes that the politicization of beef has become more strident in recent years. Cow protection and veneration movements have a long legacy, dating at least to such activities in northern India in the colonial period (Pandey 1983; Gundimeda and Ashwin 2018). But, as he notes, they are resurgent in a violent form at a time when meat eating has increased exponentially and beef has become a polyvalent signifier of minority cultural defiance (for both Dalits and Christians) and of upward social mobility for many people across different faiths.

But this project is not about just food and faith, or meat and politics. Staples observes the dietary, technological, pricing, and medical factors that have shaped the food landscape and placed meat, including both chicken and beef, in new places in new ways: in the market, in the cuisine, and in the regulatory environment for food safety and export. His attention turns to factory food and novel forms of processing and vending that have shortened the distance between eating practices in the village and in the city. His patient fieldwork takes him to beef markets, including clandestine ones, and his interlocutors show him their awareness of health and environmental pollution issues associated with the consumption of red meat.

Staples takes deep interest in the self-doubt, complexity, contradiction, and willingness to adapt that ordinary beef eaters display and describe. It is this feature of this book that sets it apart from the other writing—often strident and polemical—that fails to discern and portray the social dynamism and shifting values or stakes of eaters of beef, its producers, and those who make political causes around beef cattle. Reification of categories such as beef eater and vegetarian has long limited cultural and sociological studies of food and identity in South Asia. India has witnessed a dramatic spread of food processing industries since the 1980s, the proliferation of fast food, and a newer, growing concern with food toxicity, diet and health, and organic agriculture. This has meant that in urban centers, surely, but also across rural India, a variety of factors and preferences have challenged ordinary people to be creative in identifying food with social rank, to link food and purity, and ultimately to use food to declare their sense of self.

Given the growing evidence that meat consumption and its large-scale industrial production is a serious cause of environmental degradation and a significant contributor to global climate change, some may be tempted to make radical proposals for regulating meat in many forms. This work will serve as a salutary reminder that enduring solutions will be found in understanding human relations to animals and food, and in studying the material conditions in which human and nonhuman lives remain entangled and interwoven. In that sense, one of the most admirable accomplishments of this work is the way it takes long-established traditions of studying hierarchy and exclusion in South Asia, or foodways more generally, and places them in conversation with recent approaches to new materialism, posthumanism, and human-animal relations in sociocultural and environmental anthropology.

K. SIVARAMAKRISHNAN
Yale University

ACKNOWLEDGMENTS

At a time when the Indian state has been clamping down on those who dissent from its stance on cattle and when self-appointed vigilantes have deployed increasing violence against those who trade in or consume beef, acknowledging my friends and interlocutors in India who have made this book possible is something of a double-edged sword. I thus use pseudonyms, as I do throughout the book, or initials, to protect those mentioned here, but I hope that they, at least, will know who they are.

To the man I have called Das, my long-term research associate, I owe a great deal. He was there throughout my last two periods of fieldwork, discussing the findings as we went along and directly collecting data in the form of food diaries and village surveys, as well as helping to organize my itinerary. As a lifelong vegetarian, he also went beyond the call of duty to accompany me to interview cattle traders, brokers, butchers, and beef sellers as they went about their everyday business. His unrelenting zest for finding out new things about the society in which he lives and his willingness to talk with anyone, quite aside from his fluency in several Indian languages, were invaluable qualities in sustaining my own enthusiasm throughout sometimes challenging fieldwork. He helped prompt me to ask the questions that needed to be asked. In common with other friends in Anandapuram and Hyderabad, he has also been a willing correspondent in the months following the fieldwork and as I wrote this book, answering emailed queries on everything from the average weight of local cows to the caste backgrounds of brokers, revisiting some of the butchers we worked with several times to double-check on the finer points of slaughter techniques.

Other friends have been similarly helpful in providing instant responses on WhatsApp: recipes, photos of fuel cakes fashioned out of cow dung, and explanations of common idioms have all been forthcoming just when I needed them, both extending the fieldwork beyond my presence in the field and enabling feedback on my analysis in ways that were simply not possible even ten or fifteen years ago.

To the late Sambrajamma (my first cook in Anandapuram), to F, to K, and to all the others who fed me and shared their recipes, their culinary expertise, and their thoughts on food over the years I am also indebted, as I am to the butchers and meat sellers of Bhavanipur and of the markets and side streets of Hyderabad, as well as to all those who helped and befriended me in Anandapuram. Many of them gave freely of their time to put on record stories that they felt were not currently being told. Several also were willing to take me to the places where cattle were slaughtered and sold. Others kept food diaries, or spent hours talking to me in forensic detail about their shopping, cooking, and eating habits.

My old friend EC warrants special thanks, not only for many hours of fruitful, detailed discussions about my material but especially for providing a constant source of links to news reports on all matters bovine and for serving as a conduit through which information and the opinions of others have also been channeled. Her feedback on a draft of my manuscript was invaluable.

Institutionally, in the UK, I am grateful especially to the British Academy, whose small grant (SG161306) covered the airfares and fieldwork expenses for my two most recent visits to India, as well as funding a trip to the Annual Conference on South Asia at the University of Wisconsin, Madison, in 2017 to share (and shape) first thoughts on my data. Thanks also to Ronnie Johnson and June Costard in the research office at Brunel University London for administering the grant and for guiding me so patiently through bureaucratic hoops that were otherwise difficult to navigate. I am grateful to Brunel more generally for giving me the two terms of research leave I needed to write this book.

At the 2017 Madison conference, just months after completing fieldwork in India, I was fortunate enough to be part of a one-day symposium organized by Cassie Adcock and Radhika Govindrajan, titled "Cow, Buffalo, Bullock: Bovine Politics in South Asia." I benefited a great deal from questions, feedback, and related papers from the organizers and my fellow contributors, Sahana Ghosh, Kathryn C. Hardy, Nayanika Mathur, Barbara Ramusack, and SherAli Tareen. Naisargi Dave and Parvis Ghassem-Fachandi, our discussants, and others who participated in the preconference also offered invaluable insights. It was while I was at Madison that I had the initial meetings with Lorri Hagman, executive editor at the University of Washington Press, that led to this book being published. I thank her and her colleagues for their enthusiasm, good humor, and straightforward guidance throughout.

Back in the UK, my most consistent source of support has been through Nkumi, a small, close-knit writing group of anthropologists and sociologists working on food that meets monthly at SOAS in London. Over the past year or so, in addition to being exposed in that forum to some of the most thought-provoking new academic writing on food that I could ever have hoped for, I have also had the opportunity to present several draft chapters of this book. A big thank-you to Nora Faltmann, Katharina Graf, Elizabeth (Lizzie) Hull, Jakob Klein, Anne Murcott, Johan Pottier, and Sami Zubaida for their detailed scrutiny and always constructive comments and criticism on early renderings of parts of this book, as well as for sharing their own work. I owe particular thanks to Anne Murcott for generously providing a careful reading of my initial proposals for the book and for being such a close correspondent and source of support throughout the process of writing and rewriting it; and also to Harry West, not only for establishing the Nkumi group in the first place and later inviting me to join it but also for giving valuable feedback and encouragement in response to first drafts of my funding proposals for the field research on which this book draws. It would be hard to overstate the importance of this support network in bringing this project to completion; it would otherwise have been a much slower and lonelier process.

Useful feedback has also been forthcoming at the various other seminars and workshops at which I presented aspects of the material over the last two or three years, and I am grateful for all the invitations to give papers, which I was happy to accept. These include departmental seminars at the Universities of Manchester, East Anglia, and Roehampton; at the Anthropology in London Day at University College, London, in 2016; and, over 2018, at seminars at SOAS and Brunel. At SOAS, particular thanks go to Paul Basu—who chaired the seminar—and to Richard Fardon, Fabio Gygi, Marloes Janson, Kevin Latham, David Mosse, Edward Simpson, and others for their questions and comments. At Brunel, I am grateful to Isak Niehaus, who organized the seminar at which I presented a chapter, and to probing questions from Andrew Beatty, Liana Chua, Eric Hirsch, and Will Rollason. Peggy Froerer and Liana Chua also warrant additional mention for their help in peer-reviewing the British Academy application that ultimately made this project possible.

Elements of the research have fed into other publications along the way, reflections on which have also informed the current book. It was working on a paper for a special issue of the journal *South Asia*—coedited by Caroline and Filippo Osella (2008b)—that first got me thinking about meat eating in India; working with Jakob Klein on *Consumer and Consumed*, an edited special issue of the journal *Ethnos* (Staples and Klein 2017a)—which in turn drew on a panel we coconvened at the 2011 conference of the Association of Social Anthropologists (ASA) in the UK—drew me in even further. Jakob also invited me to write a chapter on food and caste in India for the handbook he edited with James Watson (Klein and Watson 2016), and I am deeply appreciative of his always thoughtful comments and suggestions both as an editor and as a coauthor. Kiranmayi Bhushi, with her specialist, interdisciplinary knowledge of food in South Asia, was likewise a valuable interlocutor as I further traced attitudes toward beef eating in South India for an essay in her recently published anthology (Bhushi 2018). Although none of the chapters in this book directly replicate this previous work, they draw and expand on it extensively.

In the writing of this book, I have also leaned on several South Asianist colleagues for their own fieldwork insights and for pointers toward what to read. Thank you, Henrike Donner, Michele Friedner, and Atreyee Sen in particular, and thanks also to scholars I have not yet met, such as Kalyan Das, Estelle Fourat, Suraj Jacob, Jacob Lahne, Balmurli Natrajan, and Christy Spackman, all of whom corresponded with me or shared relevant articles at just the right moments along the way.

I am indebted to the two anonymous readers for their feedback on an earlier draft of this book. I warmed to them not only because of their kind words and their enthusiasm for the project but also because of their thoroughness, fine attention to detail, and thoughtful suggestions. Remaining flaws are, of course, my own, but this certainly became a better book from responding to their comprehensive feedback.

Finally, thanks to my family, Becky, Theo, and Felix, for being there throughout. Stanley has also been a willing walking and running companion through the whole process: the hours of thinking time I spent with him away from my desk each day were often the most productive ones.

SACRED COWS AND CHICKEN MANCHURIAN

Introduction

Sacred Cows and Chicken Manchurian

CATTLE seemed to be everywhere. At least, they did once I became consciously on the lookout for them in the small corner of coastal Andhra Pradesh, South India, that I have been visiting for the last thirty-five years. I saw them on the main road when I went out to run in the misty early mornings when it was still relatively cool, being directed on their way to patches of grazing land and watering holes; I passed them while they were still resting, tethered to poles or trees alongside village dwellings. Sometimes—two abreast—they were pulling carts packed full of straw, manure, or other agricultural loads. There were nearly always small herds of buffaloes huddled together at the railway crossing when I, like them, was waiting at the barrier for a train to pass. They were kept in check by their herders, who, almost to a man (and they were, for the most part, men), brandished long sticks and wore white shirts (towel draped over one shoulder) and lungis. If they had anything on their feet at all, they wore rubber flip-flops or dusty leather sandals.

The animals waited patiently, tails languidly swatting away the flies, seemingly at home among the jumble of pedestrians, cyclists, auto rickshaws, motorbikes, and trucks. In the case of the white, humped zebu cows (see figure I.1) considered by many so iconic of India, they were more likely spotted wandering alone, unhindered, or lying in the road, impervious to the vehicles whose drivers navigated carefully around them. In the market they could be found in corners, munching away on the piles of okra, green beans, and gourds that had been discarded especially for them; inside the soft drinks shop or the bakery, I watched them edge slowly toward the counter while the proprietors, well accustomed to the drill, gently tried to lure them away with offerings of food (figure I.2).

1.1   A humped zebu cow, tethered and ready for sale at a major cattle market.

Even when one could not immediately see them, there were signs of bovine presence all around: the fragrant splats of excrement that punctuated every track into the village; circular dung cakes, for fuel, drying on walls; and the rich, earthy smell of their warm bodies lingering in the air. In some of the village households I visited, their dung was diluted with water and

1.2 A wandering, small-town cow goes trader to trader in search of offerings.

swept across interior floors to keep insects at bay; sometimes it was even mixed into the very fiber of the mud walls as insulation. Cattle products also permeated nearly every repast: melted ghee (clarified butter), drizzled onto *mudda pappu* (a plain dal, usually made with split pigeon peas); milk, thick with cream, enriching small glass cups of sugary tea; and the curd or buttermilk that, mixed by hand into rice, marked the final course of a meal. More controversially, in plenty of Christian, Dalit, and Muslim households on Sundays, their flesh also appeared as the center of the meal: a special dish to differentiate the holiday from the rest of the week, and themselves as particular kinds of people. The presence of cows, oxen, and buffaloes was, in short, a constant in rural South India.

Given the centrality of bovines to pastoral life, it is perhaps unsurprising that consumption of beef—particularly the flesh of the cow, but also, as will become clear, that of the water buffalo—has regularly sparked controversy in the subcontinent. One might well describe the cow as "a fundamental symbol" (Yang 1980, 585) or a dense metaphor (Pinney 2004, 205): an entity so embedded in the common pool of experience in India that meanings attributed to it are widely shared and understood, albeit contested. Often invoked as a motif of deep-rooted communal difference between Hindus and other religious groups, Muslims especially, their meat simultaneously represents a violation of sacred taboos and a celebration of marginalized identities. In certain circumstances, beef consumption—and beef eaten in particular ways—might even be seen as a symbol of cosmopolitan sophistication.

Following the landslide election of the Hindu nationalist Bharatiya Janata Party (BJP) government in 2014, however, the relatively peaceful coexistence of these apparently contradictory representations has come under increasing strain. Reports of cattle-related violence, particularly in some of the northern states of India, have been widespread. News reports and debate on social media suggest a growing polarization of views. On one side were Dalit (former Untouchables or, to use the state's own categorization, members of Scheduled Castes), Muslim, and Christian activists protesting at what they saw as a threat to their beef-eating heritage. On the other were Hindu fundamentalists rallying, sometimes violently, against those who ate the flesh of the "holy cow," ox, or buffalo.

This book offers an anthropological take on what it is about the contemporary moment that has led to the apparent turn away from the hitherto secularist approach of postindependence Indian governments, a move that started to become noticeable back in the 1990s, although its roots can perhaps be traced even earlier.[1] *Sacred Cows and Chicken Manchurian* attempts to bring nuance to existing accounts by journalists, historians, and others by charting how nonactivists—a wide category of people who position themselves neither as cow protectionists nor as pro-beef activists, on whom more shortly—navigate the current febrile political climate in their everyday lives. Doing so effects a shift away from an unduly simplistic binary opposition drawn between those who oppose the slaughter of cattle on the one hand, and those who view beef consumption as a fundamental gastronomic right on the other. Such an approach enables me to document the vital but frequently overlooked ambivalences that exist between these two poles. It attends, for example, to the views and experiences of those who sometimes eat beef but who see slaughter as problematic, as well as those who would never eat beef but who do not necessarily object to others doing so, and who in some cases, as I discovered, are implicated to greater or lesser degrees in the beef trade.

What role did the shared consumption of beef—or of meat more generally—play in the forging of both positive and negative identities, and how, if at all, was that changing with the times? How effective were claims relating to the positive attributes of beef at challenging the apparently hegemonic view that those who ate it were low-status and polluting? How were what people described as "modern" practices of eating, including, for example, Chinese-inspired dishes like chicken or cauliflower Manchurian—from which this book takes the second part of its title—or Western-style pizzas bought from takeaway carts, having an impact on the kinds of meat and other comestibles that were being eaten? And how did they affect the *ways* in which they were consumed? The multiple, and perhaps conflicting, meanings attributed to beef and the animals from which it comes at any given moment tell us something about what is going on in Indian society in more explicit ways than might otherwise be obvious. This is crucial, because identifying those meanings *and* the points at which they change helps us to discern the central fault lines running through contemporary India: the socioeconomic, political, and religious divisions; the dominant ideologies that motivate them; and the contexts within which these ideologies gain traction.

In attending to these questions, this book offers an ethnographic exploration of the current situation as it is experienced by people on the ground, and also locates it comprehensively within the wider foodscapes of the region. That is to say, this book is not only about cattle slaughter and the eating or not eating of beef, or even meat consumption more generally. It is also about placing—and consequently, better understanding—practices in respect of beef in relation to wider shifts and vacillations in Indian foodways. The cost and availability of different kinds of food, as well as changes in the technologies via which it is processed, distributed, stored, purchased, and consumed, all have varying degrees of impact on the significance of beef—and its capacity to have meanings attached to it—in the diets of particular families. Such changes include, for example, the availability of industrialized, packaged foods that did not previously exist, and new ready-made foods on offer outside the home, such as the Chinese-inspired dishes that are now served from takeaway carts even in small towns.

A DEVELOPING INTEREST IN BEEF AND COW POLITICS

My reason for starting to pay special attention to bovines—or more precisely, to how humans relate to them, as meat in particular—was not their omnipresence. If anything, the fact that they were such a taken-for-granted feature of the Indian landscape meant that I had ceased, over the years, to take much notice of them at all. My interest, rather, was stirred when, back in the late 1990s, I first encountered beef on the menu at dinners to which I had been invited. Even then, given that food was peripheral to my research interests, it would probably not have unduly aroused my curiosity had it not been for the fact that I was a vegetarian, and so found myself having to refuse what I had been offered. Food, while usually a pleasurable backdrop to my social encounters, was, as I saw it then, merely a means to access and sociality. Shared meals provided a context in which to speak to people, to develop relationships, and to observe people in their domestic environments. Consequently, I was initially puzzled that, in a country renowned for its plant-based diet, anyone should have been surprised by my own eating habits.[2] Forms of vegetarianism are, after all, commonly recognized practices for Jains, Buddhists, and certain Hindu castes, and even many of those who ate other kinds of meat drew the line at beef consumption. That the cow is viewed as sacred in India was, I assumed, a truth universally acknowledged.

Certainly, if anyone I met in India found my food preferences in any way worthy of remark, they had no difficulty in finding categories in which to classify them. "Oh, in his own country, is the *doragaru* a Brahmin?"[3] I recall an elderly woman once asking my research assistant, on hearing that I did not eat meat. And during the years when I ate fish but did not eat other kinds of meat, village friends jokingly referred to me as a "Bengali Brahmin." While Brahmins were not supposed to eat meat at all, fish consumption was said, at least by my Andhra informants, to be central to Bengali identity. My point here is that vegetarianism, while perhaps less ubiquitous than commonly assumed, is not an alien concept in South India.

It was against this background of acceptance of dietary differences that the dogged insistence by Victoria-Rani, a Christian teacher I knew, that I should try some of the beef curry she was offering me caught me off guard. Not only did she offer me, a dinner guest at her house, the beef dish; she also urged me to try it without at first letting on what it was. She was then disappointed when I politely refused, even when I tried to explain that I was happy with the vegetable- and lentil-based dishes also on offer. Why, I pondered afterward, was she so keen to tempt me with something she knew I did not eat, and why would she be offended—in a social setting full of vegetarians—by my refusal to partake? After all, having spent an hour or more with me almost every morning over the past year as my Telugu teacher, Victoria-Rani was well aware of my food preferences. It was also noteworthy that although I was offered beef in similar circumstances at several other Christian households over the year I spent in India in 1999 and 2000, this was something new. Prior to then, I had never, in fifteen years of traveling to India, knowingly been offered beef in someone's house.[4]

This was the event that stirred my initial interest in food as a topic of anthropological inquiry, and that began the quest that led to this book. As I explored the questions it provoked in the years that followed, a number of explanations emerged as to why my teacher, Victoria-Rani, behaved in the way that she did. First, there were the sensory pleasures of beef: why, in her logic, would I deny myself something so delicious and wholesome when my own religion (assumed to be Christianity) and status (as a foreigner) did not require me to do so? Second, eating beef would also have identified me as an ally. As a Madiga, the beef-eating leatherworker caste, previously dubbed Untouchable and now, in the state's nomenclature, a Scheduled Caste, she saw herself as one of "the people Hindus always treat very badly." Dalit, the more politicized term for people from Scheduled Castes—used by activists but seldom, if ever, by my own informants in Andhra Pradesh—literally translates as "oppressed" or "broken" or "scattered." The sharing and enjoyment of beef—albeit privately and away from the gaze of non-beef-eating Hindus—resisted the notion that its consumption was inherently linked to impurity and low social status.

To Victoria-Rani, my vegetarianism could be read as a political act: an implicit acceptance of the sacred status afforded by higher-caste Hindus to the cow, and, by association, of her Hindu-defined impurity. I appeared to be siding with a Hindu ideology that, as Victoria-Rani saw it, oppressed her and others like her. To have partaken, by contrast, would have been to recognize—and in doing so, reinforce—her positive identity as a Christian, a religion in which there was no taboo prohibiting eating beef. It would also have signaled solidarity in her struggle against oppression.

This does not, however, explain why beef has become significant *now*; the association with beef eating and low social status is, after all, long established, yet questions about my own willingness to eat it had not been raised in the previous fifteen years that I had been visiting the area. One explanation was that, by the late 1990s, Christians and other minorities in Andhra, Muslims in particular, were feeling under threat in ways that they had not in the recent past. The case of a Christian missionary in the neighboring state of Orissa (now Odisha) who had been burnt to death, along with his children, by Hindu extremists in January 1999 was a regular topic of discussion during my first major period of fieldwork.[5] Following a spate of local church bombings, there had also been a police presence outside nearby churches on Sunday mornings, reminding Victoria-Rani and others that Christianity, as well as Islam, was seen in some quarters as un-Indian.[6] Indeed, it was only a year earlier that the BJP, part of the Sangh Parivar, or "family" of Hindu fundamentalist organizations,[7] had emerged for the first time as the largest party in India's 1998 general election. Such electoral success gave a boost to the right's vision of *Hindutva*, or Hinduness: what the nationalists articulated as the revival of an Indian culture untainted either by Mughal rule or by colonialism.

This "saffron wave," as anthropologist Thomas Hansen called it, was in part a consequence of successful organizational work done by rightwing Hindu parties over a prolonged period (see, e.g., Jaffrelot 1996). It was also because its message struck a chord both with the growing middle class and the poor masses. The first group, the middle class, was fearful of its fragile dominance being threatened, in a globalizing world, from the outside; the Hindu poor, meanwhile, were seen as taking solace in the majoritarian rhetoric about cultural pride and national strength that the BJP and other regional nationalist parties were renowned for. It was in this context that the BJP emerged as "the most resolute defender of India's national pride and its national interest" (Hansen 1999, 3). A key part of this imagined Hindu culture, supposedly rooted in the ancient Vedic texts, was reverence to that most fundamental symbol of the Indian nation, the cow, leading the new BJP-led government to press for greater compliance with a provision in the Indian constitution for states to enforce bans on cow slaughter. In so doing, they constituted beef consumption as a battleground on which identities might be fought over. To be a vegetarian, in this context, placed me in an unexpectedly uncomfortable position, albeit one that triggered interesting lines of inquiry and of self-reflection.

I was particularly concerned, when I returned to coastal Andhra for short visits—six to eight weeks at a time in 2009, 2011, and 2013—to find out what other people who ate beef thought about it. Given the vitriol that Victoria-Rani and others had expressed in relation to Hindu cow protectionism back in 1999 and 2000, I had expected other Christians I interviewed a decade on to take similar, perhaps even bolder, positions vis-à-vis beef eating. But a curious thing happened. Each time I followed up on my beef-related inquiries over those visits, my interlocutors—as if to keep me on my toes—seemed to change tack. People who, like Victoria-Rani, had encouraged me to eat beef in the past no longer bothered, or told me it no longer agreed with their bodies. "At my life stage," Mariamma, a Christian who had also regularly offered me beef during my earlier visit, told me, "beef is too heating for my body; I can't digest it in the same way. Sometimes I will take [it], but mostly now"—she gestured to the serving dishes filled with pulse and vegetable preparations that filled the space on the table between us—"I take simple food like this." Others—more confusingly still—told me that it was, of course, morally wrong to slaughter cattle and Hindus were right to take a stand against it, but that yes, they sometimes liked to eat beef on Sundays. "What can we do? We need to eat something, no?" was a common response from those I asked about it, often delivered with a shrug of the shoulders and a sheepish smile. Still others, who opposed both cattle slaughter and the consumption of its flesh, readily confessed to selling their own animals when they were no longer able to produce milk; although they seldom said so, who would buy them, other than meat traders? What, I asked myself, was going on?

My initial frustrations at this shifting landscape gave way, over time, to the realization that any attempt to discover, definitively, what bovine animals and their products mean within India, even at a single point in its history, is doomed to failure. Meaning, as the literature in the anthropology of food has been pointing out for some time, does not inhere permanently in objects: animals, foodstuffs, or, for that matter, anything else.[8] Meaning is attributed in social interaction. That interaction—as anthropologist Jack Goody (1982) set out so eloquently in his seminal study *Cooking, Cuisine and Class*—occurs within an intricate web of changing circumstances, contexts, and scales that continually alter the possibilities for attributing new meanings and modifying old ones. While this insight certainly complicates social analysts' task—their job, to be sure, can never be deemed over—recognizing the potential for such fluidity of meaning is in itself vital. It also allows us to explore the contradictions and ambivalence with which those meanings intersect. As the social theorist Ashis Nandy puts it, referring to food more generally, "The crucial issues that have come to dog Indian cuisine are not radically different from the questions that dog Indian cultural life in general" (2004, 10).

So, to reiterate the question: What *was* going on?

The shifts in attitudes toward cows, buffalo, and their beef among those who eat it, while never homogenous, to some extent mapped onto wider social changes in India as a whole. In particular, the change from the BJP-led government, in power from 1998 to 2004, to a more secularist Congress-led one helped to account for why those who ate beef no longer felt the need to defend it so vociferously. Bovine symbolism—the capacity of the cow to serve as a rallying cry for Muslims and Christians, as well as a motif of purity for Hindus and Jains—was muted. By the onset of the second decade of the century, however, when the BJP was again in the ascendency, attitudes, even in South India where support for Hindu nationalism was less embedded, could be seen to be changing. A beef festival at Osmania University in Hyderabad in 2012, for example, and the violent protests against it (one student was stabbed) provoked a polarized online debate.[9] Elsewhere in the city, tensions rose when beef was thrown onto the walls of a Hanuman temple, by, it later transpired, Hindu extremists in a bid to foment communal unrest.[10]

When the 2014 general election campaign began in earnest, corruption, the economy, and protecting women's safety emerged as key issues. However, Narendra Modi, leader of the BJP and the soon-to-be prime minister, also put debates about cattle slaughter at the core of his campaign. "Those at the Centre want a 'Pink Revolution,'" he told a rally in Bihar, referring to the then-Congress-led coalition government. "When animals are slaughtered, the color of their flesh is pink. Animals are being slaughtered and being taken to Bangladesh. The government in Delhi is giving subsidies to those who are carrying out this slaughter."[11] The subsidies and tax breaks for slaughterhouses introduced by the outgoing government, Modi claimed, led to the mass killing of cows and buffaloes. With the BJP's landslide election in May that year, the mood was clearly changing once again. By the time of my most recent fieldwork trips in December 2016 and July and August 2017, it was evident from press coverage that anti–cattle slaughter protestors had been encouraged by the shift in the Indian government's tone. One of the most widely publicized cases was that of the beating to death in 2015 of a fifty-year-old Muslim man, Mohammad Akhlaq, in a village near Dadri, by a Hindu lynch mob that suspected him of storing beef in his refrigerator during Eid al-Adha, but there were plenty of references in newspapers and blogs to other beef-related skirmishes.

Much of the reported violence was taking place in the so-called "cow belt"—the northern states of Haryana, Uttar Pradesh, Bihar, and Madhya

Pradesh—but it was by no means confined to it. Hyderabad butchers I worked with, who at the end of 2016 spoke of vigilante attacks as something happening elsewhere, were, by mid-2017, reporting their own firsthand encounters with violence. Fear and anger had become palpable, at least in Hyderabad if not in the coastal regions of Andhra Pradesh. One of the most recent in a stream of government initiatives had been the introduction in May 2017 of regulations—subsequently withdrawn at the end of the year—to ban the sale of cows and buffaloes for slaughter through animal markets.[12] The proposals met with vocal resistance from some states—notably Kerala and West Bengal—and a legal challenge from the Madras High Court in Tamil Nadu. Nevertheless, the government's attempts to take control from the Centre, and what some considered to be its half-hearted condemnation of the vigilante groups to which its hard line gave encouragement,[13] marked a further shift from what many of my interlocutors described as the hitherto "live and let live approach" that had been favored by the more secular Congress Party–led Government of the previous decade.

But this was not just a struggle between two opposing political ideologies, nor, as it will become plain, does it aid our understanding of the situation to categorize the central actors as either pro-beef activists—drawn from the Muslim, Dalit, and Christian populations—or, conversely, pro–cattle protectionist Hindu fundamentalists. First, there were other things going on alongside the ideological battles, sometimes intertwined with them, one affecting the other, sometimes not. One of these factors was the changing technologies via which meat was produced, and the impact these had on cost, taste, and availability. As my own research made clear, when those technologies led to the availability of cheaper chicken, as the industrialization of broiler-chicken rearing did, those who previously preferred beef in many cases shifted their allegiances on economic grounds. Developments in infrastructure, such as a more stable electricity supply or the availability of lower-cost generators, in tandem with innovations in packaging materials, also created openings for new kinds of food products that previously were not available in small towns. Transitory takeaway stands, as well as restaurants of various kinds, alongside long-established canteens and messes, had expanded exponentially in the area where I worked over the past twenty years. Such changes helped to recalibrate, in ways small and more significant, the everyday diets and food-related practices of my interlocutors.

Environmental concerns, and with them worries over the health effects of what people called the "medicines" given to livestock to make them grow bigger and faster, likewise influenced choices. The people I worked with were mostly aware, in a general sense, of criticisms concerning the ecological consequences of the Green Revolution. So too did they partake in wider discussions about food and health, whether rooted in Ayurveda, biomedicine, or pop-science reports accessed on the internet. Concerns about high-blood pressure, "sugar" (diabetes), or "gastric troubles" all affected what people ate at different points in their lives, suggesting that few people were ever simply meat eaters or not; a large number ate it sometimes and sometimes not, helping to account for changes in what my interlocutors told me as I returned to them over the years.

My research participants' choices were also shaped by their relative position within the household: a child, while their tastes might be more likely to be indulged, had no direct authority over what was purchased at market.[14] Similarly, because it was usually men who went shopping, women might have fewer options than their husbands or adult sons in deciding what meat, if any, the family would consume—although, as the likely cooks of their husbands' purchases, they might well have had more say in how the meat was prepared for consumption. Although the women I knew cooked dishes they thought their husbands, children, and other household members might like, precisely what they made from the ingredients available was often left to them to decide. Options for the elderly might be similarly constricted. One man, for example, who had followed a vegetarian diet for his entire adult life, told me how, at the age of seventy, he had started eating meat, including beef, partly because his doctor (who, to complicate things still further, happened to be a Hindu and did not eat beef) had recommended it, to improve his strength. But it was also because his son and daughter-in-law, who purchased and cooked the food, respectively, "chose" to eat it.[15] In short, understanding the decisions—if that is what they are—people make to eat or not eat meat cannot be deduced simply on the basis of their caste and community affiliation, nor can their attitudes toward it be read only in relation to changing political moods. What does it even mean, for example, to be a nonvegetarian in a context within which one can seldom, if ever, afford to buy meat, fish, or eggs?

How people navigated through these multiple meanings—contributing to or reshaping them as they went—is a core part of this book. Instead of focusing our intention on declarations by those in favor of more stringent cattle protection or their activist opponents, who speak up instead for the "culinary rights" of those who want to celebrate the consumption of beef as an integral part of their identity, what happens if we take seriously what those who express more ambivalent, complex views toward it say? That is what this book seeks to do.

PLACES AND PEOPLE

For my first bout of official fieldwork in 1999 and 2000, I was based in a self-established and self-run leprosy colony, Anandapuram (a pseudonym), in coastal Andhra Pradesh. It was a community of around one thousand people spread across around three hundred households, most of them living below or around the official poverty line. I had been visiting it since 1984, both as a volunteer and, later, to conduct research for an undergraduate dissertation. By the time I began my PhD fieldwork in November 1999, which focused on the social implications of leprosy, I already knew many of the people there very well. Inhabited largely by converts to Christianity who made their way there via missionary leprosy hospitals, the ordering of houses in Anandapuram, unlike villages elsewhere in the region, bore no relationship to the inhabitants' original caste or religion, and intercaste marriages were very common. Of the 232 marriages I recorded in a survey in 2000, 128 were intercaste or intercommunal (Staples 2007, 138). Self-run as a colony since early settlers established themselves as an association in the 1960s, there had also been an unusually high foreign presence in the village since the late 1970s. First to stay there long-term was an Australian monk, who set up a number of income-generation and social-welfare programs. His work was continued by a British nurse, who expanded on the projects that he had begun and started new ones, and there were numerous volunteers and others, like me, who passed through in the years that followed. From the late 1970s until the mid-1990s, there was always a foreigner involved in the running of the colony's programs. That these various differences all left their mark is, perhaps, self-evident, and I drew out and explored some of the particularities of Anandapuram in my earlier work (e.g., Staples 2007).

Using research findings from such a community to make more general claims about the meanings of eating or not eating meat in India might, not unreasonably, be challenged. But the material on food I collected there over the years is useful for at least three reasons. First, as relatively new converts to Christianity, from across castes, my interlocutors' attitudes toward eating beef serve as a useful comparison to those of longer established, almost exclusively Scheduled Caste Christians that I met elsewhere. Examining the differences between Anandapuram's beef consumers and those from other places in the region might in itself be informative. Second, while always remaining aware of its limitations, the very richness of my data, some of it dating back more than thirty years, provides a unique perspective on dietary change among a particular group of people in recent times. For all their differences, after all, Anandapuram's residents were also embedded within the wider local contexts in which they shopped, cooked, and ate. Third, my long-standing relationships with people in the community were invaluable in establishing new contacts with people *beyond* the confines of the colony who also informed this study.

Several of those I worked with took me to visit their natal homes, sometimes for several days at a time, during which I learned a great deal about how commensality was done elsewhere. I spent, for example, a week in one village, with a dominant-caste, landowning family, whose Dalit laborers were fed on disposable leaf plates outside the main house. I spent a similar amount of time in a Madiga hamlet of another village, where buffalo hides hung in the sun to dry and where beef was a desired item on the menu. And I stayed with a large Muslim family—thirteen people sharing two small rented rooms—in a provincial town, where preferences for beef, as well as for other foods less eaten in the villages, were also expressed. The differences in these domestic setups related not just to the consumption of meat: there were also important variations in menus and styles of eating, influenced by locality as well as religion, caste, and class status. Other visits out from Anandapuram took me to the community's makeshift begging settlement in Mumbai; my field notes are replete with observations of shared meals there, as well as records of conversations about the availability of foodstuffs and eating habits in urban, coastal Maharashtra compared to those of Andhra, more than six hundred miles away on the opposite coastline.

I also worked with people from the local town, Bhavanipur (also a pseudonym)—Victoria-Rani, my beef-eating Telugu teacher, among them— whom I met either through friends in Anandapuram or because they worked in or visited the village. From itinerant vegetable sellers, snack vendors, and builders to doctors, teachers, and social workers, movements *into* the village as well as out of it had increased significantly over the past thirty years. Anandapuram was not the bounded, isolated community one might imagine a leprosy colony to be (at least, that was my own perception before arriving there for the first time) but instead interconnected with multiple other places. Through those incomers I got to know a range of people from Bhavanipur and the surrounding hamlets, whose experiences were arguably more typical—if there is such a thing—of quotidian life in the region. Few of them would be described as rich, and none were of the "small but important class of consumers characterized by its multiethnic, multicaste, polyglot, and Westernized tastes" that anthropologist Arjun Appadurai describes (1988, 6), still less of the "sophisticated super-elites" he refers to, from the major cities. Many of them were, nevertheless, wealthier than their Anandapuram neighbors. Several families, for example, owned at least some arable land in their natal villages, and nearly all lived in brick-built dwellings, owned or rented, with three or four separate rooms. Conspicuous evidence of their drift toward middle-class sensibilities—and, in some cases, membership, at the lower rungs of that elusively defined class—was evident in the presence of consumer goods such as dining tables and chairs, televisions, and refrigerators.

During my most recent field trips, in 2016 and 2017, I also worked specifically with beef sellers and others involved in the meat trade in Bhavanipur's market, all of them Madigas or Muslims, again relying on friends from the leprosy colony to forge the initial contact. It was beef-eating friends, for example, who got word from their contacts when cows were to be slaughtered clandestinely for sale in other towns in the district, and who accompanied me both to witness those slaughters and to purchase meat, for themselves and to sell to other households that partook. The locations of these transient, informal slaughterhouses—a clearing in a wood, or a secluded domestic compound—would not have been accessible to me without the long-standing relationships I had developed over the previous thirty years.

One family to which I was particularly close and had known from my first visit had moved to Delhi in the mid-1990s. My social obligation (and desire) to visit them meant my subsequent research field trips always started or ended (and sometimes both) with a visit there. Although these trips were intended to be social rather than a segment of my research program per se, the discussions—as well as the shopping, cooking, and eating—that I engaged in with them in their new city also came to inform my field notes. The parents, of my own generation, had grown up in rural Andhra, the children of small-scale farmers, who remembered a time—pre–Green Revolution—when millet, not rice, was the staple food for families in their respective villages. Their own children had been educated in Delhi, one of whom had gone on to take a degree in catering management and to work in high-end hotels, and who had embraced a more cosmopolitan diet. Their different perspectives, shared across the dinner table or in the restaurants frequented by the younger members of the family and their friends, offered additional insights into dietary changes and continuities.

Beyond Anandapuram and Bhavanipur, alongside fleeting trips to natal towns and villages, Delhi, and Mumbai, my current work also draws significantly on research I conducted in Hyderabad. I lived in the city with my family for sixteen months in 2005 and 2006, conducting postdoctoral work largely focused on the anthropology of disability. As had been the case in Anandapuram, however, references to food and to eating featured heavily in my field notes. Miriam, a Roman Catholic woman who sometimes ate beef, was employed as a cook and maid for the apartment we rented from an interfaith nongovernmental organization (NGO) based in the city, and she taught me and my partner how to shop for and cook what she saw as the key dishes of the area. Her presence is still felt in our own home in the UK more than a decade later, with the recipes we wrote down then in a school exercise book (the pages now annotated with traces of tamarind pulp, groundnut oil, and squashed lentils) continuing to inform our weekly menu. When my research interests later veered specifically toward food, it was to Miriam and others we had met during that earlier visit that I initially turned.

With the help of Das, my research assistant, in 2016 and 2017 we also met butchers, brokers, and others for whom beef was an integral part of their everyday lives (even when, as was sometimes the case for the brokers, they did not eat it themselves). Through our beef-seller contacts, we also attended cattle markets, long bus rides away, in order to trace the journeys cattle took from the cowshed to the serving dish, and to tease out how what the animals meant or represented changed along the way. In the same way that other commodities are transformed by, or transformative of, the contexts through which they pass, so too are cattle and the other parties involved changed along the way.[16]

Taken together, these diverse settings, emerging as they did out of serendipity as much as preplanning, offered windows onto a unique range of everyday perspectives on cattle, on beef, and on food and eating more generally. Although some of those we worked with, such as the meat sellers, had a vested interest in keeping up to date with stories of vigilante attacks and government action on cattle slaughter, for the most part my interlocutors would not describe themselves as activists. We did not seek to work with those directly engaged in perpetrating violence against those who traded in beef, nor did we spend time with those who organized beef festivals or other events aimed at defending the gastronomic rights of those who wished to eat meat derived from cattle. There is, to be sure, important ethnographic work to be done with these groups, and there are interesting questions to be asked about their respective roles in contemporary democracy and the Indian state. The perspectives of both, however, have been well reported upon (and sometimes, perhaps, caricatured) in the press and in social media, occasionally represented more directly through blogs and YouTube videos. Although I have read and watched a great deal of this material, my interest has been to give greater weight to the voices of those not only less heard but also more widespread, and to interpret what they said in the richly layered contexts in which they were embedded. These were the voices of those who chose to eat or not eat beef but who, most of the time, took more ambivalent, more nuanced positions on the issues than those on either side of the debate as it was represented in everyday discourse. I regard those voices not as fixed but as shifting in tune with the world around them. Such people are not easily pigeonholed, either by caste or by community or even within the new classifications that have arisen out of more recent work that interrogates class.[17]

What I am imagining here is a different kind of middle, a middle that has long been there but that has not necessarily been thought of in those terms. Most of the people I worked with were not middle-class, new or old, in the ways that scholars have come to define it, even as their tastes and aspirations were shaped by it. Rather, in terms of meat eating, those I worked with were representative of a large and amorphous group sandwiched between the two dominant, but not necessarily elite, fuzzy-edged groups of activists, protestors, vigilantes, and politicians that have, until now, received the most attention.

METHODS AND ETHICS

My key tool, as for most social anthropologists, has been participant observation: the "deep hanging out," as Clifford Geertz (1998) called it, of ethnographic fieldwork. That is to say, most of my interlocutors were not just people I interviewed and then moved on from. They were people I lived alongside and, in many cases, built relationships with over the course of many years. I asked them questions and recorded their answers, to be sure, but I also ate routine meals with them, traveled with them, and attended their weddings, daughters' first menstruation celebrations, and sometimes their funerals. Feasts marked all these occasions. Other meetings, such as those with the "cutting men" responsible for the slaughter of cows and buffaloes or the brokers who mediated deals between farmers and meat traders, were necessarily more fleeting. But even when I relied largely on interviews, these often developed organically over the course of several meetings. Those meat sellers whom I met only in their shops, for example, were visited at least three times: first, to establish contact; second, if they were willing, to conduct a more detailed, semistructured interview, unfolding as

I observed them going about their daily routines, customers sometimes chipping in with their own perspectives; and third, to follow up on what they had said, or to check anything that I was uncertain of.

In addition to my daily field notes—kept in a diary format—and the interview data I collected during the periods on which I worked consciously on food (in 2011, 2013, 2016, and 2017), I drew on the notes I made during visits from 1999 onward, all of which included copious references to food, as well as memories and informal recordings (such as letters, personal diaries, and recipes) dating back to 1984. In 2011, I conducted food-focused interviews with fifty-two households in Anandapuram and Bhavanipur, and in 2013, I also carried out a full village survey of eating habits in the former. On my last two visits, in 2016 and 2017, I persuaded twenty families to keep food diaries for me, recording everything they ate over periods of two weeks. On those same trips I also undertook a survey of eateries in Bhavanipur and along the half-mile stretch of highway that connected it to Anandapuram, the very acts of looking and counting, and sometimes talking and eating, leading to further qualitative insights. Collectively, these fragments formed a rich source from which to begin making sense of contemporary dietary choices in South India.

I also tried to be attentive not only to what people said and did but also to their sensory experiences and the emotional responses they evoked in relation to the world around them, to engage in, as anthropologist Chenjia Xu (2019) termed it concerning the rise of the "foodie" in China, "participant sensation" as well as in participant observation.[18] I was as interested to learn how they *felt* about animals and the consumption of their flesh as I was to know their thoughts and actions in relation to those matters. This was significant because the positions people took were informed not just by abstract thought but also through their senses, and how they became attuned to them in everyday life. Visceral responses to the smells of bovines and their products or to the taste and mouth-feel of their meat were inseparable from the intangible ideas that people had about them. The love and affection that cattle owners expressed toward their animals—something that the anthropologist Radhika Govindrajan (2018) brings out so effectively in her descriptions of human-bovine relationships in Himalayan villages—was not just an instrumental response to the ritual and economic value of the cow, the way that the anthropologist Marvin Harris (1966), for example, was prone to see it. Rather, their feelings of kinship emerged out of prolonged proximity to the physical warmth, the earthy smells, and the particular sounds their animals made, as well as to the sensory enjoyment of consuming their dairy products. To paraphrase Donna Haraway, humans and their animals "became together" (2008, 19).

I did not, of course, have direct access to what the various sensual or emotional responses of those I worked alongside actually felt like. Even if we smelled the same aromas or ate the same foods, our bodies—through their embodied histories, what Pierre Bourdieu (1990, 52) called the *habitus*—likely responded to them in unique ways. The heat of chili powder, for example, is felt more keenly on the tongues of the uninitiated than on those that have tasted it with every meal all their lives. And the creamy, salty taste of English cheddar cheese, once so delicious to my own taste buds, was—as I learned—universally repulsive to the friends in a South Indian village with whom I tried to share it some years ago. They were the same things, but they evoked different sensory experiences for different people. Not only did the same substances taste different to different bodies, they also provoked other thoughts and sensations—Proustian evocations of pleasurable meals shared, for example—that are particular to the broader webs of context within which an individual consumer is enmeshed.

The anthropologist Richard Wilk (2017, 279) put it well in a passage reflecting on childhood memories of consuming chicken soup when ill. Subsequent bowls of chicken soup, he says, "can only be experienced through a sensory memory, not just its flavor, but its emotional associations, the warming of the belly, the clearing of the sinuses, and the feeling of healing. The real soup is its archetype, not warm stuff in the bowl on the table." Even if our sensory experiences could be matched—and certainly the longer I spent with people, the closer together they were drawn—capturing them in writing is another matter altogether. It hardly needs to be said that a written description of a sensation, however evocative, is substantially different from the literal experience being described.

Nevertheless, what I *was* able to do was to be alert to the emotional responses my interlocutors displayed, like the unchecked expressions of disgust on the faces of some of them at being asked whether or not they ate pork, to take note of them, to ask questions, and, over time, learn to make sense of them. Such fine-grained observations, documented in context, can, as anthropologist Andrew Beatty (2019) recommends, be contextualized and made sense of through the narratives within which they are played out. Emotions, like the corporeal senses with which they are connected, "tell a story and belong to larger stories."[19] And while my thinking on this is inevitably also informed by those scholars who try to capture how sensory experience shapes quotidian political engagement,[20] and while I try in my writing to convey a sense of what things *felt* like as well to explain what they meant, I remain acutely aware of the problems inherent in such an approach.

That brings me to the broader issue of ethics. Here, my key concern—as for other ethnographic research, but heightened in this case because of the rising levels of violence perpetrated in relation to cattle slaughter and the sale and consumption of beef—was in ensuring that those I worked with were not put at increased risk because of me. I would hope that a more subtly textured study of everyday experiences in relation to eating or not eating meat might, in itself, be productive of a dialogue less enflamed by communal and other tensions. Certainly, some of those I spent time with on this project spoke to me precisely for that reason: because they wanted their voices to be heard, and they felt no one else was listening to them. Nevertheless, some of them were well aware of the risks they faced. One Hyderabad butcher, for example, while happy for me to quote him and keen to identify his shop in anything I wrote—safely located, he felt, within a Muslim area—did not want me to take any photographs that identified his face. In an attempt to give that protection, I have used pseudonyms for people and places—other than large cities, which it was futile to attempt to disguise—and have changed or omitted other details that might identify specific people. This offers no guarantee, of course, but it does make it difficult to attribute the particular words or actions I document to particular, named individuals.

THE ANTHROPOLOGY OF FOOD AND EATING IN INDIA

This book is a contribution both to the anthropology of food *and* to the study of food within the related disciplinary fields of history and sociology, as well as, more particularly, to the growing body of specifically Indological contributions to the field. Both Krishnendu Ray and Tulasi Srinivas (2012b, 13), in their edited collection of essays on the impacts of globalization on South Asian foodways, and Kiranmayi Bhushi (2018, 3), in a recent anthology intended to capture how India is being transformed through food practices in the contemporary moment, usefully identify a number of discrete but overlapping categories into which the study of food in India might heuristically be divided. In short, these are bodies of work rooted in agroscience, concerned with improving crop yields; nutrition and public health; development economics, emerging from studies of colonial engagement with food and famine; food science; historical analysis of classical texts; and cultural aspects of food and eating.

Anthropological contributions, clearly, fit most comfortably into the "culture" strand of this work, even as it makes sense sometimes to visit and to utilize contributions from food studies' other constituent parts. In the introduction to their masterful recent handbook on food and anthropology, James Watson and Jakob Klein (2016) trace the subdiscipline's history, noting that while food and eating feature in many of the classics—from Marcel Mauss ([1925] 1990) and Bronisław Malinowski (1935) to Claude Lévi-Strauss (1966)—there was little that placed food center stage prior to the late 1970s and early 1980s, with the notable exception of Audrey Richards's (1932; 1939) work on hunger and diet in what is now Zimbabwe. The same might be said for the anthropology of food in India. Descriptions of public dining and what it said about the relative status of the diners, it is true, had their place in the monographs of the so-called village studies era of the 1950s and 1960s.[21] M. N. Srinivas (1952), for example, used the strategic dining practices of the Coorgs of South India, with whom he conducted fieldwork, to illustrate his notion of Sanskritization, the process via which lower castes sought to improve their social standing by adopting the ideologies and practices—those relating to food and eating among them—of their higher-ranking peers. Exploring the problem of putatively higher castes being polluted by food prepared by those of lower ritual status, and the strategies they might deploy to avoid it, had also been a preoccupation of earlier scholars.[22]

It was though the work of Chicago anthropologist McKim Marriott and French structuralist Louis Dumont that commanded the most enduring attention in respect to caste and its relationship to eating, at least from the late 1960s. Marriott, in summary, depicted food transactions as a kind of tournament, during which players sought to gain "dominance over others through feeding them or securing dependence on others by being fed by them" (1968, 169; see also Marriott 1976). Dumont (1980), by contrast, developed a more abstract theory of caste, elaborated through the oppositions he drew between purity and impurity on the one hand and status and power on the other.[23] For Dumont, food exchanges were ultimately less significant than marriage when it came to understanding caste order (Khare 2012, 244). This is not the space to rehearse in detail the positions of the two theorists and the debates they engendered;[24] for current purposes, suffice it to state that for both of them, as for many other anthropologists of that era, their interest in food was predominantly as a means of explicating their theories on caste. As Sidney Mintz put it, writing about the study of food in that time period more generally, "It was not the food or its preparation that was of interest, so much as what, socially speaking, the food and eating could be used for" (1996, 4).

If one were to change the word "food" to "cow," Mintz's words would be equally apt to describe the literature that was emerging, at around the same time but in a different anthropological silo, on the cow's status in India. Chief among these contributions, at least in terms of shaping the debate, was Harris's (1966; 1985; 1989) argument that the protected status afforded to the cow in India was a consequence of ecological, rather than ideological or religious, factors. It was not, he suggested, that Hindus avoided slaughtering cattle because of *ahimsa* (the religious doctrine of avoiding violence to other beings); rather, *ahimsa* is powerful precisely because of the material rewards that observing it confers. To put it crudely, Harris's thesis was that, in order to survive, a religious doctrine or a cultural practice also had to make rational, economic sense. The debate that followed was less about the empirical realities of human-bovine relationships—Harris, by his own admission, had never stepped foot in India (1966, 51)—and more to do with what one made of Harris's cultural materialism, a theory rooted in Marxist evolutionism. For several critics it was altogether too reductionist, too selective in its use of data, and too dismissive of the role that ideological belief and emotion play in social relations.[25] It also failed to recognize that the neat distinction between "religion" and "economy" does not hold in the Indian context, where the two realms have been shown to be inseparable (Adcock 2010). But whichever position one took vis-à-vis Harris and his interlocutors, the argument was not really about cows but about wider theory.

Meanwhile, food was finally beginning to be considered a topic worthy of anthropological study in its own right. The first single-authored monograph on food in Hindu society appeared in 1976: R. S. Khare's *The Hindu Hearth and Home* (1976b), published in the same year as his related collection of more theoretical papers, *Culture and Reality: Essays on the Hindu System of Managing Foods* (1976a). Drawing on his fieldwork with the Kanya Kubja, orthodox Brahmins in Uttar Pradesh, the findings presented in *The Hindu Hearth and Home* might well have been remote from the experiences of lower-caste (or less economically established high-caste) diners, but the book was valuable in at least two respects. First, it offered a wealth of detailed empirical data that had not previously been documented; second, it extended discussion beyond public commensality, where it had become too firmly rooted, into the realm of food in the domestic arena. As such, Khare's book offered rich material not only on shared dining between groups but on the neglected areas of cooking, utensils, ingredients, and food sharing within the home, opening up an array of possibilities for future study.

The decade that followed, as Watson and Klein (2016) confirm, was when food studies in anthropology really began to blossom. It was with the publication of Jack Goody's pioneering work comparing what lay behind national cuisines, *Cooking, Cuisine and Class* (1982), and Mintz's now classic monograph, *Sweetness and Power* (1985), that the anthropology of food witnessed a shift from studies embedded in either symbolic or materialist paradigms toward more historically and ethnographically grounded work (Watson and Klein 2016, 3). Both books were instrumental in drawing attention to the relationship between material practices, power, and meaning. They also prefigured a new turn to the material a couple of decades later—arguably ignored for too long, as theorists tired of the structural Marxism within which Harris's earlier invocation of the material was embedded (Coole and Frost 2010, 3). Like Goody and Mintz, the so-called "new materialists" recognized that the symbolic must be grounded in the material, that matter is not simply passive or inert (10), empty vessels into which symbolic meanings might be poured. Rather, in line with ways of thinking inspired by Bruno Latour (2005, 2010), we should recognize that matter has agency in itself, an approach that emphasizes the active, self-transformative, practical aspects of corporeality as it participates in relations of power (Coole and Frost 2010, 19).[26] If we apply these insights to our study of the relations between cattle and other animals, both with human beings and the wider world around them, it becomes clear that "animals condition political and cultural possibilities not just as immaterial metaphors but as particular actors with complex lives, histories, and characters" (Govindrajan 2018, 89).[27] The symbolism of the cow takes its meaning through human entanglements with the actual bodies of cows.[28]

Goody and Mintz, in addition to leading us out of the cul-de-sac into which Harris's vision of materialism had arguably taken us, recognized, through food, the transnational links that shape social relationships. Appadurai's (1988) exploration of the growing numbers of cookbooks and what they said about the changing foodways of India's major cities reflected parallel moves in the anthropology of food in India. Going further than his previous writing on "gastro-politics" (1981), he demanded that we look beyond caste and traditional taboos in understanding urban middle-class relationships to food. "As food emerges from its traditional moral and social matrix," he argued, "it becomes embedded in a different system of etiquette—that of the drawing room, the corporate gathering, the club event, and the restaurant" (1988, 8).

As the anthropology of food became more firmly established, its turns reflected, or led, those of anthropology more generally. It witnessed a shift from the structuralist explanations that framed the debates between Marriott and Dumont, for example, to those that, after Appadurai (1988) and others, reflected not only the changing theoretical concerns of anthropologists but also corresponding shifts across the world. These included the impact of globalization on what had once been thought of as bounded cultural spaces, new nationalisms, and, particularly relevant in India, the sway of economic liberalization on the food people sourced, cooked, and ate, as well as its significance.

Within India, despite its particularly rich gastronomic range, there have been relatively few monographs that focus specifically on food post-Khare. Those that have been produced tend to focus on particular regional cuisines and eating practices in urban centers[29] or Indian food in the diaspora.[30] The apparent reticence of others to join them is perhaps because of, as food studies scholars Ray and Srinivas suggest, "the burdens of the long-festering discussion on caste and commensality that had dominated Indian sociology at least since Louis Dumont's *Homo Hierarchicus*" (2012b, 13). It is certainly true that our long enchantment with caste—and a focus on commensality rather than the other aspects of food that Khare drew attention to—obscured alternative forms of social relation, class among them, for too long. We were, it seems, too eager to dump caste in favor of examining the growth of a cosmopolitan middle class, and not only because, as they note, it led scholars to pay less attention to Khare's sustained input than they might otherwise have done (1976a, 1976b, 1992, 1994, 2006).

Vital though it is to take seriously the growth of the middle classes, as well as to attend to the foodways of Indians in the diaspora, such an emphasis has obscured from view the enduring impact that caste and community play in what people eat, particularly in villages and small towns, and its social implications. This is significant because relegating caste to the realm of "heritage," while the real politics goes on elsewhere, has enabled dominant groups to continue exploiting low castes and the non-Hindu "other" through food taboos, more or less unnoticed (Gorringe and Karthikeyan 2014). The denial of nonvegetarian diets in public or institutional spaces, for example, has been presented merely as sensitivity to the cultural values of Hindus (despite a significant majority of them actually being nonvegetarian), rather than violence, structural and symbolic, inflicted against those who eat meat (Osella 2008, 4). Veena Shatrugna, previously of the National Institute of Nutrition in Hyderabad, remarked in an interview that India's nutritional experts have tended to come from vegetarian castes, and their advice has thus been skewed in favor of plant-based dietary recommendations.[31] Vegetarianism has subsequently been institutionalized in the public distribution system (which provides key foodstuffs at subsidized prices for those on low incomes) and the more recent midday meals program for school children.

Much of the literature suggests that a broad change has occurred in culinary and gustatory practices and what they mean: a shift from eating habits shaped predominantly by caste to those dominated by the sensibilities of a globalized middle class. Insufficient attention, however, has been paid to contemporary foodways in village settings (despite something of a return to village studies in South Asian ethnography more widely[32]) and to those of city dwellers beyond the middle class. In beginning to address these gaps, I explore the ways in which caste and community continue to dominate the food choices of my friends and acquaintances in India, even as they are refashioned by what is going on in the world beyond them.

Sacred Cows and Chicken Manchurian focuses on meat consumption and, within that, the eating of beef in particular. Other ethnographies and collections have focused on meat,[33] but with the exception of a special issue of *South Asia* on the veg/non-veg divide (Osella and Osella 2008b), very little scholarship turns the spotlight on meat in India. With at least twenty-eight human deaths—and many more injuries—attributed to disagreement over whether bovine slaughter should be permissible in India reported since 2010,[34] attention to the problem of the kind that only a detailed, ethnographic approach can provide is long overdue. An ethnography of eating and not eating meat is also a timely intervention in a more general sense, because the worldwide industrialization of meat production has been changing eating habits in new and sometimes unexpected ways (Watson and Klein 2016, 9).

MATERIAL SYMBOLS

This book also pays particular attention to the materials in and through which meanings are conveyed, shaped, or negotiated, as in the work of Harris, Goody, Mintz, and the "new materialists." For followers of the structuralist anthropologist Claude Lévi-Strauss (1963)—whose theory drew heavily on structural linguistics—it was mostly the relationship *between* symbols, rather than their materiality, that gave them their particular meaning. As is the case for language, the relationship between the symbol and the thing it represents is often arbitrary. Some of the material symbols in the following chapters might well be thought of in much the same way. The dusty china tea cups that make an appearance in chapter 2, for example, were significant not because they were intrinsically more valuable than the glass or stainless-steel beakers but because of the contrast between the two kinds of drinking vessel. My hosts often had only one china cup (sometimes only a plastic replica of a china cup) but several metal or glass ones; serving a guest with a cup that was different from the others signified difference and more importance. In a similar way, the very chewiness of meat, usually encountered only weekly, if that, contrasted against the softness of more regularly consumed vegetable and dal dishes, was a key part of what marked it as special and celebratory (or conversely, as taboo). The contrast, or the relationship between the meat and vegetables, was, one might argue, more significant than the things themselves, even if that contrast was manifest through material differences.

In many other instances, however, there are very specific relationships between the things I describe and what they have come to represent. Bovine animals and their products—each with their own distinctive smells, sounds, textures, and tastes—are central here. From the warmth of a cow's breath and the mouth-feel of her milk, to dead or dying bodies under the knives of the "cutting men" or the wafts of a beef curry from a pot bubbling on the stove, what cows and buffaloes come to mean at different times is intrinsically bound up in their viscerality. But plenty of other materials come under the spotlight too. Caste and class identities, for example, play out in very concrete ways, not just through the different kinds of food people eat—whether they eat or do not eat meat, for example—but through an array of much more subtle changes in how those foods are prepared and eaten. The subtlety with which dishes are spiced, whether those spices are finely or coarsely ground, and how they are served and eaten all convey messages about those who prepare and eat them, and can also be manipulated, in some cases, to affect social mobility. The locations and paraphernalia that accompany the serving of food are likewise communicative. Everything from cups, plates, and bowls—and the very materials they are made from—to the tables, chairs, tablecloths, and floor mats on which meals are served, consciously or otherwise, convey and shape meaning.

The capacity for things to take on particular meanings is constrained or extended by the wider contexts within which they come to exist. If the capacity of particular objects to convey honor relies on their rarity, for example, that capacity becomes diminished if and when those objects became more commonplace. At times, however, material changes might in themselves be utilized to articulate the more abstract consequences of change. Evoking the simplicity of earlier cuisine in relation to the complexities of modern eating, for example, was one of the most powerful ways my interlocutors expressed their thoughts and feelings about the confusions and contradictions of life in the contemporary moment.

TWO RECURRING ISSUES

One conundrum I encountered when developing this book was the issue of writing about meat as a non–meat eater, particularly in a context where vegetarianism is so politically charged. The other was the problematic distinction, and blurring, between cows and buffaloes, the two animals from which beef comes. Dealing with them here is not meant to imply that they are no longer problematic; rather, it is to provide some useful background.

Vegetarian Dilemmas

Vegetarianism, for me, was a personal choice, one which arose, in part, out of my realization during those first visits to India in the mid-1980s that a nonmeat diet was even plausible. Had I not been a vegetarian (and, for some years, a pescatarian), my interest in what it meant to different people to eat meat in India would not have been piqued, as the earlier retelling of my dinner with Victoria-Rani suggests. Ironically—given the affinities I developed with my beef-eating interlocutors—it was also through conducting this research that I eventually switched, in late 2017, to a vegan diet. My constant internet searches for cattle- and beef-related information and academic papers had, presumably thanks to the search engines' algorithms, also exposed me to numerous videos depicting the alleged cruelties of the dairy industry, which, in turn, alerted me to stories about the treatment of other animals. Although I never interrogated these sources with the same voracity that I would have applied to materials for an academic publication, they were enough to convince me—having already become inured to watching cattle being slaughtered in real life—that killing an animal was not necessarily the cruelest act one could perpetrate against it. Indeed, having seen at close quarters animals being killed in a village setting, I might have almost, had I still desired it, been convinced to eat their meat, at least in particular circumstances. Although this did not (yet) happen, it still felt incongruous *not* to eat meat while continuing to eat animals' other products, and that is why I also stopped eating them after my return to the UK in September 2017.

Nevertheless, while culinary choices were inextricably intertwined with my research trajectory, *not* eating beef while working with beef eaters undeniably presented certain difficulties. Das, my research assistant and a Brahmin by birth, despite being a convert to Christianity who was married to a beef-eating Madiga woman, had always remained strictly vegetarian. There was a moment in December 2017 when, sitting in the corner of a cramped beef shop in Hyderabad, we were both struck by the apparent absurdity of our situation. The shop owner, as he answered my questions, continued to chop up the large hunk of meat on his block, his cleaver sweeping dramatically through the air and flecking us, as it did so, with fragments of bone and droplets of bovine blood. Das glanced toward me at one point and caught my eye. "How *did* we come to be doing this?" he asked sardonically, before shaking his head with slightly amused resignation. In truth, however, by then we were used to it. Whatever visceral reactions the sight and smell of raw meat might once have evoked for either of us, they had ceased to be a problem.

Our vegetarianism did, however, present other concerns.[35] First, it created a certain distance between us and some of our interlocutors. Another of the Hyderabad butchers we knew, for example, had, at one point, expressed an interest in inviting us to dine with him at his family home, a sure breakthrough in establishing lasting rapport. After Das told him we did not eat meat, however, the invitation was diplomatically and, it turned out, permanently, put on hold. It was not, I am fairly sure, given his subsequent manner, that he was offended. He had, after all, been very pleased to have the opportunity to offer his take on meat eating and cattle slaughter, and he continued to take pleasure in joining us to drink tea on the bench outside his shop and talk about his work. Rather, coming from a Muslim family of meat sellers who ate meat every day, my assumption was that he was now uncertain what he could feed us that would, at the same time, be appropriate food with which to honor his guests.

My second concern was that, having not knowingly eaten beef in India since the mid-1980s, I had little memory of its taste or its mouth-feel, nor had I felt its impact on my stomach or on my digestion. When people told me about the differences in flavor and texture between cow and buffalo meat; tried to explain their preference (or otherwise) for beef over chicken, goat or, fish; or described its succulent, sweet flavor and prized chewiness, I had to rely on their descriptions and my own imagination. I had no direct, material experience to help me contextualize their words. I could see and smell it, in all its forms, and I even felt it between my fingertips, but I never ingested it.

In the end, the pros and cons of my position as a vegetarian among the meat eaters, as it were, were fairly evenly balanced. Being a vegetarian was a useful provocation: it teased out other viewpoints as much as it suppressed them, in the same way that being outside a situation more generally can help an anthropologist to capture perspectives insiders cannot. It was also an occasional hindrance. The personal discomfort in navigating the tensions my position sometimes created was also productive, forcing me to reflect in ways that I might not otherwise have done. And my keen appreciation of other regional specialties that people fed me—*gongura patchidi* (an Andhra-specific green leaf chutney) especially—seemed to make up for any deficits in meat consumption.

Of Cows and Buffaloes

Cows and water buffaloes—the two key sources of *goddu mānsam* (beef, in Telugu, the first language of most of my informants)—are clearly different beasts. Indigenous zebu cows have played a role in Hindu cosmology since the Vedic period (c. 1500 BCE), with the sacred cow concept established as early as 400 CE (Lodrick 2005, 61). Gandhi dubbed the zebu "a poem of piety" (1954, 3; cited in Korom 2000, 188), revered, in everyday discourse, as a symbol of motherhood. The water buffalo, by contrast, has sometimes been represented in contradistinction to the cow: as the Dalit is to the Brahmin, so, in scripture and in common practice, the buffalo is to the cow (Narayanan 2018, 335–36). While the consumption of the buffalo is taboo because it is considered impure, eating the flesh of the cow is proscribed because of the animal's elevated symbolic status.

Even among cows, some are more holy than others. Shankar Lal, president of the Akhil Bharatiya Gau Sewa—an affiliate of the Rashtriya Swayamesevak Sangh (RSS), the Hindu nationalist organization that spawned the ruling BJP—reportedly suggested, in 2015, that Indians should only drink milk from what he described as "virtuous breeds."[36] In particular, he warned that the milk of Jersey cows—a breed of cattle brought into India under British colonial rule, so ripe for symbolic appropriation as "other"—might even lead those who drank it into criminal activity. In an article reporting on the RSS's plans to construct cattle shelters across the country, Lal was quoted as saying, "For a crime-free Bharat [India], it is necessary that our children drink only Indian cow's milk because it makes them *saatvik* (virtuous). By drinking the milk of Jersey cows and buffaloes, their minds get harmful ideas, which make them criminals."[37] Lal's provocative sound bite resonates with more nuanced distinctions drawn by central Himalayan mountain dwellers. For them, while Jersey and hybrid cows have style (*style-wal goru*), their milk—despite being more plentiful—is thinner and less nutritious, and their dung and urine more watery. Their local *pahari* cows, by contrast, are associated with moral, physical, and spiritual strength (Govindrajan 2018, 72–77).

What at first appears to be a clear separation between cows and buffaloes, and a hierarchy of breeds within the former category, is not quite so straightforward, however. My own interlocutors did distinguish, at least some of the time, between *eddu mānsam* (buffalo meat) and *āvu mānsam* (cow meat) when they were discussing their preferences. Some Madigas, for example, by virtue of their birth-ascribed status as leatherworkers (even if they never entered the trade), claimed a particular affinity to the buffalo, arguing that its meat was particularly well suited to their constitutions, but did not eat the flesh of the cow. Muslim informants, by contrast, tended to prefer *āvu mānsam*, in part because of *eddu mānsam*'s tainted association with low-caste impurity.[38] Christians, if they (or their recent ancestors) were converts, retained a preference for buffalo if they were from Dalit castes (as the majority of them were); others, like a Hyderabad Roman Catholic family I knew well who had grown up in a Muslim part of the city, expressed surprise that anyone would eat anything *other* than *āvu mānsam*. The reality, though, was that all the butchers I met, whichever populations they served, sold the meat of whichever animals they could source most easily and at the most competitive rates; for the most part, during my fieldwork, this seemed to be buffalo. When people purchased beef, they never, in my experience, questioned the butcher about the provenance of the animal; if they asked for the meat by name at all—hardly necessary, since the sellers sold only one product—they used the generic *goddu mānsam*, in Telugu.

As in Telugu, in Hyderabadi Hindi there were also different terms—*gaa'ay ka gosht* and *bhains ke gosht*—to distinguish between cow and buffalo meat, respectively, but it was far more common, in Hyderabad, for customers simply to ask the seller for *gosht* (meat).[39] Although this enabled customers to assume that the meat came from where they expected or wanted it to come from, it also signaled an awareness, among some of those I worked with, that sellers might also mix buffalo, cow, and ox meat together. Once the skin was drawn back from the animal, despite my informants' claims to be able to tell the difference, by appearance and by taste, it was difficult to discern with certainty which meat came from which animal. There were reports in October 2017, for example, suggesting a sharp rise in shipments of cow meat being passed off as buffalo through southern Indian ports, where enforcement of legislation on the export of beef from cows was seen as less stringent. The provenance of the meat—as had been the case with the meat found in the fridge of the Muslim man beaten to death in Dadri—was impossible to confirm without laboratory tests.[40] This potential confusion between the two sources of beef worked both ways. As a Hyderabadi butcher who had had two consignments of meat violently seized by protestors as they were transported to his shop from the slaughterhouse told me, the vigilantes had not stopped to ask what kind of meat it was before they contaminated it with phenyl and thrashed the truck drivers.

I raise these examples simply to flag the uncertainties in trying to draw a distinction between the meat of cows and buffaloes, particularly when state legislation often restricted the slaughter of both kinds of animal. It was also the case that castes and other groups who did not eat beef, even when they ate other kinds of meat, treated buffalo and cow beef as one and the same thing. Consequently, and reflecting the fact that my interlocutors were likewise often hazy about what animal the meat they purchased, cooked, and ate had come from, unless a specific distinction is called for, in this book I use the term "beef," or its vernacular equivalents, to refer to the flesh of buffaloes, cows, and oxen.

CHAPTER ONE

Differential Histories of Meat Eating in India

HINDUISM, my old friend Kandaswamy explained to me, gives recognition to the cow because of the abundance of life-enhancing materials she provides: "milk, ghee, dung, all kinds of good things." Buffaloes contribute similar products, he went on, and both animals are vital for working the land or pulling ploughs or carts:

> They look after us, so if we kill them, one day there might not be enough animals left to do all that for us, and then we'd face problems. That's what Hindus think. People saw cattle as a gift from God and so thought they should be protected. It's all written there in the Dharmaśāstras, but we need to give practical reasons if people are going to follow commands. Historically, we once ate everything—cows included—but with changes in knowledge and the situation, ideas also change, and we needed rules to stop the slaughter of important animals, and religion provided them for us. Hindus created the anti–cow slaughter rules and they were good for that time in history. Policies, whether they come from religion or whether they come from the government, need to meet the needs of the time. Otherwise they won't work, or they won't be followed. So, in more recent times, for example, we started saying that cows could be killed when they are no longer useful. It's a practical regulation, and what is useful will also change. Once, we needed buffaloes to pull the ploughs in the fields. Now, we have tractors, so once they can't give us milk, what else can we do with them?

Kandaswamy was a seventy-year-old man who was well known in Anandapuram for his articulacy and knowledge of Indian history, and whose views on issues of the day were regularly sought out. He was responding to my questions, back in 2011 (three years before the BJP was reelected to power), on cattle slaughter and campaigners' attempts to limit it. Part of his answer strikes me as uncannily like one that a student well versed in Marvin Harris's (1966; 1985) theory of cultural materialism might have given. The Marxist slant to Kandaswamy's interpretation was, most likely, a consequence of exposure to Communist Party activists in his village during his youth, something he had talked to me about in the past. Like the other older men who gathered to chat and enjoy the evening breeze on the patch of open land by Anandapuram's fishpond, Kandaswamy was not formally educated. And like most of those I quizzed about cattle and beef that summer, he had formed an opinion based on fragments drawn from multiple sources and experiences. In common with his male counterparts in Anandapuram, he read the regional newspapers, or listened to others reading them aloud in the teashops in the mornings. He also tuned in avidly to the radio news every evening before bed. Others, paying more or less attention, watched the news bulletins on the television sets that, by then, had become a common feature in most Anandapuram houses. When news stories caught the public imagination, they also became topics of what was described as "timepass" discussion among villagers, men especially.[1]

Conversations about cow protection and beef eating do not occur in a vacuum but are informed by people's past knowledge and experiences, which are molded by caste, community, and class affiliations. They are also informed by what they remember from lessons, if they had attended school, about Hinduism and Indian history; various media; and, in the case of Anandapuram, because it is a Christian community, anything picked up from sermons broadcast from the church. In terms of bovine politics, reflections are additionally shaped by more visceral experiences of subsisting alongside, and sometimes rearing, cattle, in addition to the gustatory encounters that form their dietary practices. In terms of the particular relationship between cattle and diet, many people I spent time with referenced the gradual shift from the milk they imbibed at their mothers' breasts to that of the cow or the buffalo. This was how a lot of my interlocutors, even if they ate beef, explained the widespread reticence to slaughter them. "The cow is like a mother to us and we shouldn't really kill it, so it's a good thing not to slaughter them," one beef-eating woman told me. The symbolic link between cows and motherhood was thus at least partly grounded in the materiality of milk and what were understood as its life-enhancing properties, whether it came literally from human mothers or from bovine animals. Milk's material qualities—its pure white color, its sweet flavor and rich mouth-feel, and its very perishability—all shape how the substance is understood and experienced, and consequently, its capacity to carry meanings. Connected to strength, milk serves as a metaphor for power, of both the individual body and the Indian nation (Wiley 2011). And while it remains very important throughout life, both materially *and* symbolically, milk is eventually supplemented—as children grow up—by rice, the other food par excellence.

No one claimed to remember, directly, their first cooked rice—carefully massaged into tiny balls by their mothers' right hands and pushed into their mouths with a gentle flick of the thumb and forefinger—although they recalled their own children and grandchildren being fed in that way. Later, watery dal, soft vegetables, and curd or buttermilk would be added to the rice, again mixed by hand. If the family was nonvegetarian—as most in Anandapuram were—the gravy from meat and fish dishes, forensically sifted for bones, might likewise be massaged in. As their taste buds adjusted to the chili and the salt, the proportion of accompaniments to rice slowly, almost imperceptibly, increased, and they learned gradually to mix the rice and the *kūra* (curry) with their own fingers.

When people like Kandaswamy were young, meat for rural peasant farmers was a rarity, eaten once a month, if that, and usually reserved to mark special events. Typically, it was hand-reared chicken or occasionally goat, whose sinewy flesh, and the fragrant masalas within which it was cooked, stood in stark contrast to the softer vegetable and lentil preparations, more simply seasoned with salt, chili, and turmeric, that were eaten every day. Chickens were most often kept by the household, traded between neighbors rather than sourced, as nowadays, from the market. Goats were less common than chickens but likewise domestically reared. Back then, people recalled, beef was cheap, much cheaper than chicken. Those who ate it, those born into Dalit castes or Muslims, were said to grow strong on it, because it suited their particular constitutions. For those who engaged in the heavy manual work associated with those castes, it also—as pro-beef Dalit activists argued—offered them the protein they needed to fulfill their roles. Embedded daily practices such as these helped to shape, alongside knowledge gleaned from other sources and honed during discussion with those around them, the kinds of answers people gave when I solicited their views on cattle slaughter and the consumption of beef.

REIMAGINING THE PAST IN THE PRESENT

The backdrop against which recent behavior has evolved is the historic relationship between animals (especially cattle), food (especially meat), and identity. However, it is not simply that the past informs the present but also that the past is manipulated and rethought in ways that deliberately change both the present and the future. Understanding this context entails a return first to the Vedic texts of some 3,500 years ago and what historians subsequently made of them, then a jump—with brief stops along the way—to the 1880s onward, during which records show a growing gulf between cow protectionists, who sometimes reference that earlier Vedic history, and those who wanted to continue slaughtering and eating beef. In the 2010s the history of cattle slaughter again became a pressing issue in India.

This backdrop offers not a comprehensive narrative but an illustration of how previous interpretations of the past are reimagined to particular effect, and how these narratives inform the worldviews and practices of contemporary people. Even when my informants had not read the Vedas or listened to the reported words of, for instance, Gandhi—which was certainly the case for the vast majority of them—our conversations made clear that those sources, often in heavily mediated forms, fed into their everyday perceptions of the world around them. The messages they gleaned from them—combined with their more immediate experience—formed part of their habitus.[2] The following overview is intended not to unmask Vedic reality but to sketch out how representations of that history have been applied to contemporary concerns.

VEDIC REFERENCES TO CASTE AND FOOD

The roots of caste—or, at least the "book view" (Béteille 1991, 8) of it—might be traced back to the Vedic period, to some point between 1500 and 1000 BCE, the epoch defined by a shift from the Harrapan culture of the Indus Valley to that of the Aryan peoples.[3] Creation stories in the Rigveda, the earliest of four bodies of work collectively known as the Vedas, religious texts that were scribed over that period and constituted the scriptural roots of Hinduism, describe the four categories (or *varnas*) of humanity emerging from the sacrifice of Purusha, primordial man. According to the Sanskrit text, "The Brahmin was his mouth, of both his arms was the Rajanya [the Kshatriya] made. His thighs became the Vaisya, from his feet the Sudra was produced" (Griffith 1896, 469).[4]

The fifth category of persons—the Untouchable, now rendered Dalit or Scheduled Caste—is not mentioned in those early texts, although there are numerous subsequent myths to account for their later arrival at the bottom of the social hierarchy.[5] Others have speculated that the category might have emerged to account for foreigners and outsiders who were not incorporated into the four-*varna* model; reference to wheat in subsequent texts, for example, is "contemptuously described as food for the mlecchas (outcasts)" (Achaya 1994, 34), which could have referred to the Harappans, whose civilization the Aryans had replaced.[6] And particularly pertinent here, the Vyāsasmṛti—a subsequent law book that draws on the Vedas, thought to have been written in the early part of the first century CE—makes a direct link between untouchability and cattle slaughter: "A cow killer is untouchable (*antyaja*) and even by talking to him one incurs sin; [the Vyāsamṛti] thus made beef eating one of the bases of untouchability from the early medieval period onwards" (Jha 2002, 114).

References to food more generally in the Vedic texts are copious, although they tend to relate to what is good to eat in general, rather than specific categories of people. Scholars have documented in some detail the food and drinks recorded in the Vedas and subsequent texts up to around 700 CE (Prakash 1961), and have provided encyclopedic treatment of Indian food and eating (Achaya 1994). Barley was initially the major grain eaten by the Aryans, followed a little later by rice, eaten with curds, ghee, sesame seeds, mung beans, *masha* (*urad dal* or black gram), and meat preparations. The lotus stem and the cucumber also warrant mention, and other vegetables—including the bottle gourd, lotus roots, and bitter gourd—appear in the later Vedas (Achaya 1994, 33–35). Consistently high status was given to rice throughout the ancient literature, suggesting that—as in present-day South India—it remained the ideal even when it was not available (M. Smith 2006). From gifts of puffed rice in the Ramayana and venison served with rice mixed with ghee and milk in the Mahabharata to *annaprasana*—the ceremonial first feeding of rice to babies, sweetened with jaggery (cane sugar)—rice appears as "an edible metaphor that represented prosperity, social status, and ritual purity" (482).

Despite sometimes mouthwatering details of other comestibles, however, it was meat of various kinds that occupied the pride of place in Vedic gastronomic musings. There was, most historians seem to agree, no outright ban on the consumption of cattle, with some Brahmins eating it, some of the time, at least until the twelfth century CE (Jha 2002, 143). Meat eating more generally was considered by the Indo-Aryans as part of the cosmic order: a "dog-eat-dog world" (B. Smith 1990, 177). Supernatural entities fed on sacrificial oblations, humans ate animals, animals ate plants, and plants fed on the rain. In the Vedas, religious studies scholar Brian Smith observes, eating "was simultaneously an act of nourishment, a display of wealth and status, and a demonstration of domination over that which was eaten" (178). Certainly, in the Rigveda, where food as a generic category is mentioned, by my count, at least 124 times (with copious other references to particular comestibles), it is usually in relation either to making sacrifices of it to the gods or requesting them to bestow an abundance of it upon us. Although in many cases the food itself is not specified—beyond being holy, sacred, dainty, or sacrificial—allusions to milk, butter, or meat are especially common and mirror the importance, if not necessarily the meanings applied to them, of those materials in the present.

References to the cow are particularly notable. The animal is mentioned a staggering seven hundred times in the Rigveda alone (Srinivasan 1979, 4), with reference made to the value of its dung as fertilizer (L. Gopal 1980, 90), as well as to its other products as food and offerings to the gods. Later accounts concur broadly with earlier readings of the Vedas[7]; although the cow was afforded an elevated position, it was not at the time they were written considered sacred.[8] Rather, the status of the cow was related directly to its economic and sacrificial uses. Brahmins, it was said, "ate readily of the consecrated beef" (Korom 2000, 187) during this period,[9] and direct references to the sacrifice of animals continues in the literature at least until 800 CE (Achaya 1994, 53–55). When the killing of cows *was* subject to religious prohibition, it was more likely because they were seen as the rightful property of Brahmins rather than because they were worthy of protection in their own right (Lodrick 2005, 67). Textual records of what might be good or otherwise to eat might, of course, fail to represent what was actually eaten by most people, but archaeological records do confirm that cattle were a major source of food for people of the Indus valley in the Vedic period and earlier, as were their milk and other dairy products (64).

More explicit prohibitions began to emerge in the Dharmaśāstras, the Hindu law books that were penned by Brahmins in the centuries that followed, and that also elaborated on the roles of each of the *varna*s, which began to be subdivided into *jati*s, or castes. In some texts, for example, lower castes (and women) are forbidden to use *panchagavya*, a purificatory cocktail of cow dung, urine, milk, curd, and ghee (Jha 2002, 131–32). To offer some perspective, however, the Manu Smriti (Laws of Manu), produced around 200 BCE, noted that the killing of bovines, while sinful, was less so than consuming alcohol.[10] In a similar vein, when told that eating beef was sinful, the Upanishadic sage Yāgnavalkya apparently responded, "That may well be;

but I shall eat of it nevertheless if the flesh be tender (*amshala*)" (Kosambi 1975, cited in Achaya 1994, 55).

The idea of the cow as an object of veneration appeared to have first gathered traction a few hundred years earlier, around 500 BCE, with the development of Buddhism and Jainism, both of which promoted *ahimsa*, the doctrine of nonviolence to all living things (Korom 2000, 188), which virtually all of my interlocutors in the present, even when they admitted to not following it, made reference to. According to Ambedkar (1948, 104–9), leader of the Dalit Buddhist movement during the independence struggle, when Brahmins gave up beef, they did so pragmatically, as a means of taking the moral high ground from Buddhists, who had simply drawn the line at animal sacrifice, not meat consumption. Although *ahimsa* had become established doctrine by Brahmins by the fourth century CE, even then popular practice was often at variance with this (Lodrick 2005, 61).

Subsequent travelers to India, however, commented on the vegetarian habits found there as early as 500 CE. According to Persian scholar Al-Biruni, who visited India in the eleventh century, beef was forbidden for Brahmins, in part because its "thick and cold" qualities were incompatible with Brahmin digestion, although even then they continued to eat other kinds of meat.[11] Cattle slaughter for meat was widespread at least until the twelfth century (Jha 2002, 143), with records of sacrifices in some areas persisting well into the nineteenth century. In summary, while there were moves away from openly subscribing to or condoning beef consumption over the course of several centuries, the consensus of historians seems to be that these developments were much later than is given credit for in everyday discourse or in the political rhetoric of contemporary nationalists. In the earliest Vedic texts, meat eating, including beef, was clearly an acceptable Brahmin practice.

It was not just *what* was eaten that taxed the Indo-Aryans, however, with the later law books elaborating in detail on rules concerning *how* one should take food. Diners were implored to eat sitting down on the ground, alone, in silence, and facing either east or north, for example (Achaya 1994, 64). There were also rules covering how to be a good host, fasting, what to eat during pregnancy, and acceptable festival food. A key distinction, and one that remained notable in eating patterns recorded in the ethnographic monographs of the village studies era in Indian anthropology, was that drawn between *kaccha* foods (usually those boiled in water) and *pucca* foods (if cooked at all, more likely fried in oil or ghee).[12] The former category of food, because it was seen as absorbing the moral qualities of the cook during preparation, posed particular risks if prepared by someone of putatively lower moral substance—that is, someone of lower caste—than the diner. There has been significant discussion of commensality and its importance in India,[13] and on the relationship between food, eating, and caste (Staples 2016, 76–81). For our present purposes, then, let it suffice to note a broad correlation between the elaboration of detailed rules concerning the slaughter and consumption of animals, cows included, and those concerning food preparation and eating more generally. In both cases, at least in terms of their subsequent interpretation over the centuries—and as one might expect in texts authored by Brahmins—the link between caste distinctions, food and commensality begins to become apparent.

CATTLE IN COLONIAL TIMES

Even though it seems unlikely that they went away in the intervening years—which included two centuries of the Moghul dynasty, from 1526—bovine issues subsequently became noteworthy again in recorded histories in the late nineteenth century. This interest might, in part, have been because Hindu perceptions of the cow were at such variance with those of the beef-eating colonial officials who recorded them, coupled with the not unjustified fear that resistance to pro-cow sentiment might damage the British Raj's capacity to govern. But the resurgence of cow protectionism also had much to do with the flourishing of Hindu reform movements, such as the Arya Samaj, founded in 1875 by Swami Dayananda Saraswati. These movements, in turn, blossomed through the improved communication systems of the time, including the railways, the telegraph, and the press.[14] In short, we can see the confluence of divergent contributory factors to create an "ecological niche" (Hacking 1988, 2): an environment in which it was conducive for cow protectionism to become embedded in everyday life. The cow, in this period, was reconstituted as a key symbol in the growth of Indian nationalism—and cattle protection a cause around which, the British feared, Hindus could unite—against a beef-eating British (Gould 2004) and minority Muslim population (Robb 1986, 292).

The Arya Samaj, which called for a return to the Vedic principles that it argued were being ignored by a corrupt priesthood, also popularized cow protection, a cause taken up by a variety of organizations. "The original Gaurakshini Sabha founded by Dayananda," historian Ian Copland notes, "focused initially on propaganda, disseminated via local branches and itinerant preachers called *gauswamis*, then shifted to direct action, which included operations to liberate cattle intended for slaughter and abusing and roughing up Muslim 'cow killers'" (2014, 421n58). The latter activity—which resonates with stories I collected from beef sellers in 2017—helped spark, as Copland also discusses, a series of "cow riots" in northern India during the 1890s. One of these was the Basantpur riot in rural Bihar in 1893, provoked by a Muslim-led procession of cattle intended for slaughter through the Saran District. On the broader impact of cow protection activities, historian Anand Yang noted, "Although initially at least the message of cow protection was phrased in eclectic terms, increasingly the issue was seen as defining people's relationships and activities. Under the *Sabha*'s influence, many everyday routines took on a different order. In many villages, Muslims were refused access to wells" (Yang 1980, 588).

Comparable disorders were reported in Delhi in 1886, in response to the sacrifice of 450 cattle by Muslims during Eid al-Adha, and elsewhere in India over the next decade, as orthodoxy over the cow seemed to spread eastward, from the Punjab and into Bengal.[15] The issue remained a live one into the next century, with, for example, the increased influence of the Cow Preservation League in Calcutta during the 1920s (Copland 2014, 241). The league, along with the cow protection movement more generally, was responsible for a growing number of *pinjarapole*s and *goshala*s (cow protection sanctuaries and societies) that began to spring up across India. What is also noticeable about Dayananda's approach was its emphasis on the economic, or practical, value of the cow. Although the separation of the economic and the religious into discrete realms has rightly been identified as a facet of Western categorizations rather than a universal one, Dayananda was likely aware of this in making the case for cow protection in the terms that he did (Adcock 2010, 304). Given the colonial government's reluctance to interfere in religious matters, framing objections to cattle slaughter in utilitarian terms— that they did more good alive than they did dead—made sense. But for the Arya Samaj, these benefits were not only secular. They drew no distinction between the "economic" and other reasons for protecting cows (Adcock 2010; 2018).

Mahatma Gandhi drew on some of the same arguments. But for him, love of the cow was also a facet of his broader challenge to colonial gastropolitics, which included disrupting associations of meat eating with masculinity and superiority and vegetarianism with effeminacy (Premanand Mishra 2015, 81). Although in his youth Gandhi had been inspired by Swami Vivekananda's oft-invoked prescription of "beef, biceps and Bhagavadgita" (Roy 2002, 66) as an antidote to colonial accusations of Indian effeminacy, he later argued that colonial subjugation would better be overcome through valuing vegetarianism as a cultural practice (Premanand Mishra 2015, 85). As such, despite condemning violence against Muslims who consumed beef,

Gandhi became firm in his support of cow protection, describing it at one point as *the* "central fact of Hinduism" (1999, 374). In the same passage, he went on: "Cow protection to me is one of the most wonderful phenomena in human evolution.... Cow protection is the gift of Hinduism to the world" (374). Although he was also critical in his writings of the way in which cows were treated by his fellow Hindus, some have argued that it was through Gandhi's pronouncements on the matter that the cow's status as holy finally became implanted in the minds of the Hindu population (Korom 2000, 188–89). Anthropologist Frank Korom speculated that "perhaps it was the rupture created by colonial rule that facilitated the need to 'invent' the cow as a Vedic object of veneration" (2000, 189). Certainly, the BJP leader Narendra Modi made regular (but selective) references to Gandhi's rejection of meat in his own promotion of vegetarianism and, while chief minister of Gujarat in the early 2000s, in clamping down on Muslim-owned slaughterhouses in Ahmedabad. He omitted, however, the latter's injunctions against violence toward Muslims (Ghassem-Fachandi 2012, 154–56).

Whatever the causes—and it seems likely that they were multiple—it is clear that the cow veneration of the late nineteenth century reflected a recasting of a Vedic past to deal with present-day issues and the problem of British rule, and in particular to subvert their logic that superiority was rooted in meat eating. This manipulation of bovine history continued into the postindependence period.

BOVINE POLITICS IN POSTINDEPENDENCE INDIA

Cow protection clearly remained an issue after 1947, with a clause inserted into the draft Indian constitution requiring future governments "to 'take steps' to prevent 'the slaughter of cows and calves'" (Copland 2014, 422). Many states did implement legislation between the 1950s and 1970s, albeit with varying provisions.[16] Some, for example, drew a distinction between buffaloes and cows (with the slaughter of former remaining legal), while others treated the two animals the same, and some permitted the slaughter of animals over a certain age or if they had a contagious disease. Kerala and West Bengal—with their large beef-eating populations—took no heed of the directive, and the central government declined to use its powers to impose a national ban. This was in part because the new prime minister, Jawaharlal Nehru, was opposed to any such move (Copland 2014). He was consistent in his commitment to maintaining a secular government. In a speech at Bhilsa toward the end of 1952, he confirmed as much when he told those present that he would "never allow a central legislation to ban cattle slaughter"

(S. Gopal 1997, 211). Three years later, he also threatened to resign if a private member's bill banning cattle slaughter was passed (it was rejected, 96 to 12).

The early part of Nehru's daughter Indira Gandhi's premiership, from 1966 to 1968, was a time during which the hitherto dominant Congress Party was seen as "visibly ailing" (Copland 2014, 413), while the Hindu right—the relatively newly formed Vishwa Hindu Parishad (VHP) and the Shiv Sena, as well as the older Bharatiya Jana Sangh (BJS, a precursor to the currently ruling BJP)—appeared to be making some headway as a political force. A significant part of the right's attempt to mobilize the Hindu electorate was around the old, but never resolved, issue of cow protection (Copland 2014). And although Indira Gandhi, in common with her father, was initially dismissive when the BJS did well in the "cow belt" states of North India in the 1967 general election, there was a noticeable shift in her approach toward appeasing the religious sentiments of the Hindu majority. She set up a committee to explore the feasibility of a ban, a move that played well with the core Hindu electorate, even though the committee's membership was, in the end, intentionally weighted more heavily in favor of those who opposed an all-out ban. Members drawn from the Sarvadaliya Gorasksha Maha-Abiyan Samiti (SGMS)—the Committee for the Great All-Party Campaign for the Protection of the Cow—resigned in protest, but Gandhi's committee was allowed to "muddle on" (Copland 2014, 429). With the immediate concern of a general election over with, Gandhi appeared happy to leave the contentious cow issue unresolved.

A decade or so later, the BJS-supported Janata coalition government that took power after the post-Emergency election in 1977—India's first non-Congress-led government—likewise faced pressure from the SGMS, as well as an indefinite fast by Gandhian Vinobha Bhave to demand an end to cow slaughter. It subsequently vowed to get cattle protection firmly on the statute books, although it was defeated at the polls in 1980 before any legislation was passed. The BJP deputy prime minister L. K. Advani likewise promised the SGMS that his government would act on cattle slaughter in 2002, but he was prevented from doing so by his party's coalition partners. Under the Congress-led coalition government of 2004–2014, the issue once again appeared to have been sidelined, although there were certainly signs, particularly toward the end of that period, that eating beef remained an incendiary issue in Indian society. In areas of communal or caste tensions, there were growing levels of resistance from those who wanted to defend the right to eat beef, as well as a hardening of cow-protectionist views.

In 2006, for example, there were objections to a Dalit Students Union beef stall at the annual Sukoon festival at Hyderabad Central University from both the university administration and the Akhil Bharatiya Vidyaarthi Parishad (ABVP), a student organization associated with the BJP, on the basis that publicly serving beef might stir caste tensions and cause offense (Gundimeda 2009, 130–32).[17] The administration finally came around to the Dalits' point of view, in part because they were supported by the majority of students, but, as Sambaiah Gundimeda pointed out (133), it was clear that beef and cow politics were once again being invoked in the pursuit of wider political goals.

A few years later, in 2012, a comparable beef festival at Osmania University—also in Hyderabad—sparked stronger protest from opponents. A one-hundred-strong group of protestors from the ABVP (now, it seemed, gathering in strength), was reported to have marched toward the site of the festival, where one student was stabbed,[18] two vehicles were set alight, and the police were attacked with stones before fighting back with batons and tear gas. According to the ABVP, the festival was "an evil design by Western countries to split the Indian students"—locating beef eating as a colonial imposition that had been warded off by the nationalist freedom fighters of the 1940s. The Vedas and other ancient texts were not, so far as I am aware, directly referenced, although implicit in the protests—and in subsequent online discussions—was the suggestion that *not* eating beef was a Hindu value which predated both the British and the Mughals. In a separate incident at around the same time, beef was thrown onto the walls of a Hanuman Temple at Kurmaguda in Madannapet, also in Hyderabad, by (as it later transpired) Hindu extremists, apparently in an attempt to foment communal tensions in the area.[19] When four suspects were arrested within two weeks of the incident, BJP activists were reported to have staged a dharna (fast) to protest at what they considered police harassment of Hindu youth.

But it was really a couple of years later, just prior to the 2014 general election in India, that the spotlight was turned more forcibly to the issue of cow protection by the central government. In the run-up to the election, Narendra Modi, the BJP leader and soon-to-be prime minister, promised to crack down on beef exports and to review subsidies and tax breaks allegedly enjoyed by beef export traders. India was, after all, by now one of the world's largest beef exporters. The bulk of subsequent action, however, while certainly encouraged by the BJP's rhetoric, seemed to be occurring at the grassroots level. A year after the BJP's landslide election victory, reports were that violence in relation to cow protection had ratcheted up. In the first week of August 2015, for example, there were newspaper reports of three separate incidents in different locations across Delhi. Ten people were injured in Khajuri Khas Village, in northeast Delhi, when residents attacked a truck carrying cattle, while three similar attacks on five lorries in Mayur Vihar, farther south, took place the next day. On August 4, a suspected cattle thief was reported to have been lynched in the southwest of the city. Concerns about transporting cattle—whether they were on the way to the slaughterhouse or otherwise—appeared to be spreading across the "cow belt," with three attacks in Uttar Pradesh across the course of just one month.[20]

In September 2015, media attention shifted southwest, to Mumbai. The BJP-led state government and the municipal corporation had ordered the temporary closure of slaughterhouses and meat shops for four days in a show of respect to Jains during their Paryurshan Parva festival (which, somewhat ironically, given the protests it invoked, translates as the festival of "forgiveness" or "coming together"). The high court stayed implementation of the ban on the basis that rules could not be made simply to appease one section of society, although Dinesh Jain, a BJP leader in an area heavily populated by Jains, implored the local population to "support our sentiments."[21] The local Shiv Sena, a regionalist party whose views often mirrored those of the BJP, was on this occasion opposed to the ban, apparently because the Jains were outside their Marathi-speaking support base.[22] To the Sena, Jains were as much outsiders as were Muslims (see also Holwitt 2017).

It was, though, the mob killing of a fifty-year-old Muslim man, Mohammad Akhlaq, during Eid al-Adha that year, that received the widest press coverage so far. Akhlaq was murdered in his village of Dadri, Uttar Pradesh, after rumors spread—allegedly started by a local militant Hindu—that he had stored cow beef in his refrigerator. When the son of Sanjay Rana, a local BJP worker, was arrested a few days later for being involved in the murder, Rana both claimed his son's innocence and demanded that Akhlaq's family be prosecuted for cow slaughter. Keen to shore up his party's cow-protectionist credentials, a Congress Party leader, Digvijaya Singh, made clear that his party was also supportive of antislaughter legislation, noting that it had already been in place in many states for a long time.[23] On the other side of the fence, a professor at a college in Kerala was criticized for defending on Facebook a student beef festival hurriedly convened on campus in protest against the Dadri lynching, and—in a further sign of authorities' nervousness at rising tensions—six of the students involved in the festival were suspended.[24]

Almost simultaneously, in Jammu and Kashmir—a Muslim-majority state—the Supreme Court put on hold an order banning the sale and consumption of beef that had previously been passed by the state high court.

The state government had expressed concerns that any ambiguity in the ruling might leave room for "vested political interests to exploit the situation by disrupting communal harmony, amity and peace in the state, or leave the scope to alienate the people of the state from the national mainstream."[25]

Modi, the prime minister, faced mounting criticism for what was seen as his failure to condemn the vigilante attacks, only breaking his silence—as a news piece in *The Indian Express* put it—in August 2016, a month after Dalits had been flogged by *gau rakshak*s (cow protectors) for skinning a dead cow in Gujarat.[26] Modi commented that protestors would achieve more by clearing up the plastic waste on which cattle often feasted, which, he said, was killing more cows than their illegal slaughter. In the same way that Indira Gandhi had sought to appease those opposed to cow slaughter ahead of important elections, it was suggested by opposition leaders cited in the same article that Modi realized the necessity of keeping Dalit and Muslim voters on his party's side.

By the time of my 2016 and 2017 fieldwork in India, bovine-related news stories had become common in the press, with the English-language dailies in Hyderabad, coastal Andhra, and Delhi regularly reporting tallies of injuries caused by vigilantes. Legislative tussles also continued, with the Supreme Court rejecting a petition in January 2017 to impose a nationwide ban on cattle slaughter, on the basis that it would be unconstitutional to interfere with state laws on the issue.[27] In May, the government changed tack, attempting to restrict the sale of cattle for slaughter through new regulations made under the existing Prevention of Cruelty to Animals Act of 1960. The new rules did not ban slaughter per se but rather banned the *sale* of cattle for slaughter at *shandy*s (agricultural markets), a move that, if enforced, would amount to much the same thing.[28] All of the butchers and meat sellers I worked with in Hyderabad, for instance, relied on cattle markets as the source of their beef. Almost immediately, the Madras High Court granted an interim stay on implementing the new rules, particularly Rule 22(b)(iii), which "required a person bringing cattle for sale to the market to furnish a written declaration that it would not be sold for slaughter."[29] In July, the Supreme Court extended the stay to all states, and the government announced plans to revise the rules to deal with objections. By the end of the year—in common with previous attempts over the years to impose a nationwide ban on cattle slaughter—the regulations had been withdrawn.

Nevertheless, as my own informants' stories made clear, difficulties in legislating against cattle slaughter on a national basis did not serve to control decentralized attacks carried out by vigilantes. Hyderabadi beef sellers who, as late as December 2016, had been talking about violence from cow protectionists as a feature of the northern states, by July 2017 were describing their own experiences at the hands of self-appointed *gau rakshak*s, which, again, appeared to be ignored by the state authorities. Indeed, the state scarcely needed legislation when vigilantes were prepared to act as an unofficial "cow task force"—particularly when they appeared immune to prosecution (Jaffrelot 2018). In Maharashtra, for example, state-appointed animal welfare officers had all been former *gau rakshak*s.

At the same time—perhaps because of the ennui that continual reporting of barely differentiated attacks on those suspected of transporting cattle for slaughter had induced—media attention seemed to be turning to some of the other, often perverse, implications of what was going on. One of these strands discussed the hit to the Indian economy that a fear-induced reduction in the beef trade had brought about. With incidents of cow-related violence up significantly, it was unsurprising that for those for whom there was a choice, dealing in beef was a less attractive prospect than it once had been.[30] Beef exports had dropped by 11.5 percent since 2014–15.[31] At around the same time, a professor of economics at Jawaharlal Nehru University (JNU), Vikas Rawal, hit the headlines with his prediction that the nation might have to invest over 1.5 times more than its current defense budget to care for the rising numbers of unproductive cattle caused by a reticence to slaughter them.[32]

A second strand of news stories, particularly noticeable during my second trip to India in 2017, were those with an ironic, or sometimes even farcical, edge. There were, for example, several articles documenting the problem of unproductive cattle, which would once have been sold on via brokers into the meat trade, simply being abandoned and encroaching on other farmers' crops, including by those who might otherwise be expected to support cow veneration. Mohan Tiwari, a Brahmin farmer in Dunbar village in Madhya Pradesh, for instance, was reportedly driven to kill a cow in frustration after it continually entered his field. Similar tales came out of neighboring Uttar Pradesh, where difficulties in selling non-milk-producing cattle had led to comparable problems of stray animals eating crops. Even where cow shelters were available, they struggled to keep pace with the increasing numbers of cows they needed to accommodate. In Chhattisgarh, a BJP panchayat (village council) leader, Harish Verma, was arrested after the mass starvation of cattle in three shelters he ran came to light. Describing the scene at one of the shelters in August 2017, a journalist for the *Indian Express* reported: "Inside the shed, at least 15 carcasses lay rotting, and upwards of 200 emaciated cows, their ribs protruding, herded together on a thick bed of dung, urine and sludge. No fodder or source of water was visible. Seeing humans at the gate, the animals stumbled forward expectantly" (Ghose 2017).

More than two hundred cows were said to have died at Verma's shelters over the previous week alone, although he claimed any problems were a consequence of inadequate government funding.[33] Other stories—by now a well-worn trope in the cattle politics genre—told of Brahmins slaughtering cows to incite communal violence against Muslims, who would be blamed for the animals' deaths.

The situation, in summary, remains unpredictable, particularly with those who might otherwise be counted on as pro–cow protectionists beginning to suffer the unintended consequences of unmitigated veneration. With the BJP elected back to power in 2019, it is difficult to predict how cattle politics might play out, even in the short term, although if the recent past offers any guide to the future, centralized legislation might well remain elusive.

CONCLUSION: COMPLEX HISTORIES

One could read much of the above historical genealogy as an example of classic sociological "unmasking" (Berger 1963), the process that social scientists often utilize—or perhaps even have an inbuilt predilection toward—to "negate a belief, action or statement by showing it to camouflage something unacknowledged" (Baehr, forthcoming). Indeed, accounts such as D. N. Jha's *The Myth of the Holy Cow* (2002), as the very title makes clear, set out to do precisely that, and for broadly the reasons that most social scientists do: to challenge an existing mode of domination. For Jha, exposing Hindu fundamentalist claims that the cow's sacred status is rooted in the Vedas as false also makes a mockery of the suggestion that beef eating was a practice that arrived along with Islam, and for which they can therefore be blamed (2002, ix). Compelling though Jha's argument is—and well grounded in an extensive exploration of the Vedic literature—my aim here is somewhat different, and I take seriously objections to "unmasking" on the basis that, among other things, it "underestimates the lay actor's grasp on the world" (Baehr, forthcoming). That is, I have no interest here in taking an objective position on whether the cow might legitimately be considered sacred or whether it is a status erroneously arrived at by stealth; my concerns are only with exploring the positions those I worked with took in relation to the cow's status, why they took them, and how they managed them in relation to broader contexts on an everyday basis. In short, the question is not whether the cow *should* be venerated, but why, how, and to what effect it is (or, conversely, is not). It is these more fine-grained positions that are missed by some of the wide-angle-lens shots offered by commentators.

Exploring the details of what historians, political scientists, and, in the most recent cases, journalists have said about these things—and the connections between them—enables us to go beyond debates that have been framed in terms of an opposition between economic reductionists on one side and those who take ideological explanations more seriously on the other. Politics has played a role, at various scales, in the ebbs and flows of bovine status over the centuries, not as *alternative* explanations that displace claims about the economic or religious significance of cattle but—as accounts by people like Kandaswamy, whose remarks opened this chapter, demonstrate—as *additional* layers of elucidation. The separation of religion, economics, and politics into different realms might be seen as a particular feature of Western intellectual discourse, rather than a set of distinctions that people in India make on an everyday basis.

Cow-related violence has seen an upsurge since the BJP's electoral landslide in 2014, even if the latter event might be understood as part of the same nationalist phenomenon rather than a cause, in itself, of the former. Vigilantism in the name of the cow has often been portrayed as a break with a postindependence secular past during which there was a broad acceptance that different communities within India had different practices relating to cattle and beef, even if tensions did periodically boil over. Examining the political maneuverings apparent in the historical record, however, suggests that the present is in some ways more continuous with the past than it is sometimes credited as being. With the benefit of hindsight, for example (and the help of Copland's [2014] analysis), we might argue that it was Indira Gandhi's appeasement of those who demanded nationwide legislation preventing cattle slaughter in the mid- to late 1960s that paved the way for the current situation. Certainly, communal rioting was seen to increase in the late 1960s (Jaffrelot 1998, 71).

Going back much further, the historical evidence is also suggestive that when Brahmins *did* stop eating beef and sacrificing cows, it was not simply a response to the cow's objective qualities; it also had to do with getting the moral upper hand over the Buddhists and Jains. And for all Mahatma Gandhi's injunctions against violence against Muslims, his evaluation in 1921 of cow protection as the "central fact of Hinduism" (1999, 374) certainly helped to embed cow veneration as a symbol of the nationalist cause in the run-up to independence. Reference to the cow was a useful shorthand for distinguishing not only between a Hindu majority on the one hand and Buddhists, Jains, Muslims, and Christians on the other; it also distinguished them from their colonial rulers. Marking such distinctions, as political scientists have argued, is an important tactic in uniting a group, whatever their internal differences might be, against a common cause (Basu and Kohli 1998).

Later, too, the cow was invoked as a marker of distinction between higher-caste Hindus and Dalits, for whom beef eating was a source of celebration. But even here, the conflicts that ensued in response to beef festivals were not straightforward clashes between those with opposing beliefs about the rightful status of cattle, a battle of culinary rights versus Hindu sentiment. They were also about student organizations and their politics (Gundimeda 2009). In particular, the Student Federation of India, which lent crucial support to the Dalits' beef stall, was motivated by electoral calculations on campus. Keeping the Dalit electorate on its side also helped to ensure that key positions in the student union were retained by the upper castes (134–35).

One of the reasons why cattle have constituted such a central motif to communal struggles of various kinds is, I suggest, not just because of historical precedent and representation but also because of the visceral, quotidian experience that people had of bovines in everyday life. When I asked my interlocutors questions about the rights and wrongs of cattle slaughter and beef eating, for example, their responses (and particularly those living in the countryside) were not so much philosophical musings as grounded in their daily experiences of bovine animals and their products. Such material proximity to cows and buffaloes—long established in the region—has enabled effective political appeals on the basis of emotions such as "sentiment," the term used by BJP leader Dinesh Jain in appealing to beef eaters and sellers to respect his call to close their operations for several days during the Paryurshan Parva festival in Mumbai. The more general denial of nonvegetarian diets in public or institutional spaces similarly are cast as polite appeals to non-Hindus to be sensitive to their non-meat-eating heritage. Why, after all, should cow-venerating Hindus, often also reliant on bovines for their dairy products, dung, and labor, be required to suffer others eating them in front of them? But seemingly innocuous events such as the ban on beef during the Commonwealth Games in Delhi in 2010 or the notice displayed in the staff canteen at *The Hindu* newspaper, reminding employees that "non-veg food is not permitted in our Canteen premises as it causes discomfort to the majority of the employees who are vegetarian" (Gorringe and Karthikeyan 2014, 20), are actually anything but.[34] Imposing dietary restrictions enables organizations to reinscribe caste discrimination in more palatable terms. The institutionalization of vegetarianism as the norm, in a society where between 60 and 88 percent of the population identifies as nonvegetarian, is clearly political.[35]

These are some of the complexities that underpin the historical contexts in which beef eating and cow protectionism have become reanimated in contemporary Indian society—and, in broad-brush terms, the political fault lines of caste and community that determine the directions they take. What, then, does it mean to follow a nonvegetarian diet in coastal India? Only by locating meat within the contexts of people's day-to-day diets can we begin to make sense of the importance of meat, in both material and symbolic senses, to those who eat it.

CHAPTER TWO

Everyday South Indian Foodways

WHAT does it even mean to be a nonvegetarian in contexts where the cost of eating meat, fish, and eggs renders them a relative rarity? Although at least 60 percent of Indians identify as meat eaters, according to the most recent Organization for Economic Cooperation and Development (OECD) figures, the average Indian consumes only 3.1 kilograms of meat per year. This compares to a global average of 23.1 (OECD, 2017).[1] In the United States, at the other end of the spectrum, people ingest, on average, an annual 97.1 kilograms of beef, pork, poultry, and lamb. Even allowing for what statistics might hide—or the fact that only certain kinds of meat are included in the OECD's data—being a meat eater in New Delhi is clearly very different from being a meat eater in New York. Throw into the mix the observation that many of those who *do* consider themselves vegetarian in India might sometimes eat meat, and the stark dichotomy drawn between the vegetarian and the nonvegetarian in India looks to be on very shaky ground. Consider, for example, the meat dinners clandestinely consumed by putative vegetarians in the darkened restaurant booths of Gujarat (Ghassem-Fachandi 2012); the all-male, whiskey-charged barbecues of the otherwise-vegetarian Yadavs (Michelutti 2008); or the Anandapuram households I encountered where non-meat-eating women sometimes flavored their rice with the gravy of their husband's nonvegetarian curry. That the veg/non-veg divide in India is a sociopolitical distinction as much as it is an absolutely literal one almost goes without saying.

First, examination of *what* meat eaters actually eat in coastal Andhra and Hyderabad, as well as changes to their foodways over the recent past, shows that although meat is important, materially *and* symbolically, routine diets are predominantly vegetarian. This is significant in situating meat—and the different kinds of meanings that it can be made to bear—within daily life.

The practices and politics of meat consumption, especially beef, can be made sense of only in relation to the wider diets and categorizations made around food in the region. It helps to explain, for example, the apparent ease with which diners shift from one type of meat to another, or between eating or not eating meat at all, in relation to the circumstances in which they find themselves. Second, and drawing on this detailed ethnographic material, the social meanings that food can carry are contingent on a wide arc of material and historical circumstances. The symbolic is to a large extent preconfigured by the material. Third, the processes by which foodways shift can themselves communicate attitudes about wider social change. As structuralist thinkers might have put it, we need to look not just at foodstuffs or at meals in isolation but at how they relate to one another or over time.[2] Even the most apparently unremarkable aspects of my friends' diets in South India were shaped by convergences of multiple, not obviously related, factors.[3]

EVERYDAY DINING IN COASTAL ANDHRA

Amaravathi's family—Madiga caste, converted to Christianity—is prominent in this study because of its relative typicality, both in terms of what it consumed on a day-to-day basis and in terms of variations between particular family members over time: what people reported as dietary norms were often circumvented by changing situations.

Morning: Tea, Milk, Breakfast, and Snacks

In Amaravathi's house, the day would begin at around 5:30 a.m., with tea that her husband Jonathan or their adult son Raju collected in a stainless-steel vessel from the tea shop, run from the lean-to veranda of a two-room house, similar to their own, at the end of their street. There were five or six such shops operating at any one time in the village, several of them doubling as breakfast shops, sellers of sweets and cigarettes, evening snack stalls, or, in the last year, "curry points"—vendors of takeaway bags of vegetable or pulse-based side dishes (*kūra*) to be served with rice. The second round of morning tea was prepared in-house, once a family member had gone to buy a sealed plastic bag of pasteurized milk, either directly from one of the dairies in Bhavanipur or, for a few rupees more, from one of the village's own *kirana* shops (convenience stores). Tea in coastal Andhra, always served sweet and milky, was made by adding it—usually a fairly low-grade, commercially available tea powder—to a pot of boiling milk and water as it bubbled on the stove, followed by the sugar.[4] The latter, these days, was mostly white and granulated, purchased at subsidized rates from the village ration shop. In the recent past, the use of *belam* or jaggery—a concentrated, golden-colored and syrupy-flavored cane sugar, purchased in solid hunks or tennis ball–sized spheres—had been more common. Ginger, cardamom, or cinnamon might also occasionally be added to render "special" or "masala" tea, although this was unusual in Amaravathi's house.

The ready availability of tea and instant coffee—the latter also prepared milky and sweet, nowadays with sachets of powder such as Bru or Nescafé, rather than the locally roasted and ground South Indian beans that were once ubiquitous—was also relatively new for many. Two or three decades previously, I was told, tea and coffee were regularly drunk at home only by wealthier people. "We worked as maids in other people's houses," a Mala woman in her mid-fifties told me, "so we all went out early for work in the mornings, and there was never tea, sugar, milk, or that kind of thing in the house." Nor, she added, were tea shops as common as they had become: "They arrived later, after I left that village to get married thirty years ago." The availability of milk was also regionally variable. Even when milk had been easy to come by, however, as it was in Anandapuram, it was only in the last few years that manufacturers had started to produce tea powder, as well as other consumables, in low-cost, single-portion sachets. These were available from the same local shops as sealed plastic packets of toned (semi-skimmed) milk, also a relatively new innovation. This meant that even those without access to enough cash to purchase a larger quantity of tea could now access it at least occasionally and at short notice.

Milk for Amaravathi's one-year old grandson Joseph—son of Raju and his wife, Joshna, who lived with Amaravathi, Jonathan, and Amaravathi's mother, Shanti—was purchased separately from a small-scale buffalo milk trader who lived on the outskirts of the village. "That milk is purer. We know it's not mixed with anything, so it's best for the baby," she told me. While the institutionalized standards of commercially packaged foods have elsewhere been recorded to generate reassurance and trust,[5] Amaravathi's comment reflected an ambivalence, shared by many of my interlocutors, toward such products. Like the urban Moroccan consumers that anthropologist Katharina Graf described—families from socioeconomic backgrounds similar to those of the people I worked with—knowledge of the food's provenance and its trajectory through the food system was often more important in determining quality and safety than standardized packaging and labeling (2016, 77). Amaravathi nevertheless deemed shop-bought milk suitable for making tea with. If any remained after that, it would be given to Joshna, who was then four months pregnant with her second child.

Even for those families with fridges, like Amaravathi's, storing milk for use throughout the day was uncommon. This was partly because consumption habits had developed in the days before refrigeration was a possibility and milk needed to be drunk quickly before it went bad. Tea was prepared as a batch—that could be reheated if not immediately consumed—using a whole bag of milk. Given the regularity of power failures throughout the day, the practice also continued to make good sense.

For breakfast, the family's preference was for *idli*s, steamed circular cakes made from a fermented batter of ground rice and black gram (*urad dal*), a South Indian dish said to date back to the first century CE (Achaya 1994, 25). On the day I interviewed Amaravathi, they had purchased *idli*s freshly made from one of the breakfast shops close to their house; often, she told me, she or her daughter-in-law would make them at home. "If I grind a mixture," she said, pointing to the electric blender ("mixie") on the kitchen shelf behind her, "there will be enough of it for four or five days, so we'll keep it in the fridge and make them ourselves every day until it's all gone. Otherwise, if there isn't any, Jonathan will fetch some from the shop, or we won't bother; sometimes we can adjust with tea. We'll always make sure there's one for Joseph though; he eats it mashed up with warmed buffalo milk." The adults would eat their *idli*s with fresh chutney, usually peanut or coconut, and chili powder. Outside restaurants and tiffin stalls typically served them with *sambar* (a spicy, lentil-based vegetable stew, made sour with tamarind) and chutney, as well as additional chili powder, dal powder, and ghee.

Producing *idli*s—or *dosa*s, fried savory pancakes produced from a thinner version of a batter made with the same ingredients—was a labor-intensive task, and it was even more so during my first visits to Anandapuram in the 1980s. Then, the soaked rice and *urad dal* were hand-ground on the wedge-shaped grinding stones with circular dips in the center (*attu kallu*) that were a common sight outside people's houses. In those days one could often find a group of women from the same village street encircling a single grinding stone, each taking a turn with the *kozhavi* (giant pestle) to transform the soaked grains slowly into a pulp. Now that more households had electric grinders, the task had become easier. Several families also had fridges in which they could store the batter over a few days, so nowadays it tended to be a less communal affair than it once was, when the mixture, like milk, needed to be used up before it went bad and so was shared between several households. Many people, though, still bought breakfast from tiffin shops: some men ate them there while perusing the morning newspapers and conversing with their neighbors; others, like Jonathan, took them home, wrapped in leaves and old newspaper and tied together with cotton thread.

For other families I spoke to or who kept food diaries for me, aside from *idli*s and *dosa*s, which were by far the most popular dishes for those who ate breakfast, other options included puris (deep-fried circular flatbreads made from whole wheat flour, usually served either with chutney or a simple potato curry), chapatis (dry fried bread, sometimes cooked with ghee), or *rava upma* (a semolina-based savory porridge, prepared with mustard seeds, green chilies, curry leaves, and often peanuts or cashews). Eating the leftovers from the previous night's rice and accompaniments was also an option for some families, as was *saddi annam* (leftover cooked rice soaked in cool water overnight) or *gangi* (a thin rice porridge) with salt—the main dishes that people told me they had eaten for breakfast in their natal villages in the past. In those days, I was told, *idli*s and *dosa*s were foods eaten only at special times, such as the Hindu Atla Taddi festival, when women would make small *dosa*s and pray for the health of their menfolk, held on the third night after the full moon in Aswiyuja (the Telugu month straddling September and October). Nowadays they were commonplace, at least in Anandapuram and Bhavanipur.

Afternoon: Lunch and Snacks

After breakfast, the adults in Amaravathi's house went to work: she was an ayah (nurse) in a local nursery, Raju worked as a driver, and Jonathan, whose employment was less predictable, vacillated between coolie work (casual labor) for daily wages, taking in ironing, and occasionally officiating over other households' prayer meetings for a small fee. Unless Amaravathi had already done it, Joshna, who remained in the house with her infant son Joseph, was responsible for preparing lunch. On the day I interviewed her, the two women had cooked together; Amaravathi was gradually passing on her culinary knowledge to her daughter-in-law, who, at some unspecified time in the future, would be expected to take on the whole burden of meal preparation. Lunch was *dondakaya* (ivy gourd) fry, pepper *rasam* (tamarind water, spiced with ground black peppercorns and chili powder), and fresh *dondakaya* chutney.

"We'll always have chutney," Amaravathi told me. "Usually we'll make it ourselves, and it will last a day or two in the fridge." Less perishable chutneys or pickles—those preserved in salt and usually oil—were more likely to be purchased. Industrially prepared and prepackaged condiments, either in glass jars or, for smaller quantities, vacuum-packed in plastic bags, were now available even in some of the small shops in Anandapuram. More popular, though, were those prepared locally; the jar of red chili pickles that Amaravathi showed me came from a local man whose family prepared

2.1   Locally prepared pickles displayed for sale.

batches at home and then sold it in hand-labeled jars from a mobile cart (figure 2.1). Some of the tea shops in Anandapuram sold their own homemade chutney in a similar way, weighed out from large earthenware jars into containers provided by the purchaser. In the past, as I knew from my earlier visits to Anandapuram, chutneys were most often made at home when the key ingredients (such as mangoes, limes, and chilies) were available in abundance. Many of those I spoke to still made at least some of their pickles in this way. They would be stored in clay pots and used in small quantities throughout the year. Sometimes, when cash for vegetables, legumes, or meat was short, they constituted the only flavoring for the rice consumed at mealtimes.

The components of lunch were also dictated, to some extent, by the cooking facilities available. No one in Anandapuram had an oven, so baked or roasted food was not a possibility. Most families cooked on a small range of two gas rings, fired by a cylinder of liquid petroleum gas (LPG), acquired under a government scheme.[6] A diminishing number of households also cooked with firewood over a makeshift hearth or, as had been common before 2000, on kerosene stoves. Most of those whom I witnessed cooking would either cook the curries or the rice first—often using one ring to cook the vegetables, lentils, or meat and the other for the *talimpu* (oil-fried spices added to the curry at the end of its preparation)—protecting dishes already prepared by covering the cooking pot. And while some households prided themselves on serving me hot rice, it was quite usual—and practical, given that food was scooped up to be eaten with the fingers of the right hand—for meals to be served at room temperature.

After breakfast, Amaravathi usually did not eat anything else until lunchtime. Joshna sometimes ate a piece of fruit, maybe a banana or a mango that she would share with her son. Jonathan's parents had Banganapalle mango trees back in his natal village and, when they were in season, he would bring home boxes of them. Jonathan was also partial to a midmorning snack, particularly if he was not working or was ironing in the house. "He likes to have some *bonda*s [balls of potato fried in gram flour batter] or some savory mixture at around 10 a.m.," said Amaravathi. "He has a habit of eating things from the shop after his meals, or if there are savories or other things left over from festival times in the house, he'll eat them here. He loves sweet peanut cluster balls or *chakralu* [a fried savory snack]." Joshna admitted that she too might sometimes eat shop-bought cookies—either Britannia Good Day or Parle-G[7]—although only the leftover pieces from those that had been fed to her son, Joseph.

Nataraja, who ran a local *kirana* shop, told me that lots of adult customers bought small packets of cookies, now sealed in plastic wrapping rather than the folded waxed paper of a few years earlier, to go with their tea, in the midmorning, midafternoon or, early evening. Children, he said, mainly went for the chips and sweets, tantalizingly displayed in jars or strung up like bunting across the shop front (figure 2.2). Like the bottles of fizzy soft drinks that he also sold, such products were available now in much smaller bottles and packages than in the past, making them more widely accessible. In the case of fizzy drinks, the range—including India-specific Limca and Thums Up, as well as global brands—was similar to that of the 1980s, although following the opening up of markets after 1991, nearly all available soft drinks were owned either by Coca-Cola or Pepsi. Village-based sellers nowadays kept the drinks chilled in fridges—sometimes supplied by the drink companies—unlike in the past, when the bottles were kept only slightly cool in buckets of tepid water. "Party-sized" plastic liter bottles, occasionally purchased for prayer meetings or other events at which larger numbers of people needed to be honored with a cool drink, had also become available in the last few years, served at such events in disposable plastic cups.

If Raju, Amaravathi and Jonathan's son, was working locally, he would return to the house to eat at lunchtime. If his driving took him further afield,

2.2   A village shop, sweets and snacks displayed in jars on the counter or strung up across the shop front.

he would eat with his clients. If he was likely to return home late in the evening, after everyone else had eaten and gone to bed, they would leave him dry chapatis, cooked without oil, which he could eat with some chutney or leftover side dishes from the fridge. Amaravathi always came home for lunch and often ate with Joshna; Jonathan ate when he was hungry, either before or after her. In many households, though, the women still served the men their food, which they would eat with their right hands from stainless-steel (or sometimes melamine) plates, most often sitting on the side of one of the charpoys (beds), on a stool, or, less common nowadays, cross-legged on a mat on the floor. The women served themselves or each other. Older people I spoke to recalled that in the past it was more common to eat from an aluminum *ginne* (bowl).

Unlike the more communal Muslim dining occasions in Kerala that Osella and Osella (2008a) describe, families in Anandapuram rarely all ate together, seated in a circle on a floor mat or around a table. Even those who ate at the same time usually ate sitting alongside one another, a formation that more closely matched "the Hindu style of always leaving one or two women standing to serve and of diners eating sitting in a line, not looking at each other" (187; see also figure 2.3). While everyday meals were less formal, with diners sometimes serving themselves rather than women serving the men and eating in hierarchical order (the men and most senior family members eating first), they nevertheless retained elements of this structure, amended as necessary to accommodate changing work patterns and other commitments. "The smallest, meanest meal," as Mary Douglas put it long ago, "metonymically figures the structure of the grandest, and each unit of the grand meal figures again the whole meal—or the meanest meal." (1972, 67). Festival meals in Anandapuram—for example, to mark weddings—remained almost structurally identical to those eaten every day, with the addition of extra side dishes and more elaborate versions of the central ones, such as the insertion of *pulao* or biryani rice as well as plain boiled rice, or more complex masalas to flavor the vegetable, dal, and meat dishes (see Staples 2014, 69).

The rice and curries would always be followed, in Amaravathi's household, like most in Anandapuram, with curd. Diners mixed it into their rice with salt and, if it was particularly thick, a little water. For celebratory meals, plain curd might be replaced with a more sophisticated raita of curd, red onions,

2.3   A festive meal in Anandapuram, diners seated in conventional linear fashion.

green chilies, and coriander leaves. "We buy half a kilogram of curd a day from the dairy for thirty rupees," Amaravathi told me. "It's tastier, and smoother than if we made it ourselves at home, like we used to, and they make it there with toned milk, so it also contains less cholesterol, which means it's better for us. These days, lots of things you couldn't buy before are coming readymade." Curd was also available for purchase by the plastic cup from the same buffalo owners who supplied villagers with fresh milk.

What side dishes the family ate depended on what Jonathan, who, like most village men, did the bulk of the shopping, brought back from the market, where he would select whatever was "cheapest and best." Common vegetables included gourds and marrows of various kinds, okra, eggplants, tomatoes, potatoes and other root vegetables, green beans, leafy green vegetables, and, these days, the once exotic carrots, beets, and cauliflowers. Raju would also sometimes pick up bargains if he spotted them while on the road. Other families shopped in a similar way, some men—those with refrigerators—buying vegetables only once or twice a week from the town market and leaving the women who did the cooking to decide in which order to use them. Others, who had neither refrigerators nor the kind of cash flow that enabled them to buy in bulk, tended to purchase vegetables more regularly, at slightly higher rates, from a vegetable trolley that passed through the village every day. All those I interviewed, however, were discerning in their shopping: in addition to feeling the produce and inspecting it closely before committing to a purchase, many would travel farther afield for what they perceived to be better-quality goods. When prawns were to be served in Amaravathi's house, for example, Jonathan told me, with some pride, that he traveled six miles on his moped to buy the freshest and tastiest rather than those at the local market. For cow beef, people were prepared to travel even farther.

Evening: Dinner

As in other households, dinner in Amaravathi's house would often be a repeat of lunch, if there was enough food left over, sometimes with a vegetable side dish freshly prepared. Tonight, she told me, she would boil fresh rice to eat with what was left of the *rasam*, and each family member would also have a one-egg omelet, flavored with sliced red onions, salt, and chopped green chilies. Two or three times a week, they would supplement the vegetables with a lentil-based dish—*pappu charu* (a thin but flavorsome lentil soup with chili and onions) or a slightly thicker dal, often mixed with green leaves or another vegetable—or, as on the day I interviewed them, an egg or an egg-based dish. They would again follow the rice and side dishes with curd, a final helping of rice, and, directly after dinner, a glass each of buttermilk—seen as good for the digestion—made with whatever was left of the curd, mixed with drinking water and salt. Other families ate in very similar ways: always white rice (unless diabetes, some other ailment, or a fast demanded that they eat chapatis as an alternative), lentil- and/or vegetable-based accompaniments, pickles or chutneys, and curd and/or buttermilk.[8] A *pulusu*, or wet curry, was often preferred over a fry, because it could be used to flavor more rice.

Like nearly all families in Anandapuram, Amaravathi's family had a BPL (Below Poverty Line) ration card, which entitled them to certain quantities of highly subsidized comestibles through the Public Distribution System (PDS). In the village, this was operated through a registered "ration shop" (the official designation was a "fair price shop," although I never heard anyone in Anandapuram use this phrase) run by the elected village elders from the community storeroom. Provisions available included rice, lentils, sugar, cooking oil, and onions. Depending on the quality of the rice, which was variable across the year, Amaravathi would use it to make either *idli*s—if the rice was young, which meant the grains tended to stick together and become indistinct if boiled—or, if it was better quality, their main meals. If there was a surplus of ration rice, there was the potential for families to sell it "on the black" for a slight profit to village breakfast shops, and to use the income to subsidize their own purchase of better-quality rice from the bazaar in Bhavanipur, where they would also purchase spices and other groceries. Families with school-aged children also benefited from the government's national midday meal scheme, which ensured that children received a daily meal of rice and vegetarian accompaniments, served through schools.

Other than occasional snacks from the village tea shops, Amaravathi seldom ate ready-prepared foods from outside the home, despite the growing number of "curry points" selling small plastic bags of ready-made accompaniments for rice that now lined the main road from Anandapuram to Bhavanipur. I counted twenty-nine ready-made-food vendors on a walk to the town center, a distance of just over half a mile, one day in 2017. These included established restaurants, college messes (aimed at students, who would pay a monthly fee to eat all their meals there), and "meals hotels," at which one might eat set rice-based offerings. There were also more transitory arrangements on stalls and trolleys, including "curry points," tiffin shops (selling *idli*s, *dosa*s, and other fried snacks), several chicken *pakora* stalls, Chinese food outlets (selling stir-fried noodle dishes and cauliflower or chicken Manchurian), and, together in a row of five, Muslim-run meat biryani stands.

2.4   Dining out Western- or "continental"-style in Bhavanipur.

Purchases might either be consumed from disposable plates while standing in the street or packaged to take home. There was also a "continental restaurant"—the phrase used to describe outlets serving what were perceived as Western dishes—called Rock Starz. Its menu included burgers (chicken or vegetarian) and other processed chicken items, milkshakes, and french fries. Similar fare was available from the four "fast food centers" (figure 2.4) and ice cream parlors on the road out from the town center toward the main bus stand. Additionally, there were now restaurants offering dishes more closely associated with North India: tandoori preparations, vegetarian and nonvegetarian, including paneer (country cheese), dishes containing peas and mushrooms, and naan bread (none of which I had ever seen cooked at home).

For Amaravathi's family, with five members, it was considered cheaper to prepare food at home rather than to buy takeout. For other families, however, the small plastic bags of *sambar*, dal, *rasam*, or *perugu charu* (fried mustard seeds, curry leaves, onions, green chilies, salt, and turmeric mixed with curd) prepared en masse in domestic kitchens and made available through curry points, were sometimes cost-effective. For a meat-eating family with one vegetarian family member, for instance, on Sundays it was cheaper to spend twenty rupees on a bag of *sambar* for that member of the household to consume over two meals than to make a batch just for them. Others told me they would buy curries three or four times a month to cover occasions when time for cooking was limited. For elderly widowers who did not have relatives around to care for them, as for students living away from home without cooking facilities or, often, the skills required to prepare their own food, curry points were a more regular source of sustenance, particularly now that a couple of families had picked up on the trend and were selling bags of curries in the village. They were cheaper than eating out in a restaurant or cafeteria, and the main source of sustenance—the rice—would be still be home-boiled, which was considered less of a threat, either to health or perceived bodily integrity, than eating it cooked outside the home.

Younger people in the village were perhaps more likely to eat out than people like Amaravathi, who was 52 and well settled in her culinary habits. Even Joshna, however, who was in her early twenties, was adamant that, even as a local college student, she had not eaten out or taken snacks with her friends. The only exception, she said, was once joining her peers for an ice cream to celebrate the completion of their degrees at one of the parlors that had sprung up in Bhavanipur in recent years. Now if she wanted ice cream, she added, her husband Raju would take her into town on his motorbike, or he would buy it and bring it to the house for her. "Otherwise, if she wants something special to eat, we'll prepare it for her here," Amaravathi interjected. Both women, and particularly the older one, were very keen to assert that they, if not their menfolk, kept their eating within the household. Although contexts in which younger people could eat out or partake of cold drinks and snacks with their friends were becoming much more common, especially among incoming, lower-middle-class male students in Bhavanipur, for Amaravathi these were still not entirely respectable places for women of her own family to be seen in. Nor were novel foods necessarily positively received. "Raju brought us noodles once," Joshna said, "but I didn't like them at all; they were like little snakes." Amaravathi nodded in agreement. "If we have anything from outside," she said, "it's most likely to be egg puffs." She smiled wistfully at the thought of them. "We like those pastries very much."

2.5   Door-to-door vendors selling freshly fried savory snacks of *gari* (left) and *bonda*s.

Other families were more open to ready-made foods from outside, although even then they generally saw such items as supplementary to rather than a replacement for a meal. "Sometimes our son will bring stir-fried egg noodles from the bazaar," said Varun, a forty-year-old television repairman, who ran his business from home. "But we'll share one portion between two or three of us, so it's very light. If we buy chicken *pakora*s [deep-fried chicken snacks in a gram flour batter, usually with curry leaves and other seasonings] from a stall outside, though, we might eat those as a replacement for a curry with our evening meal." On the day I interviewed Varun and his wife, Kumari, we were interrupted—in line with their description of their daily eating patterns—by the arrival of a door-to-door vendor of *gari*s (black gram fritters), *bonda*s (deep-fried and battered potato snacks), and chutney (figure 2.5). She would come every day at around 4 p.m., and if they had money at hand and were hungry, they would buy and eat some.

Meat Eating

In terms of meat consumed at home, Amaravathi's family ate beef, chicken, fish, prawns, and—very rarely, because of the price—goat mutton. After Joseph's delivery, they had bought goat brains for Joshna; they were seen as good for her health and consequently would better equip her to feed her infant son. Pork was the only meat they actively avoided. When I asked Amaravathi why, she scrunched up her nose in a gesture of disgust that had become a familiar response when I asked others the same question. She said it was because they had never eaten it.

As for almost every family in Anandapuram, meat was eaten every Sunday or when they had visitors, and Jonathan or Raju would go to buy it from the market early on Sunday mornings, when they also purchased most of the vegetables for the week. Sometimes they would decide what to have before they went; sometimes they would just buy what looked best when they got there. Amaravathi's mother, Shanti, always expected beef. It was, she said, what Madigas of her generation had always eaten. The rest of the family, however, would often have chicken, fish, or prawns instead. "We mostly have chicken now," Amaravathi said. "Beef is costlier nowadays, and it also sells out earlier, so it's harder to get good-quality meat unless you get to the market early in the morning. To get the best, really you need to be there at 6 a.m. on a Sunday; a few years ago, you could always get it at least until 10 a.m."

She went on: "Before, most people didn't take it—it was only for Scheduled Caste people, like us, for Malas and Madigas. Now the Malas and Madigas are taking it less often, and everyone else is eating it too! I think it's because doctors have promoted its health benefits. It's good for strength. Other creatures, like goats and chickens, eat all kinds of rubbish, so beef is purer and healthier as a meat. Sheep meat also has a lot of fat, which beef doesn't have." And, mirroring the comments from other Anandapuram residents that I will discuss in chapter 5, she added, "But the government, it doesn't make much of a difference around here to what meat we eat. We eat what we choose."

Alcohol

If some families were circumspect in talking about eating beef, they were even less likely to volunteer information about alcohol consumption, although for many men in the village it formed a significant part of their daily intake. Kirthi was one of the few women to refer to it in describing her family's eating habits, telling me that her husband, Ramu, would always take ninety milliliters of cheap brandy at three points during the day to sustain him while he was begging in nearby small towns. During this time, unless people gave him food, he would not eat. It was clear from what others told me, however, that a lot of the evening consumption of fried snacks was to accompany, or soak up, alcohol, most often plastic packets of arrack or domestically produced bottled spirits, especially whiskey, brandy, and rum. There was a particular concentration of snack stands outside the one remaining bar and liquor stall in Bhavanipur, all of which did good business in the evenings. A place even more male-dominated than the meat market, the bar served drinks in small bottles for immediate consumption or to be taken away and drunk at home. Several men told me that they needed liquor to stimulate their appetites sufficiently to be able to consume rice, which in turn would enable them to sleep at night. Women did not usually drink, although there were a few, mostly elderly, women who were known to do so. In general, however, alcohol—like meat, for those who were otherwise supposed not to eat it—was an expected if not quite acceptable transgression for men only. In common with meat, certain forms of alcohol could also be used to index class and sophistication.

FOOD IN THE CITY

Overall, the diets described above were very similar to those of my interlocutors in Hyderabad. This is as one might expect, since both groups came from similar socioeconomic backgrounds. Two daily rice meals, accompanied by lentil and vegetable side dishes, were the norm, and certainly the aspiration. Unlike in rural regions of coastal Andhra, however, my Hyderabad friends had less access to fresh dairy products sold directly from cow or buffalo owners, nor, in most cases, did they have the opportunity to keep chickens and grow some of their own vegetables. Among the Hyderabadi Muslims I knew, meat made more regular appearances on the menu than among the Christians of Anandapuram—albeit in smaller quantities at each appearance—although a number of Dalit households I spent time with in Bhavanipur also aspired to eat beef more than once a week, even if they were unable to achieve it. Several Bhavanipur Mala and Madiga families, for example, recalled childhoods when they ate beef, then much cheaper than the alternatives, three or four times a week, suggesting that variations related to caste and community rather than location per se.

It was also true that a wider range of fruit and vegetables, as well as everything from industrially produced cereals, such as cornflakes, to sliced Western-style bread and bottled pasta sauces, were potentially available in Hyderabad, even though this range was hardly discernible in the diets of those I knew the best. When, for example, I visited my friend Miriam in 2017—a Roman Catholic who had worked as a cook for my family when we lived in Hyderabad in 2005 and 2006—I initially assumed that offering me branded curd from a sealed plastic tub rather than homemade curd from a steel pot was a sign of modernity, something that differentiated her dietary habits from those of Anandapuram. Only later did it dawn on me that she had purchased curd because it was not something they had in the house on a regular basis, and so—curd requiring the addition of existing curd for its preparation—she would have been unable to make it for me at short notice.[9] Neither was it available from domestic cattle owners, as it was in Anandapuram and Bhavanipur, so commercially available varieties were the only option. And although she purchased products such as dried spices, oil, and flour in sealed, commercially packaged plastic containers, there was no evidence on her shelves of the ready-made meals and preprepared flavoring pastes that occupied increasing shelf space in the city's supermarkets. The ready-to-eat cartons of paneer butter masala, tomato rice, and other side dishes displayed alongside pots of instant noodles were, based on my observations of those purchasing them, targeted at middle-class students or single office employees working away from home rather than families (Dittrich 2009, 273–74; figure 2.6).

Miriam's family's weekly diet, like Amaravathi's, was based on rice and vegetable curries, with meat as an occasional weekend treat. Like many of those I interviewed in Hyderabad, however, they were more likely to eat leftovers from the previous day rather than *idli*s or *dosa*s for breakfast, mainly because there were no roadside stalls selling them in the vicinity of their house. There were also small variations in recipes among my Hyderabadi interlocutors that reflected the city's Mughal heritage and continued Muslim influence, as well as the ready availability of particular ingredients. Fish curries, for example, sometimes came prepared in creamier, cashew nut–enriched sauces rather than the tamarind-and-tomato gravy in which it would have been served in Anandapuram. Chapatis—thin, perfectly round, and puffed up directly on the gas flame rather than the thicker, unevenly shaped breads cooked in oil or ghee that were more common in the village—as well as biryanis and dishes featuring paneer were also more commonplace. *Keema* (minced beef), unheard of in Anandapuram, was a preparation regularly requested by Muslim customers from butchers in Hyderabad; buyers would fry it with spices and eat it as a dry dish with chapatis.

In terms of preparation, while gas rings rather than kerosene stoves or firewood were now usual in both locations, pressure cookers were more regularly used in the city to speed up cooking times. Miriam's daughters, in their mid- to late teens at the time of my last visit, were also more knowledgeable than young village women, like Joshna, about what they referred to as "junk foods." One of them, fifteen-year-old Esther, confided that her favorite foods came from Pizza Hut and KFC—rare treats, even for her, but

2.6 Supermarket display of ready-to-eat meals and instant noodles, marketed toward urban office workers and students.

more known and discussed among her peers than those in Anandapuram. Organic foods, marketed in relatively new specialty shops in the affluent areas through which Miriam and her relatives passed on the way to and from work (see Dittrich 2009, 275), did not feature in any of the food-related conversations I had in Hyderabad (or elsewhere).

DECIPHERING ANDHRA CUISINE

At first glance, the diets of those I worked with in both coastal Andhra and Hyderabad, despite slight variations, not only appeared remarkably consistent but had remained so across time, at least over the decades in which I had been traveling to India: *idli*s and tea for breakfast, two rice meals with spicy vegetarian accompaniments and then curd, meat once a week and to mark festivals. Such meals were exemplars, in fact, of a core-fringe-legume pattern, with the "fringe" (the flavorsome side dish) making the "core" (the plain boiled rice) more appetizing (Mintz and Schlettwein-Gsell 2001, 41). Examined more closely, however, it became clear not only that my interlocutors' foodways were constantly changing, in small ways and more significantly, but also that even the most apparently unremarkable aspects of their diets were shaped by convergences of multiple, not obviously related factors.

The style in which Amaravathi took her morning tea, for example, was not simply a matter of personal taste, of culturally embedded preferences inculcated over time, or of the social meanings attached to the sharing of tea with particular people at particular junctures in the day, even as it was informed by all of those things. The very presence of tea in her arc of choices emerged out of connections between the colonial powers that established tea plantations in nineteenth-century India (see Besky 2014); the ecological conditions that saw the flourishing of the dark, tannic varieties of tea for which India is renowned, rather than the green teas of China (Besky 2014); and the economic imperative of finding local outlets for the poorer-quality leaves deemed unfit for more lucrative export markets. Just as New Zealand meat traders developed trade with Papua New Guinea to dispense with the fatty lamb cuts that they could not sell to more affluent markets (Gewertz and Errington 2010), so too, under the conditions of contemporary capitalism, were local markets nurtured for what might otherwise be the waste products of tea production. The fact that Amaravathi, like her fellow villagers, or like Miriam in Hyderabad, also drank it heavily sweetened and with milk referenced the British innovation of serving it that way—a combination that had developed in tandem with the rising popularity of sugar among the British working class (Mintz 1985). Sugar was a "proletarian hunger-killer" (Mintz 1979, 60), making tea a substitute for breakfast when funds for solid foods were not available.

The fact that poorer families could now afford to brew tea sometimes for themselves was made possible by the introduction of single-portion packets of tea, designed to access, as marketing guru C. V. Prahalad put it, "the bottom of the pyramid" (2009). This, in turn, had been made possible by innovations that made such packaging and storage technically and economically plausible. Economic liberalization since the 1990s—which saw the opening up of Indian markets to international companies and brands—certainly helped to extend the fronds of market capitalism ever further into the lives of even the most economically marginalized citizens. It also meant that the tea tasted different too. Nowadays it was sweetened with highly refined, white granulated sugar rather than jaggery, and was often mixed with semiskimmed, pasteurized, and commercially packaged milk from Jersey cow hybrids—crossbred for their milk yields—rather than creamy, home-boiled milk from local buffaloes. Such changes in taste might well have prompted thoughts about social change more generally. It also meant, however, that tea, like other changing products, had potentially less capacity to evoke the social contexts of the past than it might once have had (Sutton 2001).

This brief analysis of the genealogy of Amaravathi's morning tea only scratches the surface of the complex, historically contingent food systems that brought it to her cup. A comparable and more sustained analysis could be applied to every aspect of Amaravathi's diet, as well as to the processes via which it was sourced, cooked, and presented. For the present purposes, I simply wish to illustrate the point that what the people I worked with ate, mostly without thinking much about it at all, relied on a mesh of interconnections between history, technical innovation, ecology, politics, economics, and social practices. This interplay of dynamic factors also contributed to how diets had changed, as well as to how the meanings that different foods carried were liable to shift or be manipulated.

The Green Revolution of the 1960s, for example, which ushered in the industrialization of Indian farming by introducing new, higher-yielding varieties of rice and new technologies, from pesticides to tractors, had had an enduring impact on the diets of those I worked with.[10] For many, the changes of that era heralded a shift from *sangati*, a heavy porridge made from *ragi* (finger millet) or *jonnalu* (sorghum), along with hand-pounded rice, to industrially processed rice as a staple. It had done so to the extent that many of the younger people growing up in Anandapuram were not even aware of the existence of those earlier preparations. And while new farming methods had no doubt increased yields, they had also, according to my older research participants, changed the flavors and mouth-feel of what they ate. "The taste was better back then," said Abdullah, wistfully. It was common trope among people over fifty. "The smoke from the firewood flavored the food more," he went on, "and because vegetables were grown in buffalo dung, without 'medicines,' they were more natural. You could even eat raw vegetables then, and they would really taste good. Now they are more bitter."

Such comments were noticeably consistent across other parts of India (and indeed elsewhere). Farmers, herders, and artisans from comparable age groups in rural Rajasthan, for example, talked of a decline in taste and nourishment, which, as was the case for my interlocutors, they blamed on chemical fertilizers and new grain varieties (Gold 2015, 552–53). Food talk became a medium through which to critique modernity itself, even as they partook of it. But material changes in the food also changed what it meant. Rice, for instance, had long been aspired to in South India but was now metonymic of food itself: instead of asking whether I had eaten, the question people in Anandapuram asked me was "Have you taken rice?" Other foods—there only to stimulate appetite for the main component of the meal—remained secondary.[11]

Over time, the symbolic dominance of rice might again shift in relation to the material circumstances in which it is engaged. Even as recently as the late 1980s, for example, women I knew in Anandapuram spent hours shaking and sifting through uncooked rice in order to separate the grains from loose pieces of husk and stray stones that, in the intervening years, the industrialization of rice packaging had virtually eliminated. No one ever told me that they wished to return to doing that painstaking work, even if they missed the drawn-out conversations with neighbors, the tempo of which were determined by the task, that often accompanied it. But the visceral engagement with almost every grain of rice that they prepared had also made for a different kind of embodied relationship between rice and cook than that established through the more fleeting encounter of simply washing and boiling the rice that typifies contemporary preparation practices. It meant rice was more important in structuring the day, and consumption of it more valuable because of the time and effort invested in it. How rice was subsequently eaten had also changed. The ratio of rice to accompaniment had decreased in Anandapuram over the last thirty years, at least among families whose income levels had increased, and whose work had shifted from heavy manual labor in the paddy fields or pulling rickshaws to more sedentary occupations, such as driving cars or working in call centers.[12]

A related change was that the availability and consumption of snacks—from industrially produced biscuits to savory street food—had also risen in Anandapuram, Bhavanipur, and, I suspect, Hyderabad over the past two decades. Correspondingly, the dishes served to flavor the rice were less fiery than in the past, and the spices were often bought ready-ground in sealed packets rather than purchased loose and roughly pounded at home on a grinding stone, giving different textures as well as subtly different flavors to domestic cuisine. "My mother's curries had fewer masalas [mixtures of spices] than people use now," Venkatarao, a man in his early seventies, recalled. "She would only use peppercorns, ginger, curry leaves, coriander, and *carom* [chili powder], lots of *carom*. People don't have the capacity for that much chili powder anymore." Foods not only had less taste but, he implied, were now more bafflingly complicated than in the past, when a more straightforward way of life had been possible. Nevertheless—and in direct contrast to Amaravathi's earlier comment that milk direct from the buffalo herder was purer than packaged milk from the dairy—my friends in Anandapuram at the same time urged me to buy spices in sealed packets rather than those sold loose from sacks in the market, because they were less liable to be contaminated or, in local parlance, "duplicate." There was an ambivalence toward change, as things seemed to be simultaneously getting better and worse.

Other dietary changes—hinted at in the prolonged description of Amaravathi's family's dietary habits above—included a gradual shift, as witnessed elsewhere (Dittrich 2009, 273–74), toward more processed and convenience foods, from noodles, pickles, and jam to biscuits and other confectioneries. Eating outside the house or bringing into the household dishes that had been prepared outside it was also a growing trend. Meals in some households—even as they remained almost as structurally consistent as those Mary Douglas (1972) rendered into algebraic equations in her seminal essay "Deciphering a Meal"—had become increasingly sophisticated over the decades. When I was called to dine at people's houses on my most recent trips to India, for example, there were seldom fewer than three dishes on offer (a fried vegetable, a *pulusu*, and a lentil dish of some kind), even before curd, chutney, sweets, appetizers, and postprandial fizzy drinks and bananas were taken into account. In the 1980s and early 1990s I was much more likely to have been served a single curry with the rice. Published recipes—online, on TV, and in recipe books, magazines, and newspapers—had also expanded the repertoires of a number of the younger women whose houses I dined in beyond those they had learned from their mothers and mothers-in-law. Here, food had become a medium through which women (for most domestic cooks I encountered remained women) could communicate both knowledge and sophistication, as well as demonstrate appropriate hospitality.

In short, then, this documentation of daily diets shows at least three things. First, it indicates that meat, while important, played a materially small part in the diet of most meat eaters, whose routine menus were predominantly vegetarian. Second, it demonstrates that the social meanings which food can carry are contingent on a wide arc of material and historical circumstances. Third, it suggests that it was not just that food—in the sense of identifiable dishes or preparations—was meaningful, but also that the processes of change in foodways could themselves serve to communicate attitudes about wider social change.

CONCLUSION: MATERIAL SYMBOLS

Diets have changed, and continue to change, in relation to wider food systems and other, broader factors that stretch beyond either the immediate political situation in India or well-trodden practices related to caste and community. The reasons for this include, among other things, the industrialization of food production; the impact of economic liberalization and globalization; ecological change and the impact, specifically, of the Green Revolution; and technological and infrastructural developments, including the wider availability of refrigeration and of gas for cooking. Shifts in gender and kinship relations within particular families across the course of life, as well as more widely, also have had an impact on the ways in which people source, prepare, and eat food, and its symbolic value. Interactions between these crosscutting elements help to ensure that the arc of contingent possibilities from which food choices at ground level are made is continually shifting, and thus warrants our continuous attention.

The symbolic meanings of food—what it might signify—also change over time, and they do so not separately from but in relation to its materiality. Factors relating to cost, quality, and the ways in which food was sourced, prepared, and eaten, all had a bearing on what it could mean. One of the key messages conveyed through the consumption of food in contemporary Anandapuram, for example, was about social change and the ambivalence with which most inhabitants experienced it. The advantages conferred by the food system—in terms, for example, of savings in cost, time, and domestic labor, as well as packaged products sometimes seen as less vulnerable to adulteration—were tempered by nostalgia for a past when things were simpler and food apparently tasted better.

Such messages were evoked not by arbitrary or static meanings invested in the food but via the more visceral experience of tasting and feeling it. *Idlis*, for example, were said to taste different than they had done in the past, because of new varieties of post–Green Revolution grain and the fact that they were now steamed over a gas flame rather than a wood fire, which used to impart a faintly smoky aftertaste. Because the soaked rice and *urad dal* were quickly ground together in electric grinders rather than manually—and so in the more private environment of a single home rather than slowly and collectively around a grinding stone in the street—they also *felt* different in the mouth. So, while *continuities* in sensory provocations evoked memories of past events in the way that Sutton (2001) describes, subtle changes in the way things tasted, felt, and looked helped to convey—and enabled people to talk about—change in the wider social environment. On the one hand, change had put things that were not previously available within reach. On the other hand, the value of those things had in themselves diminished.

The meanings that different objects can convey, however, are not uniformly bound up in their particular materialities. Take tea as an example again. Very often, in people's houses and in village tea shops where I was known, the drink would be served to me in a tiny china cup, rather than one of the more usual small glasses or stainless-steel vessels that were also used to drink water from. It was, as I was told repeatedly over the years, a way of honoring my status and showing respect. The china cup, it was clear, was not intrinsically more valuable, and—frequently chipped and grimy from past use—was often considerably less appealing. But here it was less the cup's material qualities—despite, perhaps, its reference to a British colonial past—that enabled it to convey respect, but how it stood in contrast to other drinking vessels. Giving me something different to drink out of than other tea shop customers signified my difference in status. In a similar way, a flower-patterned melamine plate might be used to serve me dinner rather than the (intrinsically more valuable) stainless-steel plates or bowls used by the hosts.

Here, then, the cup and plate appear as signifiers fairly straightforwardly in the sense explained by Roland Barthes ([1961] 1997). However, material changes in tea and how it is drunk—the availability of single-portion packs of tea and, thanks to refrigeration and other changes in the dairy industry, a more consistent supply of homogenized milk, for example—*did* have an impact on what offering me a cup of tea in Anandapuram could mean. The fact that almost everyone could now offer it, at any time, diminished its capacity to convey a special level of hospitality to the receiver and prestige to the host, because there was no longer a social demarcation between those who could serve it and those who could not. It had become everyday, even as changes to its taste both celebrated and critiqued modernity.

Recognizing that what food signifies can and does change in relation to material conditions helps to rejoin the split between symbolism and materiality, and also helps explain changing patterns in beef consumption and the meanings attached to them. In this context, how did beef make its way into dinner pots? Indeed, given the apparent social injunctions against it, and the all-too-real risk of violence, how is it even possible for such a trade to operate?

CHAPTER THREE

From Cattle Shed to Dinner Plate

THE word in Anandapuram was that, if you wanted to be sure you were buying *āvu mānsam* (cow meat) rather than buffalo, you needed to keep your ear to the ground and be prepared to travel, at the right time, to places that were known for it. After hearing, over the years, numerous stories of arduous late-night journeys to remote spots in search of cattle and the remarkable meat those expeditions yielded, I had become somewhat cynical about whether these stories were anything more than tall tales designed to glorify regular trips in search of what was probably, in reality, only water buffalo. Could those who purchased the meat brought back by those enterprising village men be sure it was really the flesh of a cow that they were consuming, or was it the act of *believing* that it was that gave those diners more satisfaction than that gained from the *eddu mānsam* (buffalo meat) they could more readily purchase from the town's market? Questions about what people knew and did not know, as well as what they actively avoided knowing, are significant in understanding how the beef trade works in India. But in answer to the specific question of whether those white zebu cows ever made it on to the dinner plates of my interlocutors, I eventually got a definitive answer on my most recent field trip, in the summer months of 2017.

It was Anand, a now-thirtysomething son of an old friend, who finally, after I had been asking around for some time, invited me to join him and a handful of other village men (two Dalits, an Adivasi, and a Muslim) on an expedition late one Saturday night to a large village, twenty miles or so from Bhavanipur, where they planned to buy freshly cut *āvu mānsam*. It was, he told me, a "known place" for cow beef because it had a large Muslim population; even restaurateurs from the district town would send buyers there to source meat for their biryanis. Word of whether or not a slaughter would happen on a particular day or time passed informally through relatives and friends. Traveling there, it was easy to understand why stories of previous trips were communicated through tropes akin to those of adventure fiction, complete, as it was, with that sense of danger, suspense, pace, and, of course, life and death, which make such stories so compelling.[1]

The journey, with six of us packed into a yellow auto rickshaw, was along dark, deserted roads on which we were stopped, twice, by police roadblocks to check where we were going at such a late hour. The answer, which Anand had coached us on prior to setting out, was that we were on the way to attend to his relative who had suffered a sudden heart attack and was being treated at a hospital along the route. I, it was decided, should say nothing, other than to confirm—if asked—that I had not been kidnapped by my fellow travelers. Although the roadblocks probably had more to do with prevention of crimes other than beef shopping, the fact that a cover story was deemed necessary did hint at a greater awareness of the difficulties faced by the meat trade than my interlocutors usually gave direct voice to.

Finding the precise location of the slaughter was the second hurdle, since the village, as we drove through it at around 1:30 a.m., showed no signs of life. We eventually pulled up at a welding workshop on one of its peripheries, from which sparks were casting flashes of white light upward into the night sky like fireworks. Anand and a couple of the others who had accompanied us chatted awhile with the young men working there, cautiously broaching the subject of where the site we were looking for might be. They, likewise guarded, initially feigned not to know, before eventually pointing to a location—later confirmed by the *chai wallah* (tea seller) along the route—back toward the heart of the village. There was a lengthy discussion about the time we ought to get there until, nearly an hour later, we reached a consensus that it was time to move, and we were back on the road, first through the village center, then off down a narrow side road in which the darkness, save for the sulfurous glimmer of a distant hurricane lamp, seemed almost total. When the lane turned into an overgrown pathway, we continued on foot until, finally, we reached the source of the light, dramatically illuminating the still-warm carcass of a humped white zebu. My niggling doubts about whether cows were ever the actual source of my interlocutors' desires were put to rest. A second animal appeared to have already been stunned and, lying on her side with her legs bound, was having her jugular slit with a large cleaver.

Despite my initial shock at the scene—triggered by the stark contrast of the iconic animals' white bodies, picked out by a circle of intense light, against a background of complete blackness—the atmosphere was, in fact, quite jovial. The elderly man in charge, Samson, to whom I was introduced, identified himself as a Madiga and converted Christian. The two much younger men who were working for him—who had slit the cows' throats and were now busy dissecting the animals—were both Muslims. They had learned their skills, they said, from their grandfathers, although these days they only did this work on Sunday mornings, each earning five hundred rupees from it. During the week they both worked as laborers at a local factory. Their skills, at least to my untrained eyes, were impressive: each working on his own animal, they first removed the legs before carefully cutting away the skin, starting with a slit along the abdomen, and then drawing it back to create a clean, smooth surface on which to work on the flesh. Buckets of water, darkened by blood, were used regularly to wring out their cloths. The kidneys, liver, and heart were removed next, slopped into baskets that Samson carried into the open-sided thatched shed alongside them, which would later serve as the trading area.

Having spent a lot of time in butchers' shops and market stalls over the previous year, it was easy for me to recognize the paraphernalia of the meat seller's business already lined up there: meat hooks, dangling from a bamboo pole that had been strung up; a mat composed of old sacks on which to display the meat; a roll of small black plastic bags next to the scales; the glinting knives and cleavers; and a crude chopping block fashioned from a cross-section of a tree. The meat, cut from the carcass into manageable portions and laid out across the mat, would later be hacked into smaller pieces to be sold, not as cuts but, generically, as meat.

My reading of the situation was aided by the fact that, having by now witnessed several other slaughters, it was clear that the illegality of the acts being committed did not necessarily prevent them from being undertaken with care and precision. The people involved, in doing things in what was tacitly agreed to be the proper order and with what they acknowledged as the appropriate skill and respect for the animal, were enacting their own ethics of slaughter. The very bodies of the butchers—shaped through the corporeal practices of transforming an animal into meat—were finely attuned to the process. They knew, for example, how the cow's body felt to the touch, the sensation of the knife cutting first through the skin, then flesh, then sometimes sinew or bone. They knew how the animal should feel and smell as they cut it open, and how much blood would flow from it. The sequenced movements of the two butchers consequently appeared as consistent and in synch as if they had been performing choreographed dance movements. As anthropologist Shaheed Tayob's (2019) descriptions of various slaughter events in Mumbai illustrate so evocatively, there are recognized right and wrong ways of doing it. Tayob's informant's brother was overcome with nausea and vomited in visceral response to observing a slaughter at a particular abattoir, but his disgust was evoked by the *manner* in which the slaughter was conducted rather than by witnessing the killing of an animal per se. My own developing appreciation of the ethics of slaughter—despite my vegetarianism—likewise enabled me to observe the process unfolding before us that morning without adverse bodily reaction. My own body, in the same way that those of the men more directly involved in the slaughter had done over a much longer period of time, was slowly becoming attuned to it.

The current going rate for *āvu mānsam*, Samson told us as they prepared to begin trading, was 220 rupees per kilogram, comparable to that of *eddu mānsam* (buffalo meat). He always slaughtered two cows, every Sunday, never more nor fewer, although he was willing to go elsewhere if people had their own animals that they wanted slaughtering. It was not difficult to source animals from local farmers: today's cows, which would render, he estimated, around ninety kilograms of meat each, had each cost him 13,000 rupees. Assuming he sold all the meat, that left a tidy potential profit, even after paying his assistants. As he pointed out, however, there were still the costs of transporting the animals here, of renting the plot, and of paying off local police officers and others to ensure that they were left to trade in peace. "There's no real danger here," he said, waving his hands dismissively, when I asked about the risks. "Even in the police station over there"—he pointed toward the outline of a building in the distance that was slowly becoming visible as dawn began to break—"some of the officers are Muslims, so they won't bother us, other than to come and collect their own meat!" The potential danger also subsided once the skin of the animal had been removed and its body rendered into meat; for all my research participants' claims that they could tell the difference between cow and buffalo beef by sight, it was notoriously difficult to ascertain for sure the provenance of their meat without laboratory testing.

By daybreak, despite our seemingly remote location, the footpath back to the road had become noticeably dotted with people on the way to buy beef, including, I was told, those who, like us, had come a long way to be sure that what they were getting was *āvu mānsam*. While they were unlikely to describe themselves as such—and the friends I had traveled there with did not consider themselves in such terms—the customers struck me as an unexpected group of gastronomic connoisseurs; unexpected, that is, because having the cultural capital to assert what constitutes taste and discernment is usually attributed, as it is by French sociologist Pierre Bourdieu in his book *Distinction*, to the ruling class (1984, 41). Those who traveled to buy *āvu mānsam*, by contrast, generally came from among the most marginalized groups in Indian society: Muslims, Dalits, and Christians.

But if they were not going to the lengths they did because it gave them access to a foodstuff of superior taste, why would they bother at all? Chicken, after all, was now cheaper than beef and, at least among meat eaters, was considered a more respectable meat. Not to eat beef would also remove a major signifier of one's negatively construed "otherness" in an increasingly hostile environment. Stopping consumption, as the record shows, in some cases can actively enhance social status. For Paraiyar Catholics in Tamil Nadu, for example, conversion to Christianity symbolized a shift from actions perceived by Hindus to be unclean, beef eating included, to those worthy of greater respect (Mosse 1999). Catholics in the region had earlier given up rather than relished beef after conversion, in the same way that the Madiga converts gave up beef eating in the 1920s to counter obstacles to higher-caste Hindus joining them (Harper 2000, 278), and the tribal Saoras, from Orissa (now Odisha), were persuaded by Brahmins to give up beef by the 1950s (Jha 2002, 121). "To move upwards," as Jack Goody summarizes it, "meant changing one's diet, usually by becoming more vegetarian" (1982, 115). The shift toward vegetarianism might also be seen by some subaltern groups not simply as buying into upper-caste values but as spiritually transformative in itself (Desai 2008).

TAKING ON SACRED COWS

The limited social benefits to be had from presenting oneself as a discerning diner are unlikely to be sufficient to account for the flourishing of the Indian beef trade in an environment that appears so hostile toward it. How is it even possible that India remains one of the biggest exporters of beef on earth; that between 60 and 88 percent of its population identify, at least to some extent, as nonvegetarian;[2] and that beef was, at least until quite recently, apparently the most highly consumed meat product by quantity after fish?[3] Even if state rhetoric and self-styled cow protectionists have impeded growth in the cattle trade, there seems here to be a clear mismatch. How can we reconcile the facts that, on the one hand, a majority of Indian states significantly restrict bovine slaughter—cows especially, but also buffaloes—and, on the other, that beef is not only eaten but widely traded on international markets?

One of the reasons is that the stark distinction drawn between those who herald cow protectionism and those who celebrate beef consumption had been overstated by those on both sides of the debate. My ethnographic findings suggest that although the polarized voices of these two radically opposed perspectives on cattle are the most often heard, there are plenty of people who, while they might align themselves more closely with one side of the debate than the other, have far more nuanced views than the debates allow space for. In addition, many non–beef eaters are also complicit, knowingly or otherwise, in helping to ensure that the beef trade continues in spite of an outwardly hostile environment. Some of the apparent contradictions between eating beef in a country where cattle slaughter is billed as morally wrong, low-status, and un-Indian, in short, are managed through the particular ways in which meat is traded. Tracing the journeys undertaken by bovines from the cattle sheds of, very often, non-beef-eating farmers to the kitchens of those who relish it shows *how* such journeys are made possible.

In order to keep my task one of manageable proportions, I have not focused on the role played by larger companies like Al-Kabeer, which exported meat products overseas as well as sold them within India. Gaining access, even if it had been possible, would have been arduous and time-consuming, and would have diverted me from my focus on the everyday experiences of South Indian meat eaters. That said, many of those large companies also appeared to rely on the same networks and cattle markets as the smaller-scale butchers and meat sellers that I did work with, so there may be fleeting glimpses of their activities along the way. Nor, for the same reasons, do I explore the beef supply chains utilized by, for example, the major five-star hotel groups and other tourist hotels, some of which—according to contacts working as managers in some of those companies—had their own, dedicated suppliers of bovine meat to ensure consistent quality. Rather, my interest here is in the local, domestic meat trade: the small-scale farmers and cattle rearers whose animals passed through brokers, cattle fairs, and then market stalls and small shops before ending up on the dinner plates of my research participants in Anandapuram, Bhavanipur, and Hyderabad. The account at the start of this chapter represents a point along the routes of these journeys.

These narratives, woven together, challenge two dominant assumptions made in respect to cattle slaughter and beef consumption in South Asia. The first is that the Indian beef trade directly concerns only Muslims, Dalits, Adivasis, and Christians, in other words, that high-caste, non-beef-eating Hindus play no part in a process to which they are implacably opposed. This is simply not the case. The second assumption is that, conversely, respect for cattle, cows especially, is the sole preserve of upper-caste Hindus. An ethnographic approach that documents the concrete, everyday relationships, exchanges, networks, and processes through which buffaloes and cows are transformed into one of the most contested components of the Indian diet demonstrates that this too is not so. Some of the closest, most kinship-analogous relationships I encountered between cattle and their owners were between beef-eating Dalits and their buffaloes.

Given the strength of the empirical evidence against these two assumptions, how could such a stark framing of the debates along caste and communal lines have been sustained so successfully and for so long? What has been called "the anthropology of ignorance" can perhaps explain strategic acts of *not* knowing what goes on at particular junctures along the chain from cowshed to cooking pot that a number of actors are complicit in working to maintain. Managing knowledge—what one knows and what one does not know—as Clifford Geertz (1978, 29) discussed in relation to the "bazaar economy" in Morocco, is an essential component of trading.

Compared to the complexities of industrializing food systems more generally—so labyrinthine, in the case of recent European food scandals, for example, that it proved impossible to identify the source of ingredients in some ready-made foodstuffs—the journey from tethered cow or buffalo to plate in South India is usually a relatively short one.[4] Nevertheless, tracing that trajectory still exposes a network of locations, diverse actors, and processes that unsettle routinely made associations between beef and a non-Hindu other. At the same time, in the same way as other commodities are observed to be transformed by, or transformative of, the contexts through which they pass (e.g., see Van der Geest, Whyte, and Hardon 1996, 155), so too are cattle and the other parties involved changed along the way. Understanding these incremental changes, material and symbolic, from venerated animals into a sought-after foodstuff is of general interest to scholars of food. But it is particularly relevant in this case, because it is in the spaces between these shifts that my research participants navigated (and sometimes reconciled) the potential contradictions inherent in sending loved animals to their deaths, or in eating the flesh of those killed by others.

THE BEEF CHAIN

Most cattle sellers I encountered were rural, small-scale farmers or others who reared buffaloes for dairy provision (either to meet family needs or to sell to households in the vicinity), or who kept oxen to pull a cart or plow. They came from a variety of backgrounds, Hindu as well as Muslim and Christian. Rani and her husband Prasanth, for example, who sold milk, curd, ghee, and eggs to neighbors within a few streets' radius of their residence in Anandapuram, hawking their wares from house to house, derived much of their income from their half dozen buffaloes and several chickens. As Reddis—a locally high-ranking, traditionally landowning farming caste—they ate meat, but not beef, and in any case said that they would not have countenanced eating the animals they reared themselves. Chickens, at a certain age, would sometimes be sold to neighbors who, in turn, would transform them into chicken curry. The buffaloes, when they no longer gave milk, would be sold externally. Replacements would either be bred in-house, purchased from neighbors with calves they did not want, or, if need be, bought from local cattle markets. Male calves were often surplus to requirements and so sold while they were still young, in the same way as were older females no longer able to produce milk. Even those who ate beef, like my Christian friend Mariamma—whose family were from the beef-eating and traditionally leather-working Madiga caste—would not slaughter and consume their own surplus cattle. As she put it, "They are like our pets, members of our family!" So, rather than eating them, like Rani and Prasanth, they sold them on to others.

I encountered sales of cattle for meat in two main contexts in South India. The first of these, more common in Anandapuram and Bhavanipur, was through private sales from animal owners to butchers, with the formal or informal aid of a local broker. This was how Mariamma and Rani and Prasanth disposed of their no-longer-productive animals. The second context, which also involved brokers, was through sales via *shandy*s (livestock markets, fairs, and auctions), the most common sources of animals for the traders we met in Hyderabad (figure 3.1). Those who ran larger dairies in Bhavanipur, like one with more than a hundred cattle, were also more likely to take this route, since they usually wanted to shift more animals at a time than the local market could bear. These were not, however, the only contexts in which cattle changed hands. Online sales, for instance, were reportedly on the increase through websites such as OLX and Quikr (Ranal 2015). In addition, when a buffalo met its end unexpectedly (if it was hit by a train on the rail tracks, the example those I worked with always gave), it was common, in villages like Anandapuram, for leatherworker Madigas to be asked to deal with the carcass. A cobbler told me that, in such circumstances, they would call upon their caste fellows to help carry the animal into their part of the village and would then dissect and share the meat among themselves. For all the exchanges I encountered firsthand, however, private transactions or *shandy*s were the avenues through which cattle-as-meat were traded.

3.1 Apparent chaos belies a tightly run open-air cattle market on the outskirts of Hyderabad.

In towns like Bhavanipur, nearly all transactions were of the first, small-scale kind. Those wishing to dispose of their cattle would either contact a known broker or seek one out from those who waited around the tea shops in the town center every evening. Like their clients, brokers these days also came from a wide variety of backgrounds. Traditionally, though, cattle brokerage had been an occupation of those from the non-beef-eating and cattle-herding Yadav group of castes, who were often credited with having developed the particular sign language used by brokers at cattle fairs (Michelutti 2004, 46; see also 2008). In small rural communities, like the hamlets dotting the area around Bhavanipur, brokers usually operated on a part-time, ad hoc basis, helping neighbors to find buyers for their surplus cattle alongside other work (including other forms of brokerage). Once you had established a reputation for it, I was told, it was relatively straightforward: those with cattle to sell would seek you out and you, in turn, would draw on the contacts you had built up among meat sellers and others to find them a buyer at the right price. Other brokers, like those I met at major cattle markets, made a full-time occupation of it, charging (in 2017) each party around five hundred rupees per animal for their services.

From Cattle Purchase to Slaughter

In Bhavanipur, all the butchers I met in 2016 and 2017 were Hindu (or converted Christian) Madigas, and in each case were doing the work that their fathers and grandfathers had done. Rajshekar, whom I got to know the best, would purchase buffaloes nearly every day, in the afternoons or early evenings, usually within a five- or six-mile radius, from wherever his brokers directed him to. He would hire a small truck to transport the animals he purchased home, where he would keep them tethered in the small compound surrounding his house until he was ready for them to be slaughtered, then sold as beef from the family's pitch in the town's market in the mornings. Rajshekar initially told me that although they had previously slaughtered animals in the courtyard of their family house—a skill he had learned from his father—current government rules no longer allowed this. The panchayat (village council), no doubt alert to current sensitivities surrounding cattle slaughter, had recently broadcast a diktat from an auto rickshaw via a loudspeaker that slaughter should now only take place at the municipal-owned abattoir, a mile or so away, on the town's border. As we discovered, however, much of the slaughter *did* still take place, albeit more discreetly, in Rajshekar's compound, most mornings at around 3:30 a.m., more than an hour before the local slaughterhouse opened. His explanation was that it was less time-consuming than attending the abattoir and saved on both the cost of transport and the small charge imposed by the abattoir's "cutting man."

As had been the case for the cows whose slaughter opened this chapter, the animal's legs were tied together, and it was silenced by tying its mouth shut. It was then stunned with a swift blow to the head with a wooden club. Once it was lying on the ground, its throat was slit. Even though Rajshekar was not a Muslim—and so he did not, as far as I was aware, make the declaration required for the meat to be officially considered halal, that it was slaughtered in the name of God—killing the animal in this way did appear to render its meat acceptable for Muslim as well as Hindu and Christian consumers.[5] Indeed, on several occasions Muslim purchasers came directly to the house to buy meat before Rajshekar went off to his stall. After the slaughter, Rajshekar or one of his brothers, aided sometimes by his now-adult sons, would then dissect the animal in a style and order comparable to the butchers I observed in my opening example, piling the meat into the plastic woven baskets they used to transport it to market, mopping up the blood as they went and wringing their cloths into a bucket of water that, even in the moonlight, grew discernibly darker in color as the process went on. Those wanting specific parts—particularly the liver or the heart—would sometimes

3.2   One of the beef shops operating in the walled compound of Bhavanipur's market.

come to the house to obtain them before he set off to market (and, if people knew we were going, I would sometimes receive telephone calls from friends to ask if I might buy those cuts for them) (figure 3.2).

Most butchers in Bhavanipur did not have access to refrigeration, so slaughter was a daily affair, and any meat neither sold at the market nor consumed by the household would be cut into strips and preserved by drying it out in the sun. Rajshekar had a good idea of how much he was likely to sell on a given day, however, and purchased animals accordingly: a small male calf, for example, was usually adequate for midweek sales, while an older, much larger animal would be needed to satisfy demand on a Sunday morning. Those who wanted to be sure they obtained *āvu mānsam*, as we have already seen, had to be prepared to travel much farther for it.

The city butchers I encountered in Hyderabad, by contrast, tended to buy their meat—directly or indirectly—through *shandy*s, held at various locations throughout the state. The first one I attended was a weekly event, fifty miles out of Hyderabad. The adult son of Mohamed, a Hyderabad butcher we had been spending time with, agreed to accompany us there on the bus and to point us to the entrance, but he made it clear that he did not want us to be with him while he conducted his business. Unlike an auction at a comparable *shandy* we tried to visit in coastal Andhra a week or so later, where we were barred entry by security guards and warned not to take photographs, we had no difficulty in entering that first market, an open plot of several acres, well shaded with trees. There were no obvious security guards, and several brokers were happy to talk with us.

The sellers were varied, although, like the brokers and the buyers, they were exclusively men. Some represented dairy farms selling relatively large numbers of animals: mostly in the range of twenty to forty buffaloes, but sometimes as many as a hundred in a single lot. Others brought just one or two of their own domestically reared cattle. Both cows and, in greater numbers, buffaloes were available. The sellers, as far as one could tell based on their dress (dhotis or lungis and kurtas, towel slung over one shoulder, simple *chappel*s) and other signifiers, were mainly rural, Hindu farmers. The buyers were a mix of rural and urban-based Hindus and Muslims (in citywear shirts and trousers), some relatively local, some coming as far away as Kerala, where beef was more widely eaten, around six hundred miles southwest. Although cattle were being sold here for milk and draft as well as for meat, a lot of the animals we saw, several of the brokers predicted, would end up as beef in Persian Gulf countries. Some purchasers, like Mohamed's son, who had accompanied us to the fair, were buying cattle to supply their own shops; others were hoping to secure bigger numbers to prepare for export, as frozen boneless meat or processed meat products.

As had been the case at the early morning cow slaughter we attended, the atmosphere was pleasantly relaxed, contrary to our expectations. There were several stalls selling tiffin—freshly prepared *idli*s, *dosa*s, *gari*, and puris—as well as small cups of sweet, milky tea and coffee, and there was no detectable undercurrent of fear. "We've had no trouble here," a broker told me when I asked if there had been any issues with the antibeef "cow vigilantes" whose attacks were being widely reported in the press at that time. "But the danger is when those buying or selling are on the road, coming or going. Everyone has read in the newspapers about the attacks or seen them on the news." Some buyers, like Mohamed's son, had regular brokers; newcomers were approached as they entered the market along the track from the main road. In addition to the cut taken from the broker for each transaction, buyers also paid a levy of 150 rupees per animal to the leaseholder of the land, a local "big man," as the tea vendor at the entrance to the market described him. He, in turn, paid 100,000 rupees a week in rent to the municipality, which owned the land. With upwards of a thousand bovines sold at each market, the potential for profit was still significant. Buyers paid their fees at an office kiosk, where they were issued with a chit to hand in to one of the leaseholder's employees in order to exit the market with their animals. They were also issued a receipt for the animal and a copy of the permission for its sale, obtained from a district-level branch of the Animal Husbandry Department.

Mohamed's preferred method of transporting his purchases—on this occasion, eight buffaloes—back to Hyderabad was by a Tata air-conditioned van. Unlike Bhavanipur's abattoir, the state-owned slaughterhouses in Hyderabad could accommodate animals before slaughter, so Mohamed's cattle were taken there directly, while his son, like Das and I, traveled back to the city by bus. He would later go to the slaughterhouse to identify his cattle—which were marked at the point of sale—and have them slaughtered according to demand, often over the course of several days. Sometimes, Mohamed told me, they might have one slaughtered for their own shop and another to sell wholesale to other, smaller-scale butchers who did not attend the *shandy*s. Aziz, who ran a small shop in a Muslim enclave of Banjara Hills, was one such butcher. He would go to the slaughterhouse early every morning to source meat from bigger traders, like Mohamed, whose family had several shops, with the aim of opening his own shop by 8 a.m. Vans and trucks with drivers could be hired from nearby to transport their purchase—now a dead animal, dissected into four parts—to the place of sale.

Beef Sellers

For Mohamed, his main sales outlet was a covered and enclosed building rented from the municipality in a large, daily food market, which included space both to hang and prepare the meat and for a fridge and chest freezer in which stock could be kept if need be. The plot was situated alongside the others selling meat, chickens, goat, and fish, although the beef shop was harder than the others to identify because it had no signboard, and the meat was kept in the covered space at the back, out of immediate view and separated from the external market space by a short corridor. The presence of Mohamed outside, an elderly man with a white beard and lace Muslim skullcap, as well as the shop's location, were the only obvious signifiers of what might be inside, at least until one got close enough to peer down the corridor to the slab and meat hooks within, or to catch a whiff of uncooked bovine flesh.

In the case of Aziz, the smaller-scale butcher, the destination was a small shop facing onto a side road in a residential, working-class Muslim area. Here, hooks displayed meat from the open frontage, above which was a signboard explicitly advertising this as a beef shop, both in English and Urdu, alongside an ambiguous illustration of a cow (the significance of which will become clear later). Behind the hooks, working from a raised platform, Aziz rendered the meat into smaller chunks—or into mince, for *keema*, which was commonly requested by Muslim customers—on his large chopping block, which, like Mohamed's and Rajshekar's in Bhavanipur, was a cross-section of a tree trunk. Several large knives, electronic scales on a compact wooden chest—in which he kept black plastic bags that the sold meat was packed into—and a small, blood-stained plastic bin were the only other objects in the shop, a space of less than eight feet by eight feet. Whereas the fact that the market was a communal space—frequented by Hindus, Muslims, and other groups alike—appeared to demand discretion, the location of Aziz's shop in a Muslim area meant that there were fewer issues in publicly displaying the meat.

Aziz had, however, faced more problems in transporting the meat from the slaughterhouse to his shop than Mohamed. Although when I first met him in December 2016 his knowledge of attacks had been confined to film clips he had watched on YouTube, by the time we next spoke, in July 2017, the minitruck drivers he hired to deliver meat from the state-owned slaughterhouse to his shop had twice been attacked by men claiming to represent the Bajrang Dal, the youth wing of the Vishva Hindu Parishad (VHP), the World Hindu Council. The vigilantes had seized and contaminated more than 30,000 rupees' worth of beef. They had also beaten the drivers and thrown them face down into the Musi River, releasing them only after they chanted "Jai Sri Ram!" (Victory to [the Hindu deity] Ram!).

For Rajshekar, in Bhavanipur, the situation was so far much calmer. He traded from a setup similar to Mohamed's: his regular bay in the municipal market was one of ten spaces inside a walled, gated compound that separated it from other traders, and there were no permanent beef shops elsewhere in the town. Only two bays were occupied every day (except for Mondays, when the beef compound was closed) at present, although there were sometimes five or six butchers there on Sundays. The setup was even simpler than Aziz's shop in Hyderabad: a bamboo pole tied across the front enabled larger pieces of meat, awaiting cutting, to be hung, behind which was only his chopping block, a knife, the empty woven bags in which they had carried the meat to market, and the ubiquitous black plastic bags in which to pack the sold meat. Unlike in all the Hyderabad shops we visited, there were no scales—people just asked, he said, for a hundred or two hundred rupees' worth of meat, and he filled the bags accordingly. Unlike Aziz, who tried to keep his shop open all day, returning to the slaughterhouse for more supplies if he sold more meat than they expected, Rajshekar had often sold all his supply by 10 or 11 a.m.

Beef Buyers

The next link in our chain is the individual, domestic purchaser of meat. Although some of the butchers I spent time with included trade buyers among their customers—from restaurateurs to those running more modest food carts, such as the biryani stalls that lined the main highway out of Bhavanipur—the majority of them were those buying meat for consumption by their families in their own homes. Whoever those customers were, a universal claim from the beef butchers I interviewed was that there were now fewer of them than there had been before the BJP came to power in 2014. Stories of vigilante attacks were not good for business, nor was the fact that chicken, once a costly alternative to beef, was now around half the price (140 rupees per kilogram in Bhavanipur in mid-2017).

Nevertheless, although overall domestic sales had declined, butchers also concurred that the *range* of buyers had widened. When I posed the question "Who buys from you?" *all* the butchers answered in the same way: "Everyone!" They did not, of course, mean this literally, but that members of all communities and castes purchased their meat, even if their main customers remained Dalits and Christians, particularly for Rajshekar in Bhavanipur, and Muslims, for Aziz. Mohamed, who sold from a central location less defined by community, listed his buyers not just by religion but also by language group: "Muslims, Christians, Telugus, and Tamils, Malayalis—whoever comes!"

Notionally, when I asked them, Muslim customers expressed a clear preference for cow beef ("Who would eat buffalo?" was not an uncommon response from friends who seemed genuinely puzzled that I should ask them such a question), while Dalit Hindus and some Christians, depending on the wider communities within which they had grown up, tended to favor buffalo meat. Miriam, for example, was a Christian, but, having been reared in the largely Muslim settlement served by Aziz's shop, said she would only eat cow beef. Others, like Bhaskararao, a Madiga Christian convert from a village near Bhavanipur, preferred buffalo because "it's less fatty, and it is particularly suited to my body." Those like Anand and the others with whom I had traveled to purchase cow meat happily ate meat from either animal, although the relative rarity of *āvu mānsam* in their locality these days lent it a particular allure.

Purchasers of meat, whatever their backgrounds, were usually men, although it was mostly women who then prepared the meat for consumption. There was also a dominant (and enduring) narrative among traditional diners of beef, both in Hyderabad and coastal Andhra, that price increases and shortages of quality meat were because others were now increasingly buying a meat that had once been the preserve of Scheduled Castes, Muslims, and Christians. "And the [other castes] are eating beef directly too. That's why the price became so high!" was a not-uncommon refrain. "Even Brahmins will come and ask us to cook it for them sometimes," a woman from Anandapuram once told me, dropping her voice as she did so. "[They are] afraid to ask their own wives to prepare it, so they will come to us instead!" An elderly Dalit man substantiated her claims: "It's hard even to get to market in time for the beef these days," he complained. "The Reddis and the other non-beef-eating castes with their fancy motorbikes and cars get there faster and so are at the front of the queue!"

Whoever the buyers were, although some expressed a preference for the heart, liver, brains, or even lungs, most customers would simply ask for a specified weight (or rupee value) of meat, which would be diced into bite-sized chunks and tied up in small, opaque black plastic bags. Some butchers would throw in additional bones free of charge. In coastal Andhra, where my informants were less likely to have refrigerators, beef was cooked for consumption at lunchtime on the day of purchase (usually Sunday, for Christians), and the leftovers, sometimes just the gravy, were eaten on the same evening. If preparation was likely to be delayed for some reason, cooks would quickly preboil it in salted water to prolong its life for a few hours. For most people, meat was a weekly, celebratory dish, with beef, chicken, and sometimes fish prepared alternately. In Anandapuram, it was eaten privately, with family members, at home. When publicly feeding others—at weddings, for example—the meat served was always, in my experience, chicken, a meat that *all* nonvegetarians could openly partake of and therefore acceptable to serve in a multicaste village (Staples 2017, 245). Goat would also have been acceptable, but these days it was prohibitively expensive. In Hyderabad, where refrigerators were more common, several women—most of them Muslims—told me that they refrigerated the meat in a plastic box and cooked it in smaller quantities over the course of a few days. There was an aspiration, certainly among my urban Muslim interlocutors, to eat beef more regularly than on Sundays, when it was deemed essential. "We say, "Without meat, we cannot eat!"' as one woman summarized what she saw as the Muslim attitude toward beef consumption. Beef facilitated the essential consumption of rice.

OF KNOWING AND NOT KNOWING

What is interesting along this bovine biographical journey is not only the observation that actors and meanings shift as they move through what Appadurai called "regimes of value" (1986, 4), significant though this is. Actors change from, predominantly, Hindu cattle herders—many of them non-beef-eating, some of them vegetarian (see, for example, Robbins 1999, 411–12)—at one end of the chain, to Muslims, Dalits, and Christians at the other. The cattle also change, both materially and symbolically, from being kin or sacred objects to an edible source of protein, a celebration of a cultural identity, and, conversely, a symbol of a spoiled, marginalized identity (see Staples 2017). But also noteworthy is the work that various actors do, in different ways, to avoid, subvert, bracket, or deny knowledge of activity and meanings at other points along the cattle-to-meat chain. This work—what Whyte, van der Geest, and Hardon (2002) explicate as the compartmentalization of knowledge—is vital to the maintenance of a chain that otherwise appears riddled with insurmountable contradictions.

To some extent, one might argue, this work of actively not knowing might be considered a feature of food systems more generally, and there might well be some mileage in applying this kind of analysis elsewhere. If it is through the bracketing of "irrelevant organic processes" that civilized social intercourse comes to take place, as Mary Douglas ([1970] 1996) showed us, for many of us it is often through not quite knowing what goes on in farms, in food processing plants, or in restaurant kitchens that we are able to enjoy the food that we do. Many of the meat eaters I know in Britain, for example, admit that they would not wish to observe the killing of the animals that, in processed form, end up on their plates, and many I asked said they were also happier eating that which was not directly identifiable as the animal it had come from. And both the food industry and consumers might conspire to not fully know the provenance of the highly processed products that might be consumed, for example, as ready-made lasagnas or chicken nuggets (Staples and Klein 2017b).

In the case of cows and beef in South India, however, the business of knowing and not knowing takes on particular dimensions. First, given that the chain from animal to plate is often much shorter than it is in more heavily industrialized contexts, it is harder, if you buy meat from a market trader who had slaughtered and butchered the animal himself, *not* to recognize the product as coming from a dead animal than it is, say, for a supermarket shopper buying cellophane-wrapped, prepackaged meat in plastic or polystyrene cartons. In Aziz's shop or Rajshekar's market stall, for example, not only were there giveaway signs that the meat had once been an animal—skinned heads with eyes still intact, for example, or large pieces of carcass still recognizable as legs—but the metallic smell of blood and guts was also that much stronger. Second, given the politicized nature of animal-based foods in India, beef in particular, there is generally much more at stake in selling or buying at various stages in the process than there is for, say, the British consumer buying a carton of minced beef. Transactions, often, are on or beyond the boundaries of legality.

To return then to the beginning of the chain: cattle sellers, even those who consumed beef themselves, not only balked at the idea of consuming their own animals but said that they would not sell them for consumption either. "They are like brothers and sisters to us" or "they are our children!" people routinely claimed of their livestock, invoking kinship as the logic that prevented them from eating them.[6] "We rear them like members of our own family. How could we eat them?" said beef-eating Bhaskararao, who in the past had always kept at least two buffaloes that he rented out to pull a cart. "We used to sell them, mostly, when they could still be used by someone for milk." Other informants likewise claimed to be supportive of the Hindu doctrine of *ahimsa* (the injunction not to take life) while continuing to purchase and eat beef. "They kill, we eat!" was how one of my research participants described how people dealt with the contradiction between not killing animals and meat eating, a comment that, despite appearing initially contradictory, fitted well with what earlier adherents of *ahimsa* had believed (and followed much the same logic as the British diners I spoke to who likewise made a clear distinction between the killing done by others and their own consumption). The order not to kill, for the Vedic Brahmins we encountered in chapter 1, was interpreted as meaning that someone else had to conduct the slaughter, not necessarily that they should not eat the meat that resulted from the sacrifice. As this implies, the distinction between killing and eating also enabled social distinctions to be drawn between those who *slaughtered* (Muslims, in particular, but also Dalits in some cases) and those who merely *ate*.

The logic described here resonates with the notion that kinship differentiates between "conscious fields of social connection" (Campbell 2009, 162) to help us to understand relationships between the human and the nonhuman. Anthropologist Ben Campbell uses the term "kinship" to discuss how English people positioned themselves in relation to the countryside over debates about genetically modified (GM) crops, but, in regard to interspecies relatedness, kinship can also be useful for understanding human relations with animals (Govindrajan 2018). In the same way that forest fishermen in the Sundarbans relate to tigers because they share the same harsh environment (Jalais 2010, 74), my friends in Anandapuram and Bhavanipur "shared mutual substance"—by eating food reared from the same soil, drinking water from the same wells, and experiencing the same vagaries of the environment around them—with the buffaloes or cows they reared and lived alongside. Likening livestock to siblings or children, in contexts where bodily boundaries were in any case considered relatively fluid, was not only figurative. And while the networks of relationships in which people were entangled with their livestock presented a problem in terms of passing them on to others—even as it might justify the consumption of animals with whom they do not share the same familial connections—kinship is shaped as much by differentiation, exclusion, and hierarchy as it is by love and care (Govindrajan 2018, 10). Acting in ways that might not be in the direct interests of our kin, particularly when we can disguise them even from ourselves, is perhaps not as paradoxical as it might at first appear.

For vegetarian, high-caste Hindu cattle owners, the potential problems of selling their animals for slaughter were even more significant, however, since cattle were not *only* kin but also venerated. Given the limited uses of a cow or a buffalo after a certain age, to *not* know that they were being purchased for meat required a certain "wilful ignorance" (Chua 2009, 343). It was not simply that they knew and chose not to acknowledge the fact (although in some instances this might well have been the case) but that they ensured that their ignorance was maintained through the act of not asking: "Seeking ignorance is not merely a tactically empowering manoeuvre, but an admission and evasion of the potentially *dis*empowering drawback of knowing" (341). My friend Mariamma, like other cattle owners I spoke to, was emphatic in her claim that her family did not sell their buffaloes for consumption, even as she conceded, later in the same conversation, that the only use for non-milk-producing buffaloes was as meat. Sellers were not, I came to realize, denying that those who bought their animals killed or ate them, only that their families did not actively sell them for that purpose. Purchasers I spoke to recognized this need-to-not-know and were complicit in keeping their own intentions undeclared: "We don't *tell* them that's what we are buying their animals for!" one butcher told me, laughing at the very naivety of my question, when I asked him whether those from whom he bought cattle were ever reticent about selling to butchers. If they were not told, and if they did not ask, how could sellers *know* that their animals were going to be eaten?

Brokers who, as elsewhere, straddled different social worlds (Koster and van Leynseele 2018, 803) provided a further buffer between the seller and the purchaser. They too, however, often maintained an uncertainty about the destinations of the animals they helped to sell. This was particularly the case for those working in *shandy*s, which were not specifically beef markets but contexts for the sale of buffaloes and cows for multiple purposes. Two young bulls, for example, could be being bought for their new owner to train to pull a cart or a plow, just as they could be being purchased as meat for midweek sales at a municipal market. And in a changing context, where, at the time of my fieldwork, the sale of animals for meat from such places looked like it might become illegal, ignorance in such matters was increasingly worth maintaining. Some of the brokers I met speculated that around 40 percent of business at some *shandy*s was for the beef trade, but even for them, it remained a matter of speculation. They were likewise well aware that their best interests were served in *not* knowing for sure. What *was* important was their ability to know the cash value of any given animal at a glance, something which, of course, required implicit knowledge of whether the animal could still produce milk or perform labor *and* of the value of cattle as meat (see, for example, Kapur 2011), but it was a knowledge that could be bracketed from its practical application.

Even in small towns, like Bhavanipur, non-beef-eating sellers of cattle, unless they were also surreptitious consumers, were unlikely to encounter the butchers to whom they sold their animals. Butchers lived, for the most part, in Muslim or Madiga settlements, away from the streets and enclaves of higher-caste Hindus, and they traded from within walled and gated compounds inside the market. Beef sales were subsequently difficult just to stumble across: although once I started this research I seemed to encounter beef shops everywhere, particularly in Hyderabad, in my first twenty years of traveling to India, I scarcely, if ever, noticed them at all. Geography and architecture were utilized effectively to maintain the states of not knowing that the smooth running of the beef trade required. If you were a high-caste Hindu vegetarian, chances are you could avoid ever passing through the Muslim areas where beef was sold openly, and in the markets where you might buy your vegetables, it was conveniently hidden not only behind walls but, once purchased, by the very opacity of the black plastic bags in which buyers transported their meat home.

When it came to selling the meat—the transaction between the butcher and consumer—different kinds of knowing and not knowing seemed to be in evidence. Sellers could not usually avoid knowing what animals they had purchased, unless, perhaps, they were small-scale urban butchers, like Aziz, who bought their meat from wholesalers at the slaughterhouse, once it was already skinned. But sometimes they strategically forgot, or at least bracketed, that knowledge. Mohamed, for example, when I asked him what kind of beef he sold, delayed answering me by seeking clarifications: "Are you talking about the white ones or the black ones when you're talking about 'cows'?" he asked, as though the dark-skinned water buffaloes and white Indian cows were simply different-colored versions of the same animal. "Whatever is available and is good," he finally settled on as his answer, avoiding—as did the other Hyderabadi butchers I spoke to—confirming what the meat on his block at that moment was. On a larger scale, recent press reports of hikes in the quantities of frozen buffalo meat being exported through southern Indian ports have aroused suspicions that the meat being exported, much of it transported from North India, might in fact be cow.[7]

For butchers like Mohamed, clear identification of the meat he was selling was problematic either way. To say openly that it was cow meat would be to admit that they were selling illegal meat and, potentially, put off Dalit and Christian consumers who, in general, were said to prefer buffalo meat. It would also lay them open to attack from vigilante groups, and even prosecution, if the information got out. On the other hand, to say that it was buffalo—while legal, at least in some cases—would be to deter those Muslim customers who claim they cannot imagine anyone eating anything *other* than cow meat. For them, very often, buffalo meat was associated with Hindu untouchability. It was perhaps not by accident that the depictions of cattle I observed on the signs of beef shops were recognizable neither as common breeds of Desi cows nor as buffaloes. The black-and-white animal depicted above Aziz's shop, for example, is almost identical to an online image I found of a Dangi cow, which, although it is apparently native to western Maharashtra, is unlike any cow I ever encountered in Andhra, where the Ongole, or Nellore, breed is the most common. Such ambiguous imagery serves the dual purpose of identifying to potential customers what is actually on sale within, while, for those who do not want to eat or even encounter beef, it protects their sensitivities. A similar process seemed to be at play in McDonald's restaurants in Gujarat, where nonvegetarian fare, despite being identifiable by the pale orange paper in which it is wrapped, is sufficiently processed and sanitized that the sight of it causes no problem for those who would otherwise eat only in purely vegetarian eating houses (Ghassem-Fachandi 2012, 160).

Customers in Hyderabad's beef shops, in turn, were often more passive than the sellers in maintaining their ignorance, but for comparable reasons. They tended not to ask: because they knew it was too risky a question for any butcher to answer in any case, so it was not worth asking; because asking ran the risk of exposing them to knowledge that contradicted what they believed and wanted to be true; or because, in some cases, it simply never occurred to them that the meat could ever be anything other than that which they had grown up learning it to be.

It was not just that some people ate buffalo believing that it was cow, however. Restaurateurs buying cow meat from illicit outlets, for example, despite seeking it out because they knew it was why many of their customers returned to them to purchase their ambiguously named meat biryani, would not always openly admit what it was. Mariamma told me that she sometimes bought biryani from one of the stalls that lined the road out of Bhavanipur. "They try to tell me it's goat mutton," she said, confirming what they had told me when I had asked them about what meat they used. "But I can tell from the bones what it is!" For those in the know, like Mariamma, the illicit insertion of what she believed to be beef into these dishes offered a secret pleasure for the discerning palate, a reason to return. For some Christians and Dalits I spoke to, it also offered a small sense of victory over those seen as their higher-caste oppressors (see, for example, Staples 2008). For some who presented as non–beef eaters, it held a similar attraction. They could consume and enjoy a forbidden dish and, because they were not actively aware its ingredients, could not be seen to have acted immorally. And for those who genuinely did not wish to eat beef? "Well, how would they know what the bones are like?" exclaimed Mariamma. "They will just think that they are eating goat mutton. So, where's the harm?"

More problematically, vigilante groups were likewise vague in distinguishing buffalo meat, which often was legal, and illegally slaughtered cow. The fact that Aziz's drivers were most likely transporting buffalo rather than cow, for example, did not prevent them from being attacked, in the same way that no one was sure that meat found in the fridge of Mohammad Akhlaq, the Muslim man killed by a lynch mob near Dadri, was actually cow beef.[8] Not only were Hindu extremists less concerned with knowing the origins of the meat than one might expect, it appears that in some cases, they were also actively complicit in spreading misinformation. "It's not about the meat," claimed Aziz, when he spoke of the attacks on those transporting beef to his own shop. "It's about Muslims."

At the level of the state, its institutions, and its officers, a certain ignorance—or at least a failure to connect different pieces of knowledge—was also required for state-run slaughterhouses, municipal markets, and cattle fairs, from which the state took a cut, to benefit from a trade that it also, officially, objected to. The rent charged by the municipality for the land on which the weekly *shandy* I attended took place, for example, was economically tenable *only* because a high volume of the livestock traded there was for the beef market. These two pieces of information—one about the rental value of the land for a cattle market, the other about the markets for cattle—could, though, be held apart from one another, in much the same way as those selling cattle could deny to themselves and others that they were selling it for meat.

Moving in closer to those charged with enforcing state policy, the police officers whose station was near the clearing where I witnessed the slaughter of two cows could not—given the extent of the news coverage on the subject—have been entirely ignorant of the laws on cattle slaughter, confusing though they remained. Nor could they have been utterly oblivious to the activity that was going on almost literally under their noses. In this case, knowing, without making the knowledge public, about the business also gave the local police considerable power over the operation, enabling them, for example, to extract a cut of any profits or get good rates on meat for their own consumption. It also ensured the discretion of the butcher and those working for him, in the same way that the panchayat's banning of home slaughter, while not taken literally, helped ensure that Rajshekar, in Bhavanipur, carefully moderated his own activities.

Just as the law offered the vigilante groups a level of protection, given that those transporting cattle were not in a strong position to complain to the authorities—particularly as their paperwork was seldom fully compliant with current legal requirements—so too were the law enforcers able to use the system to their advantage. Andrew Mathews, an anthropologist who examined the workings of the Mexican Environmental Agency, observed, "The various forms of official ignorance, misrecognition, collusion and complicity, and acts of official ignoring . . . imply a much more complex relationship between power and knowledge than is suggested by Foucauldian studies of power/knowledge" (2005, 798). In other words, what he dubs "official ignorance"—from actively turning a blind eye, as in the case of the police officers referred to above, to the avoidance of knowing, as for the municipal authorities reaping substantial rental income from cattle markets—was as significant to power as was knowledge.[9] What the law appeared to demand happen should not be seen as a reflection of what *would* happen, or even what would be expected to happen, on the ground. Rather, the act of making something illegal helped to determine the parameters within which it continued to happen.

CONCLUSION: CIRCUMVENTION AND COMPLICITY

That cattle can at once be venerated and a significant medium of trade and, once killed, a valued source of food is sustained by the willful separation of different knowledges within the chain sketched out above. Knowledge that relates to selling one's animal, such as knowing its market value and how to find brokers to facilitate the sale, is actively separated from one's knowledge that buffaloes and cows of a certain age are usually purchased only for consumption. Likewise, sellers and consumers of meat collude in not quite knowing, all of the time, precisely what it is that they are selling and buying, enabling those with a preference for the meat of either buffalo or cow to eat the meat of the other without having to acknowledge the fact.

Cattle, and the different things they come to mean and be at various stages of their journey, along with the human agents involved at various points along the chain, might also usefully be thought of as forming a bovine nexus—something akin to the "pharmaceutical nexus" in the movement of medicines (Petryna, Lakoff, and Kleinman 2006), which includes not just the prescription and consumption of medicines but also manufacture and marketing, stages during which pharmaceuticals carried meanings quite different from those with which they later became associated (Van der Geest 2006, 308). The life course of a buffalo or cow—from its existence as a dairy-, dung-, and labor-supplying family member to its eventual reappearance on someone else's dinner plate—in the locations I worked is, in some ways, more straightforward than that of pharmaceuticals (Van der Geest, Whyte, and Hardon 1996; Van der Geest 2006; Petryna, Lakoff, and Kleinman 2006) and, indeed, much simpler than that of most industrialized foods. Despite that—or, perhaps more accurately, *because* of it—significant work needs to be undertaken by the human agents who come in and out of the animals' lives to distance themselves from those aspects with which they are not directly involved, and which in some instances would threaten their involvement at all.

Appadurai's notion of "regimes of value" (1986) is useful here in distinguishing the qualitatively different meanings that bovines take on at different stages of their biographies. The same animal that begins its life as a relatively high-status part of a Hindu vegetarian household, for example, can become transformed into a commodity. As the latter, it is first an animal brokered, negotiated over, bought, and sold before, in another regime of value, it becomes raw meat and finally the central part of a meal. In other contexts, when it is repackaged and served in international hotels and cosmopolitan restaurants, it might also serve as a marker of urban sophistication (Staples 2014). Bovines have the capacity to carry multiple, apparently contradictory meanings.

As distinct from questions about how knowledge of medicines is constituted and how that knowledge travels (Van der Geest, Whyte, and Hardon

1996, 170), in relation to bovine biographies we need also to consider how and why dissemination of that knowledge not only travels, but is circumvented, bracketed, and denied. It is in doing so that the value of ethnographic interventions into the current debates become apparent. The actors involved are complicit in working hard to bracket their own knowledge from that of others in the chain: from the cover stories my friend had us learn for our late-night meat-buying excursion to Rajshekar's initial reluctance to tell us that he actually slaughtered the animals he sold in his own compound rather than the abattoir. Even the black plastic bags that hid what was really inside, as opposed to the usually translucent ones used to carry fruit and vegetables, helped to maintain others' ignorance and to ensure that the trade ran smoothly and to everyone's relative satisfaction. What emerges, when we connect together the fragments of knowledge through which the beef trade operates, is that there is not a radical distinction between the practices of high-caste Hindu cattle lovers on the one hand and beef-eating Christians, Dalits, and Muslims on the other—a narrative necessary to sustain debates about cattle slaughter and consumption in their current forms. Brahmin cattle owners, for example, appear no less likely than their lower-caste or Muslim counterparts to sell their no-longer-useful cattle into the beef market, even if they work harder to maintain ignorance of their involvement. Those who eat beef, too, relate to their own cattle via much the same kinship idioms as vegetarian Hindus do, in some cases even keeping their own animals out of the market.

The beef trade in India thus continues despite a rhetoric that would appear to make it nigh on impossible. But why do those at the end of the chain—like the friends who traveled with me late that Saturday night in search of cow—continue to buy beef when, for example, chicken is cheaper and poses less risk of them being battered to death by lynch mobs or, less dramatically but equally enduringly, permanently demarcated as a lesser category of person? Vigilante action in relation to cow slaughter is not, as Aziz correctly surmised, just about love of the cow. Such action is also about ensuring that Muslims, Dalits, and Christians remain aware that they are "other."

CHAPTER FOUR

Cattle Slaughter, Beef Eating, and Ambivalence

GROWING up as the child of Christian Mala parents in Anandapuram in the 1980s, Prakash had eaten beef at least once a week.[1] His father, Subbarao, who died a few years ago, told me in a previous interview that he had provided beef for the family every Sunday. He went to the market himself to purchase it when he was fit enough; in later years, when he became infirm, he would ask a rickshaw puller to buy it on his behalf. If he specifically wanted *āvu mānsam*, he would ask a Muslim neighbor to acquire it, in the same way that my friend Anand had been requested to bring back bags of it to the village from the late-night clandestine excursion described in the previous chapter. "Cow meat tastes better," Subbarao responded when I asked him about his own preferences. "It has more flavor than buffalo meat does. All meat has its own taste of course, but for me, and for my wife and family, *āvu mānsam* is the best of all. Eat it two or three times a week and you'll become very strong!" Subbarao's widow, Kanthamma, still ate beef when she got the opportunity—buffalo or cow—although even for her, a once devoted consumer, it was now a rarity. Like many other women in the village, she did not go to the market herself, so she ate what her son-in-law, who lived with her daughter in a neighboring house, purchased for her.

For Prakash, now in his forties, who for the last nearly twenty years had lived with his wife and their two children in Hyderabad, beef was no longer any part of his diet at all, or at least not that he was prepared to admit to. "Why would you eat it, when chicken is so much cheaper than beef these days?" he asked me rhetorically when we last talked about it, in July 2017. "And there's also the social stigma you get with beef that you don't have with other meats." In previous conversations over the past decade, Prakash had suggested that he avoided eating beef in the city so as not to upset his Hindu neighbors, who might have objected to the smell of it cooking, but that he still savored it on the occasions he had returned to Anandapuram to visit his parents. The two rooms he rented for his family in Hyderabad were modest, but they were in a relatively smart building, the bulk of which was occupied by the higher-caste Hindu owners, on what he described as a middle-class street in a middle-class suburb. No one, he insisted, had ever expressly told him that they must not cook beef on the premises, but he felt that, even if he had wanted to, it would be disrespectful to the landlord, who he was keen to keep on his side. In Hyderabad, finding suitable accommodation in a middle-class area—vital if one's family is to have a chance of ever being seen as middle-class—is difficult, particularly for those from low-caste origins (Säävälä 2003, 237). Likewise, in Mumbai's housing developments, eating particular kinds of food increasingly means being denied accommodation in such neighborhoods (Holwitt 2017). Prakash was acutely aware of this risk, and he believed that their current accommodation provided the best base he could offer from which his own children's status might be elevated in the future.

Paying the rent and school fees had been a struggle: he had a bachelor's degree from a college in Bhavanipur, which finally helped secure him a reasonably remunerated clerical job with a city-based NGO, but he was employed on a series of rolling one-year contracts and so lived in a continuous state of tension that each year would be the last in which he had work. Nevertheless, he had resisted pressure from his wider family to return to Anandapuram on the basis that providing this background, however precarious, would enable his children to get good, secure jobs and make good marriages in the future. Not eating beef in Hyderabad, as he told it when I chatted with him informally back in 2009, was a sacrifice worth making: it meant his son and daughter, who identified at school only as Christians, were not stigmatized as Malas. "If they don't eat beef," he said, "how can anyone tell what caste they come from, especially if they are well educated?" People might speculate about their background, he suggested, but they would not like to ask directly.

More recently, however, Prakash had shifted in our conversations from talking about beef eating as a surreptitiously enjoyed treat, on par perhaps with the alcohol he occasionally drank with male friends from Anandapuram or from work, away from the gaze of the local neighborhood, to seeing it as a practice evocative of mild disgust.[2] Talking about it certainly caused him some discomfort. "When I was with my parents, they cooked it, so yes, I ate it," he told me in 2017. "But when I studied at college for my degree, my friends were not beef eaters, so I never ate it in their company, and I have avoided it ever since when I can." He recalled students from his school and college cohorts who discriminated against those who were known to eat beef, and it clearly still rankled him. He did not want to be a person from whom others refused the offer of a glass of water, for example, and was even keener that his children should not experience such indignities. Unlike some of the others I spoke to—such as my Telugu teacher Victoria-Rani, the Christian beef eater—he did not respond to these references to his caste-based polluted status with a defiant celebration of beef eating but conversely, by rejecting any practice that he felt could be used to diminish him socially. In his apartment in Hyderabad, the only meat now on the menu was chicken, which they ate almost every Sunday—in both fried and *pulusu* form—or, occasionally, fish and prawns. His rejection of beef, he insisted, was not out of any deference to the position taken on it by the BJP and their followers but rather mirrored his son's and daughter's preferences and helped to shore up the family's still-insecure status.

He was also aware of the debates about cattle slaughter and beef eating that were reported in the newspapers and on the television. "That thing in the English and Foreign Languages University," he said, referencing a mass eating of beef that had been organized at the college campus in 2010 and that had triggered counterprotests (see Gundimeda, Tharakeshwar, and Bhrugubanda 2012), "you need to understand, that wasn't about food, that was about political issues. And I agree that Muslims and others, if they want to eat beef, they should be allowed to. It's especially important for Muslims. They need to eat beef at their own festival times. But my feeling is that it's not necessary to have these university beef festivals. No one objects to people eating beef at home, so why make a big public fuss? It only makes the tensions worse. Look, some people eat snakes. Some people eat frogs. That's fine, I don't care, let them eat whatever they want. But it shouldn't be made a public issue. Should we have a frog festival? That would also cause some problems for people. Or for dogs? Chinese people like to eat dogs—especially street dogs, people say. Do we need a festival for that too?"

He went on: "So, no, I am not against beef eating. But it shouldn't be used to cause problems in the community. Cows are like gods to Hindus. And if they see people eating beef, the Hindus will get upset and then they will cause problems for the Muslims, and for us Christians."

• • •

This fragment of Prakash's story articulates well the ambivalences toward cows and beef eating that were expressed by many of my research participants, and the different ways in which food might be utilized in personal wrangles over one's status and identity on a larger stage. His narrative also helps to locate the incongruities and shifts in his position over time in relation to the varying circumstances in which, to him, those shifts make good sense. He had adapted his diet, and no doubt other aspects of his behavior, to reflect what he predicted would ensure the best possible outcomes for his family. Prakash's story also challenges the assumption that you are *either* a beef eater or you are not, that culinary identities are fixed and reproduced ad infinitum through caste and community endogamous marriage practices. They are not. Nor does the fact of beef eating, associated as it is with particular communal or caste identities, neatly map onto those identities sculpted by pro-beef, anti–*gau rakshak* activists and commentators, which, in many cases, are taken on uncritically by their opponents. Like many I spoke to in Anandapuram, Bhavanipur, and Hyderabad, direct contestation of the government's stance on cattle slaughter was not the route Prakash wanted to take, even as he expressed disapproval of it.

CHARTING CHANGING ATTITUDES

Ethnographic data on my interlocutors' foodways challenges the stark divides regularly drawn in relation to South Asia between, first, vegetarianism and nonvegetarianism and, second, within the latter group between those who eat beef and those who do not. Such divisions, in turn, have been used to map hierarchical distinctions between castes and religious communities, with the highest social positions occupied by those who follow vegetarian diets (predominantly Brahmins, Vaisyas, and Jains), followed by those who eat meat (in Andhra, the dominant farming Sudra castes, as well as the less economically powerful castes from the same *varna*), and, at the bottom, those who not only eat meat but also eat beef (Dalits, Muslims, and Christians).

On the ground, however, people's eating habits are not so easily or terminally categorized, with many I worked with moving back and forth along a continuum between the poles of eating and not eating meat, and for a variety of different reasons. Shiva, for example, despite being a Madiga, had grown up vegetarian because he had worked as a child for the upper-caste, vegetarian family that fed him. "When I was young," he told me, "my guru advised me that the killing of animals was wrong, so I didn't eat meat for a long, long time." In his seventies, however, and reliant on his son and daughter-in-law to provide his meals, he now ate what they gave him, including meat and even beef. "Before, when I was working, I was paying for the food myself, so it was up to me to choose what we ate. But now I'm old and retired, so I should eat what the family provides. My son, or sometimes his wife, will do the purchasing now. And if we sit together and everyone is eating meat, then I feel that so should I." Beef, he told me, was something he particularly relished these days, not least because his doctor—a Naidu,[3] so from a nonvegetarian but non-beef-eating caste—had recommended that he eat it for health reasons. "The doctor, he's the guru I follow now," said Shiva, with a wry smile.

Ruth, by contrast—and like Prakash, whose story I began the chapter with—had *stopped* eating beef, in her case because, after the death of her husband, she had no one to purchase it for her. Her sons did not wish to buy it from the market. "They see it as a less respectable meat," she explained, "and so now we only eat chicken." And while others, like Shiva, had taken up beef consumption for health reasons—it was particularly associated, even by those who did not eat it, with strength and stamina—many others I spoke to had either given it up or reduced consumption of it in order to control high blood pressure or because, now that they were older, they found it harder to digest. Even Mariamma, a middle-class Bhavanipur Christian who, like Victoria-Rani, had tried to tempt me with beef dishes on earlier visits, later told me she had stopped eating it because of "gastric troubles."

Meat eating shifted both across the course of people's lives—with children of vegetarian families, less bound by food rules in general, more likely to be indulged if they expressed an interest in meat eating than their elders—as well as across space. There were men and women from Anandapuram who went begging in Mumbai, for instance, who told me that they would sometimes eat beef while they were away in the city but would never consider eating it back in the village. Similarly, I knew young people who *officially* did not eat beef but who confessed to trying it when they were far enough away from home, that is, in contexts where eating it would have no discernible negative impact on their status or that of their wider families.

Others I knew, while theoretically categorizing themselves as nonvegetarian, in practice ate meat so rarely, if at all, that their diets were almost identical to those who considered themselves vegetarian. Miriam, for example, a Christian woman who lived in Hyderabad, told me she had seldom eaten meat since her husband died. This was not so much because of dietary observances followed by widows of the kind Sarah Lamb (2000) writes about, which required the high-caste West Bengali widows she described to avoid meat and other "hot" (*garam*) foods to help ensure that their passions were not aroused. Rather, in Miriam's case it was because she had neither the money to buy meat nor the sons to go to the male-dominated meat section of the market to purchase it for the remaining family members. She also now rented accommodation in an intimate block of six single-roomed houses, all sharing one latrine and a communal clothes-washing area, separated from an identical block by a pathway of no more than three meters. The majority of these properties were occupied by Hindu families, so she said she would in any case not have cooked beef there for fear of offending anyone: in such dwellings, cooking smells traveled freely between the houses. "Now," she said, "I might eat meat once in six months, if that. Chicken or beef, when I go to my brother's place."

Miriam's beef consumption was most likely less than that of the non-beef-eating woman I interviewed in Anandapuram, who cooked beef for her husband and children and who, if there was no dal- or vegetable-based alternative available, stirred some of the gravy—but never, as she protested, pieces of the meat—into her rice. What both these examples also show is the gendered, as well as pragmatic, nature of choices taken around what to eat and what not to eat. While I did sometimes observe women at the meat market, shopping in general was seen as a male occupation, and most of the women I knew were not prepared to buy meat for themselves. This was particularly so for those who would otherwise have eaten beef, since purchasing it required them to enter a separate, walled, and gated part of the market. Vegetables, by contrast, could be purchased without even leaving the village, either from a trolley that passed through every day or from the various itinerant sellers who went door-to-door with baskets of produce balanced on their heads.

Other Kinds of Meat

The distinctions drawn between different kinds of meat are also subtler than the implied one between beef on one side and everything else on the other. Pork is perhaps the most obvious other taboo meat, eaten neither by Muslims nor, in Anandapuram and Bhavanipur, by Christians. The latter group claimed that pork was banned by the Bible, that the devil resided within pigs and so, yielding only unclean meat, they should not be eaten. Visiting the natal village of one of my Madiga friends, for example, I was told that the Adivasi Erukala hamlet was even more isolated than those of the beef-eating Madigas and Malas because they kept and consumed pigs, so "no one"—even Dalits—"would want to live alongside them."[4] The reaction of my friend's mother when I asked her—following a litany of complaints about higher-caste neighbors who would only offer her water in a disposable coconut shell—whether they would share food with Erukala households was strikingly similar to that received when I asked non–beef eaters comparable questions about eating beef. "*Chee*! No!" she gagged, screwing up her face in an expression of disgust.[5] "They eat pork!"

Donkey meat was the other meat most commonly rejected by the Christians I worked with. As Christ's favored form of transport, I was told, donkeys were especially blessed. When I surveyed 242 households in Anandapuram in 2013, 191 (or 79 percent) of them listed donkey meat, almost always alongside pork, as a meat that they, or at least most members of their household, did not eat. In addition, given that many of those who did not actively mention it only referred to chicken, beef, goat mutton, and fish as meat that they did eat, I suspect there were several households who did not even consider it an option. There were others who did eat it, at least occasionally, though: some because of what they saw as its health-giving properties (it was seen as increasing "male power," or virility, as well as stamina, strength, and blood quality), others because they liked the taste. It was relatively hard to come by, which for some enhanced its appeal. There were no local shops or market stalls that sold it openly,[6] at least that I was aware of, and those keen to obtain it would have to make special journeys to villages known to cut donkeys (from which I would occasionally receive via WhatsApp photographs of butchered animals from those who had attended).

There were, however, multiple distinctions other than those drawn between beef, pork, and donkey. Ramaiah, for example, from the traditionally hunting Boya caste, told me that while his caste-fellows back in his natal village ate a range of what he described as "jungle meats" not conventionally eaten in Anandapuram—including wild boar, deer, mongoose, rabbit, and squirrel—they did not eat prawns. "There is an old story," he told me, "that our people were trapped on one side of the river and needed to get across to the other to avoid danger. At that time, the prawns rose to the surface of the water and formed a bridge, allowing us to cross. So, for us, prawns are like brothers and sisters. They saved us, so we show them respect by not eating them."

Two of my other interlocutors, one a roving Dalit pastor and the other a fixer for a local politician, had spent considerable time working in Adivasi communities along the road to the seashore and had subsequently developed a taste for crabmeat. Although many people would not eat crab because, as one of them told me, it was "not a respectable meat to eat," once you had mastered the skills necessary to extract the flesh from the claws, it was, they said, both delicious and very good for you. Both men, however, were circumspect about whether they ate beef. Joshua, the Dalit pastor, purchased it for his mother and had eaten it a few times in the past but claimed, like Prakash, not to eat it now, even when offered it in the villages he visited as a pastor.

"I tell them I can't eat it because of my blood pressure," he told me. Joshua had spent a lot of time during his youth in the houses of non-beef-eating-caste families while his parents were away begging in Mumbai, so had not, he told me, developed a taste for it. Samuel, the fixer, initially denied eating beef but eventually confessed that he did sometimes eat it, but *only* if it was *āvu mānsam*, and then *only* the heart. This preference for cow over buffalo related to the fact that his late mother had been a Muslim, but the insistence on only admitting to consumption of the heart seemed to suggest a hierarchical ordering of types of meat within a type of animal. To eat something but not *everything*—whatever that something happened to be—suggested a level of control or moderation that identified one (if only to oneself) as superior to those who drew no such distinctions.

Beef Distinctions

Most other people I knew who ate beef were less particular about which cut they consumed, although important distinctions were drawn between fried, *pulusu* (a "wet" curry, cooked in a sauce or gravy), and dried meat. A *pulusu* was the dish most commonly served for a family dinner in the home, because it best facilitated the consumption of rice. Recipes I collected, in both urban and rural environments, were surprisingly consistent in terms of ingredients, even though quantities varied somewhat. After carefully washing the meat in several changes of water, the chopped-up meat would be sealed in hot oil, usually with the addition of onions and (in a few cases) tomatoes, along with garlic, ginger, green chilies, curry leaves, turmeric, salt, and chili powder. Once the meat had been browned, water would be added to create a gravy, and the curry would either bubble away in a wok-like pan on the gas ring or, as was more common in Hyderabad, finished off more rapidly in a pressure cooker. To serve, chopped coriander leaves were a common garnish, and a couple of cooks told me they also liked to add fresh mint. Several also suggested adding ground coconut, toward the end of cooking, and/or a final masala of ground-up cloves, coriander seeds, and cinnamon. One cook liked to use ground black peppercorns sometimes instead of chili powder. Various vegetables, such as *gongura* (a green leafy vegetable), *dosakaya* (yellow cucumber), potato, or eggplant, might also be included, helping to stretch the meat further, and bones would often be added to the pot to impart additional flavor.

Fried preparations, where pieces of meat were rubbed with chili powder, salt, and turmeric and cooked in oil, sometimes with the addition of garlic, ginger, and coriander leaf, were considered less distinguished than meat cooked with similar spices in a gravy, largely because they were sometimes served as accompaniments to alcoholic drinks and were thus associated with, as one man described them, "rowdy, drinking fellows." Dried meat, both because it was cheap and had a particularly pungent smell and taste, was considered less refined and evoked the most disgust among non–beef eaters and was generally positioned at the bottom of the hierarchy.

Surreptitious Meat Consumption

In addition to the multiple distinctions drawn between those who openly admitted to eating meat and the subtle demarcations between *what* those people ate, the picture is further complicated by the very common narrative, referenced in the previous chapter, of people from non-beef-eating castes secretly indulging in the meat when they got the opportunity. Butchers were united in their claims that people from *all* communities, high-caste Hindus among them, were customers of their meat. Blaming increases in the price of beef on the fact that those who should not be consuming it were doing so surreptitiously was also a common trope, among those I spoke to in Hyderabad as well as my interlocutors in coastal Andhra. While it is difficult to test the veracity of their claims, or to estimate the extent to which those who were not supposed to eat beef actually ate it, there were a number of men I spoke to from nonvegetarian but non-beef-eating castes in all the locations where I conducted fieldwork who confessed that they sometimes ate it, often secretly, away from their own families.

Such transgressions were likely commonplace across India. Ghassem-Fachandi, for example, describes the "darkened glass and intimacy of private cubicles" characteristic of nonvegetarian restaurants in Ahmedabad, in Gujarat, which are "most necessary for the consumption of illicit alcohol that often accompanies carnivorous escapades by vegetarians" (2012, 161). In Anandapuram, I was also struck by the number of people that I knew to eat beef—sometimes because they had told me in casual conversation, sometimes because I had witnessed them buying or eating it—who, when speaking to me "on the record," chose to deny it. "Some people might think less of us if they know we eat beef," one friend told me, a tad sheepishly, when I questioned his denial. "It may not be good for our dignity."

Even those who one might be certain to take the moral high ground are, according to those I spoke to, often directly implicated in the beef chain about which they protest. Mohamed, one of the Hyderabadi butchers I spent time with in Hyderabad, for example, spoke of how cattle that were seized by vigilantes did not always find their way to the cattle shelters but were resold back into the meat market, perhaps even to be reseized. Meat that was not contaminated, he claimed, likewise found its way back into the shops.

Sometimes, he said, paying a sufficiently large bribe was enough for your cargo of cattle to be allowed on its way; this added to the price increases that end-customers were complaining about but was less damaging than an entirely spoiled batch of meat. The anthropologist Atreyee Sen, who conducted fieldwork with militant Hindu women in Mumbai (2007), told me that one of the most virulent Hindu nationalists she ever encountered during her 1999–2000 research was a woman who bought and then chopped up beef to sell to her Christian neighbors (pers. comm., 2019). The woman was apparently ardent in her *political* support for the Shiv Sena and the right's drive for vegetarianism; she certainly drew the line at actually consuming the meat herself. But she also had to make a living, and selling beef, given that she lived in an area dominated by Christians, to her made sense. Against such a variegated background, neatly drawn structural patterns that link high and low with vegetarianism and nonvegetarianism, respectively, and beef with otherness become much more blurry-edged.

AMBIVALENT ATTITUDES TOWARD COWS AND BEEF

Victoria-Rani, my former Telugu teacher, may have been more vocal than many I worked with when she insisted back in 2000 on the importance of eating beef if you were a Christian and/or a former Untouchable, but she was by no means a lone voice. *Not* to eat beef, as her reaction to my refusal of it demonstrated, could be interpreted as a snub, a tacit acceptance of the dominant Hindu thinking that normalized the oppression of those from Dalit castes. Reclaiming beef eating as part of a specifically Christian—as opposed to low-caste—identity was, in her view, a positive act, a celebration of an identity that bound her together with other Christians in India and beyond. Others agreed. Jesuit schools in Tamil Nadu—the next state down on India's eastern coastline—were said to have promoted beef eating as "a provocative, conflict-generating, dramatic act of protest and denial of shame" (Mosse 2010, 254; Arun 2004). University beef festivals in Hyderabad and elsewhere, bringing Victoria-Rani's quiet, mostly private celebration of beef out more loudly into the open, spoke of a similar refusal to have what they saw as their culinary rights subsumed within mainstream Hindu culture.

I was also aware of the same note of defiance in Aziz, the angriest of the butchers I met in Hyderabad several years later. Matching the vitriol Victoria-Rani saved for her perceived high-caste persecutors, Aziz's ire was reserved mainly for what he categorized as "the government"—municipal, state, and central all, in his mind, collapsed into one—who he said was conspiring against small, local meat shops. "Their policy is that *we* can't eat it—that means Indians, that *Indians* can't eat it—but that they still want the revenue they raise from exporting it for *others* to eat." Deeply critical of what he saw as the government's support of particular exporting companies that he told me—inaccurately, as it transpired when I checked—were actually owned by Hindus rather than Muslims, he insisted that the merits of beef were less about a *celebration* of identity than simply an unavoidable part of it. Restrictions on slaughter, on meat selling, or on its consumption were, as he saw it, simply attacks on Muslims. And like Mohamed, the butcher with a larger stall in a more central market, continuing in the business despite the increasingly hostile environment was not an active choice; it defined who he was. "What else can I do?" both men had responded identically when I asked them if they would keep trading if the situation grew worse. "Become a beggar on the streets?" Aziz suggested, dramatically, as a follow-up response.

Mohamed, who was much older, was more circumspect: "My life is nearly at an end; there isn't anything else I can do, so I shall carry on, even though profits are down." Only one of his five sons had remained in the beef business, and in his case only because he had been unable to find alternative employment after completing his bachelor's degree in commerce. The other sons each ran a chicken shop instead, a relatively more straightforward and potentially more sustainable business in the current political climate. His oldest grandson, who sometimes helped Mohamed in the shop, was to be trained in software engineering so that he could move out of the meat business altogether.

In short, then, both the lower-middle-class beef eaters of Bhavanipur I spoke to in 2000 and the beef sellers I interviewed almost two decades later were, unsurprisingly, unequivocally opposed to any government attempt to restrict cattle slaughter or the sale of its meat. In common with Prakash, however, many of those I spoke to in the intervening years took more ambiguous positions on the issues. Consider, for example, the following comments, all offered by people in Anandapuram in response to a question I posed, as part of a 2011 household survey to canvass people's views on the issue, about whether or not they thought the government was right to restrict cattle slaughter:

> Of course, killing cows is not a good thing. The cow is like a god. Chickens are only small animals, so it's okay to eat them. We don't eat beef that often, only sometimes.

> The regulation [restricting cattle slaughter] is probably correct. You shouldn't kill. But now I am eating it anyway.

> Yes, it's wrong to kill, and if we shouldn't kill a cow, then we shouldn't kill a chicken either, but we do. So no, the government is wrong to try to stop it. People need to eat.
>
> It's a good law because they are living creatures. We don't slaughter ourselves, but we do eat beef. They kill, we eat!

All of the speakers quoted above ate beef, at least occasionally, but most were relatively unperturbed by the prospect of greater legislative restrictions on cattle slaughter. Of 52 households I surveyed, roughly a third expressed broad support for regulation—even if they ate beef themselves—and another third opposed it. The remainder were uncertain one way or the other, or they offered ambiguous responses. Killing animals was, as almost everyone I asked said, considered at least theoretically wrong, but, as the last speaker quoted above demonstrates, it did not necessarily follow that eating their flesh, once they had been killed, was also considered wrong. In the same way that those who sold their cattle into the meat market distanced themselves from what their actions led to, so too did many of those at the other end of the beef chain distance themselves from the links that preceded their meat purchases. Slaughter was an issue for the butchers and meat sellers to deal with, not something with which they needed to concern themselves.

Others saw the restrictions imposed by the state as targeted specifically at Hindus, and so unimportant for Christians or Muslims to take heed of. "Hindus say you shouldn't kill, but Christians can eat both buffalo and cow meat. It doesn't say anywhere in the Bible that we shouldn't, so I don't think it's a problem," as one man put it. "The only problem is the price." Another told me, "As Hindus, you shouldn't cut or eat cattle. They pray for cows. They are like gods to them, so I suppose it's correct that they have that rule." In other words, many of my interlocutors could see a logic in what the authorities were doing, but they did not see the injunctions as relating directly to them. Indeed, for some, any such regulation was simply deemed impossible to follow and therefore irrelevant: "Whatever the rules say, as Muslims we have to eat anyway," Uzma explained to me. "At Bakrid [Eid al-Adha], it's compulsory to slaughter a cow and a goat, so we have to do it."

Christians were not as constrained by religious injunctions, but biblical rules were given precedence over state regulation in a similar kind of way. One interviewee told me, "If you read the Bible, it says that God created everything to be eaten, so we don't need these kinds of rules. But it is good to have some kind of restrictions, for example, that we shouldn't kill or eat meat every day. Moderation is a good thing. But these government laws, they are only about Hindu beliefs, so they shouldn't be there." Nor was what I read as an increased assertiveness in the messages put out by Hindu nationalist groups seen by those I worked with on the ground as particularly significant. "All this about cows, it's not a new thing," explained another interviewee. "From the beginning, the Dharmaśāstras have ruled that we should not kill them, but even those who wrote such rules—the Brahmins!—are not following them. People will write down one thing and do another thing!" The point being made by the speaker in this case was that what the law demanded in theory and what happened in practice were two entirely separate things.

What seemed like shifts in people's attitudes toward cattle slaughter and beef consumption were related to changes across time (Staples 2018). The strength of pro-beef feeling among those like Victoria-Rani in 2000 was a consequence of local Christians fearing that their religious identity was under immediate threat. A decade later, people's views seemed more ambivalent: they still wanted to eat beef, to be sure, but more because they enjoyed its taste and texture than because it symbolized a radical identity politics or a positive Christian identity. Some of them also felt that regulation of the beef market was appropriate, that only certain cattle should be deemed suitable for consumption. The change was for multiple reasons, but principally because the immediate threat from the Hindu right had been in decline since the BJP was knocked back into second place in the general elections of 2004 and 2009. When that threat began to resurface in the run-up to the 2014 election, beef once again emerged as polarizing issue, this time also attracting the attention of Dalit and Muslim activists, who organized beef festivals and other events targeted at reclaiming beef as a marker of positive identity. Away from the political hotbeds of university campuses, however, those I worked with remained circumspect about celebrating their beef-eating habits. In some cases—as for people like Prakash—they chose to give it up altogether, or to eat it but officially to claim that they did not, rather than to expose their low social status.

Not only have attitudes toward cattle slaughter and beef consumption changed along a temporal axis in response to wider changes but my research participants' attitudes have also shifted according to the centrality of certain identities at play in different contexts. All those, like Victoria-Rani, who proactively positioned themselves against what they perceived to be the government's position—and that of the vigilante groups who decried cattle slaughter—fitted into a particular stratum of the new, provincial middle class occupied by Dalits and Christians who had done relatively well. They were teachers, nurses, and clerks, and some of them, through successfully navigating the reservations system,[7] had acquired much sought-after government jobs. They were also educated, at least to degree level, and had some command of English. This gave them greater access to debates and events that were taking place elsewhere in India, in relation to which they positioned their own situations. Crucially, they also identified strongly with their local churches and saw their Christianity as firmly intertwined with their caste identities. Unlike in Anandapuram, where the community was made up of multiple castes, the congregations of the churches that the Bhavanipur Christians I knew attended were drawn almost exclusively from Mala and Madiga castes, the two main Dalit castes of the region. Eating beef, in that context, was very much bound up with an identity that stood in direct opposition to high-caste Hinduism and connected them, often across generations, to other families from comparable backgrounds.

People like Prakash came from a similar caste background and had, in Hyderabad, achieved a comparable class identity. Although he was less well established financially than people like Victoria-Rani or Mariamma, who also had small areas of paddy land back in their natal places, he was likewise educated to degree level and considered his family upwardly mobile. Critically, however, Prakash was not closely identified with a church in Hyderabad; he identified as a Christian, but he did not attend church, except when he returned to Anandapuram. His day-to-day associates, then, were not simply people like himself but work colleagues—a mix of urban, educated Hindus, Christians, and Muslims from varied caste backgrounds—and neighbors, mostly higher-caste, solidly middle-class Hindus. Within these loose networks there was nothing to gain, for Prakash, from building an oppositional identity based on beef consumption, and—given that a number of his colleagues would not have eaten beef and that some were vegetarian—there was plenty to lose.

Those like Victoria-Rani, by contrast, in proclaiming their beef-eating credentials as a positive aspect of their Christian identity, bound themselves firmly to other local Christians from the same church, built solidarity, and maintained a strong sense of self-worth. "And why shouldn't we eat beef?" asked Jhoti, a Bhavanipur Christian in her mid-twenties, one of my few interlocutors with something matching Victoria-Rani's defiance when I spoke to her in early 2017. "What people want to eat in their own homes is their own business, no? This is about Hindus oppressing us. We don't want to take beef and put it in their temples or anything like that, just to eat it peacefully in our houses. But this is a country for Hindus, and it has been since 1947. Why else did we have partition?" Living in a small town, denial of their birth-ascribed Dalit identity was not a possibility in the way it was for Prakash and others like him who had moved away to the city. Recasting beef as something status-enhancing rather than status-diminishing was thus important, and something that people with Jhoti's educational background and associated social capital were arguably more adept at realizing.

The relative ambivalence toward cattle slaughter shown by those I spoke to in Anandapuram, then, was not just a reflection of a changing sociopolitical climate. Living in a mixed-caste community, albeit one in which almost everyone ate meat and around two-thirds of the population ate beef—63 percent, or 153 out of 242 households surveyed in 2013—there was less to be gained by asserting a Dalit identity than there was from suggesting that, because they were living in a leprosy colony, the differences between them did not make a difference (see, for example, Staples 2007). In short, positions taken in relation to cows and beef were directly related to the highly specific and contingent identity politics of different beef-eating groups, and so they cannot be collapsed into one another or considered as necessarily the same.

CONCLUSION

Keen as I was to get to the perspectives of ordinary beef eaters, I had no direct contact with those cast as their direct opponents: the self-styled vigilante groups whose violent rhetoric and actions evoked terror in some of the Hyderabadi butchers I interviewed, or else elicited anger in others whose identities they threatened. Based on media reports and the wider literature on Indian vigilantism and the rise of the Hindu right, however, it seems likely that they were also motivated by an identity politics and ambivalence toward the state. Many of the people I encountered, wherever they positioned themselves in relation to beef eating, considered the state and its regulations peripheral to their everyday lives, relating to it in the fuzziest of ways. They recognized that they had to work around whatever it was the state appeared to be demanding at any given time, and certainly they were not oblivious to the effects of some of its policies. The demonetization that occurred just before one of my field trips in 2016, for example, had a major bearing on everyone's access to cash and, in the case of the smaller butchers I worked with, affected their capacity to buy stock.

Such recognition is not the same, however, as actively complying with whatever the government's demands might be. For butchers in Bhavanipur who were told that they could no longer slaughter cattle in their own domestic compounds, for example, the response was not to actually stop slaughtering animals. Rather, it was to do it earlier in the day and more discreetly than they might otherwise have done. Similarly, the legality or illegality of beef was not the deciding factor for most people in whether it would be eaten or not. All bar the most educated—such as a couple of recently qualified lawyers in Anandapuram, who helped me to clarify more precisely what the law required—tended to be unclear about where the lines between the state (and its various arms), vigilantes and activists, and other forms of authority, such as the church, should be drawn. The rules to be obeyed, wherever they came from, were those least likely to disadvantage them or disrupt their everyday lives, or those that appeared to speak most directly to the identities they claimed for themselves or had imposed upon them. Authority was contingent.

Such a situation is perhaps consistent with the outsourcing of law and order that is characteristic of neoliberalism (Sundar 2010, 114), with culpability displaced onto those who take up the causes it tacitly approves. Such blurring of lines is certainly also recognized by the vigilantes themselves, who commit themselves to direct action precisely to counter what they perceive of as the inertia of the state. For the BJP and other regionalist parties, "vigilantism is not a response to an exceptional situation, but a permanent condition of the way that the relation between party and state is organized, with the cadre and the ruling party relationship dividing up the space of civil society and the state between themselves" (115).

For those engaged at the sharp end of vigilantism itself, as ethnographic work with self-acclaimed child soldiers in the old city of Hyderabad demonstrates (Sen 2012), most of them are also motivated, as for the most vocal of my own interlocutors, by a combination of fear and comradery, by a sense of belonging in a world in which they felt marginalized and alienated.

That many of the cow protectionists are not, in the end, so very different from the beef eaters perhaps makes the existence of Hindu fundamentalist beef sellers or moral disapproval of animal slaughter by meat eaters less paradoxical than they at first appear. Attitudes toward cattle slaughter and beef eating are both nuanced and fluid, refined in relation to intricately negotiated identities and contexts. And while caste and community affiliations are indubitably the most significant of the broader identities to which people attributed their eating practices, their food choices were also shaped in relation to class, gender, age, family position, and education, as well as a range of external factors. Distinctions between eating and not eating meat are better plotted along a continuum—along which one might also shift position over time and according to circumstance—rather than as a binary opposition. And on the meat-eating side of the scale, we need to make far more complex distinctions than those routinely drawn between beef on one side and chicken, mutton, and fish—the default "respectable meats"— on the other. Doing so muddies the waters and challenges conventional wisdom, but it also enables us to start better understanding culinary decisions taken in a changing sociopolitical climate.

CHAPTER FIVE

Health, the Environment, and the Rise of the Chicken

I CAN still remember the first time, back in 1984, that I ate meat in Anandapuram. It was chicken, consumed just days after my arrival in the village at a wedding feast, where it was served up alfresco, on leaf plates laid out on narrow tables for the higher-ranking guests or on raffia mats on the ground for everyone else. Picking out the chewy meat from the gristle, most of it still attached to splintered chunks of bone, exercised my fingers and jaws in ways that a daily diet of dal and well-cooked vegetables could not. Pulling or gnawing the flesh from the bones and separating it from whole pods of cardamom, shards of cinnamon, or spiky cloves also demanded an attention and a dexterity that brought a focus to the food. The act of eating it, and its distinctive feel and flavor, forced me to savor its specialness in a way that everyday dinners did not. The latter were consumed more rhythmically, the food shoveled in and swallowed quickly to sate hunger. But after the labor demanded by the wedding feast, the fingers of my right hand, stained yellow with turmeric and fragrant with spice, provided a sensory reminder of the chicken curry long after it had been consumed. I can no longer recall, if I ever knew, whose wedding it was that I had attended that day, nor do I have more than the haziest memory of the watery *sambar* that was poured over the rice once the meat was eaten, or even the fiery *gongura patchidi* that always lent its distinctive tang to the boiled white rice at village weddings. But I do remember that chicken.

◆ ◆ ◆

Meat, for those who eat it, is as vital in the forging and maintenance of relationships as *not* eating meat is for those identified as vegetarian. The shared eating of meat, as in the vignette above from a wedding in Anandapuram, is as much about unifying people as it is about the separation and hierarchical ordering of diners that many classical ethnographic accounts interpret such commensal events as being concerned with.[1] As Appadurai phrased it, "Food in South Asia is prone to be used in social messages of two diametrically opposed sorts. It can serve to indicate and construct social relations characterized by equality, intimacy, or solidarity; or it can serve to sustain relations characterized by rank, distance, or segmentations" (1981, 507). Shared nonvegetarian meals among those I knew in Anandapuram were almost exclusively of the first sort.

Meat also draws its specialness from the contrasts that can be made between it and other components of the everyday diet. A day on which meat is eaten demarcates that day as different from the ordinary. To channel a linguistic metaphor of the kind used by Barthes or by Geertz (1975), with his well-worn notion of society as text, eating meat could be seen as a form of punctuation.[2] For militant vegetarians, on the other hand, eating meat, beef especially, stood in for negative otherness. My Muslim butcher friend Aziz was only telling part of the story, however, when he located the meanings attributed to meat entirely within the realms of the symbolic. His comment—"It's not about the meat. It's about Muslims."—made the point that current reactions to the beef trade were not explicable simply in terms of cattle's putative sacred qualities but related to wider social prejudices. However, retention of meat's symbolic position as representative variously of specialness and sacrilege *did* also depend—as the vignette above suggests—on its materiality. Meat's sensory qualities in terms of flavor, smell, texture, and chewiness, as well as its cost, accessibility, and status in relation to a range of external factors, all contributed to what meat could be made to mean at any given time and place.

But meat was not only understood, and experienced, in relation to other kinds of food in a very general sense, with meat meals marking the rest period between one week and the next or signaling major events in the course of life. Nor was consumption of it wholly shaped by the political contexts which overdetermined discussions both about meat in general and beef in particular. Shifting attitudes concerning whether to eat or not to eat beef, then, cannot be plotted simply in relation to the ebbs and flows of Hindu nationalist fervor, with meat's changing consumption patterns indexing levels of resistance to, fear of, or compliance with government lines. Rather, a penchant or otherwise for eating beef was also shaped by economic, environmental, health-related, and aesthetic concerns—some local, some global—which, in turn, fed into the capacity of beef to carry particular meanings. "My informants' perspective on the cow," as I wrote elsewhere, "was not simply oppositional to that of the high-caste Hindu; rather, it was flexible and contingent" (Staples 2018, 74).

RECENT CHANGES IN MEAT-EATING PRACTICES

A flattening-out of practices among those who ate meat in Anandapuram or Bhavanipur was the most notable change in relation to meat eating over the past forty years. In the past, while members of Dalit castes, Malas, and Madigas recalled eating meat, and especially beef, several times a week, dominant Sudra-caste diners insisted that, back then, they only ate goat or chicken—and never beef—at festival times. In the case of the latter group, their diets had been supplemented more regularly in some villages by the small fish that were once bountiful in the water of the paddy fields (and subsequently expelled by pesticides introduced to protect the rice). These days, despite variations in recipes and other dietary tweaks that might denote status differences, including the inclusion or rejection of beef as an option, for both groups meat tended to be a weekly affair. No one in Anandapuram or Bhavanipur (and almost no one I knew in Hyderabad) admitted to eating pork; a few occasionally ate donkey meat. Other options, from "jungle meats" to cat or crabs, catered to specialist tastes (informed by identity) and/or medical requirements. Changes in how and which meat was consumed, however, were not only a matter of what was going on politically.

DECLINE OF THE GOAT

Goat, first of all, had become less widely eaten in the area I worked because, like the small fish that once filled the paddy fields, ecological change meant that it was now harder to come by. Common land, where goat herders might once have taken their animals to graze, had been diminished by the new building developments that had dramatically changed Bhavanipur's skyline over recent years. A new flyover had recently been completed to help deal with the noticeable increase in traffic through the town, and the construction of several new residential blocks suggested a gradual increase in population. Neighbors who had previously kept a few goats to fatten up and sell to others in the village no longer did so, they told me, because it had become too expensive to feed them. "Before, there was lots of green land around where goats could eat," Mohandas, who lived a couple of streets away from me, explained. "Now all the land is taken up, and farmers are using lots of pesticides to keep the goats away. If they eat that stuff, they get sick and die, so that has also meant a drop in the goat population. If you lose a goat, it's a big loss. If you lose a chicken, it's a loss too, of course, but not such a big investment."

Among the higher castes, who in the past had only eaten meat at festivals, the shift toward more regular consumption of meat also demanded a cheaper option than goat. "Forty years ago," my elderly friend Venkata Reddy told me, "when we ate goat, or even chicken, the meat would come from within the village. There would be a *dandora* [a proclamation by the village announcer, often accompanied by a drum to draw attention as he marched through the lanes of the community] that one of the goat herders planned to cut an animal, and if we had money or something else he wanted to exchange for it, we would go and get some. Maybe it would happen a few times a year. That's how it worked." And although there were still shops in the market that sold goat mutton, it was double the price per kilogram of either chicken or beef. Goat mutton thus remained desirable, but out of reach for most of my interlocutors.

RISE OF THE CHICKEN

Fish, prawns, and other animals were also occasionally consumed by those I worked with. Some of them, like the "jungle meats" eaten by Ramaiah, were sourced informally and on an ad hoc basis; others, like the prawns marketed by the shrimp hatcheries that now dotted the coastline and employed several women from Anandapuram who would previously have worked in the paddy fields, were now commercially produced. But among meat-eating preferences, one creature stands out: the chicken. Although chicken has long been common as a nonvegetarian option in coastal Andhra—the bird is thought to have first originated in South Asia, as long ago as 3200 BCE (Wood-Gush 1959)—the ways in which it is eaten, and the very bird itself, have changed dramatically over the last forty years. These changes, in turn, have had a significant impact on beef and goat consumption, as well as on meat-eating patterns more generally. Chicken, more than any other meat, had made a difference. The fact that many of the recent changes I describe below resonate with global shifts in poultry distribution and consumption—heralding the emergence of what Jane Dixon called "the global chicken" (2002, 164)—offers compelling evidence that there is more than Hindu nationalism, important though that is, at play in shaping India's contemporary meat-eating practices.

Local Change and Chicken

When Ramaswamy, a chicken seller who had been running a business on the same site since 1980, started trading, his was the only chicken shop in Bhavanipur's market. Prior to that, chickens were much more likely home-reared country breeds, purchased, like goat meat, from neighbors rather than the market. Now there were ten shops at least, as well as others, some of them more transitory, that seemed to have sprung up on the main road out of town to capitalize on passing trade. In 2017, I counted four chicken shops on the half-mile stretch between Anandapuram and Bhavanipur's town center, as well as six more—some of them operating alongside the shops selling the raw meat—that sold chicken-related products. There was a cluster, for example, of four chicken *pakora* stalls, selling battered and fried snacks to a mixture of students passing time after classes and farm laborers as they returned home hungry from the fields. Some ate them there, standing at the roadside, some took away the food to eat as a side dish to the brandy or arrack they would later pick up from the liquor shop, and others bought them to take home as a peripheral item to eat with the evening rice meal. There was also a restaurant that advertised itself exclusively as a "Chicken Biryani Centre."

Other outlets also sold chicken alongside other dishes. The Chinese stalls, for example, served chicken as well as egg-based and vegetarian preparations—either as what they called chicken Manchurian, a Chinese-inspired version of the chicken *pakora*, served in a soy- and chili-based sauce—or in nonvegetarian stir fries, often cooked with egg. A number of tandoori and other nonvegetarian stalls and restaurants also sold chicken as the default nonvegetarian option. Meat dishes served at Rock Starz—the air-conditioned fast-food joint—were also centered around chicken. In addition to various burgers, all chicken-based, its menu offered chicken nuggets and fingers, hot wings, chicken lollipops, popcorn chicken, and boneless strips. It was, according to Das, my research assistant, "the closest you'll get in Bhavanipur to Kentucky Fried Chicken. That's what it's trying to be." Improved electricity supply and the relative cost-effectiveness of generators that enabled such outlets to maintain refrigeration made this a possibility in ways that it simply would not have been even twenty years earlier: the outlet could buy readymade frozen chicken products, in themselves relatively new innovations, from wholesalers and cook them on demand. To ensure that all tastes were catered for, the menu also listed a dizzying array of more than thirty chicken biryanis, curries, and Chinese-inspired dishes to choose between, the majority of them marketed as snacks rather than alternatives to the meals one would eat at home.

Back in the early 1980s, however, there were few opportunities in Bhavanipur to eat outside the home, aside from the tiffin stands which sold *dosa*s and *idli*s, and a few utilitarian canteens and messes that sold "plate meals" or "full meals" (with limited or unlimited rice, respectively). There were even fewer places to eat nonvegetarian food. When Ramaswamy first began trading in 1978, he sold only eggs, sourced in towns within a fifty-mile radius and transported back to the market on the train or sometimes by bus. "There were no plastic trays then," he recalled. "I'd buy up to a hundred cardboard trays, each with thirty eggs, and pay the bus conductor something to let me keep them in the gap near the driver's seat at the front of the bus. The farms, then, only kept chickens for egg production: there were no broilers in those days." In the late 1970s and early 1980s, if you ate chicken in that area, it was most likely from an Aseel breed, one of the hardy, brown-feathered varieties that some families still reared, in very small numbers, in Anandapuram. People reared their own, to sell to neighbors; if you wanted chicken back then, I was told, the best way was to go house to house until you found somebody ready to sell you one. Such "country" birds, as they were also referred to, were almost certainly the source of the chicken I ate at the wedding feast I described in my opening vignette.

Chicken after the Green Revolution

Things began to change in India with the introduction of large-scale intensive poultry units in the wake of the Green Revolution in the 1960s, a time when the Food and Agriculture Organization of the United Nations also began promoting broiler chicken farming in India as a good source of cheap protein for the growing population. Subsequently the production of broiler chickens, white-feathered, fast-growing, and plumper than their "country" counterparts, had increased at a rate of up to 10 percent per annum.[3] The effects of these shifts, however, only started becoming tangible in places like Bhavanipur from the 1980s. "After 1980," Ramaswamy told me, "we sold eggs and chickens too, but broilers. Now we don't sell eggs, except for wholesale. Chickens are my main business. We did try raising our own chickens, but there wasn't really any profit in that, from the numbers we reared. Also, sometimes we made a loss, especially if the chickens got sick and they died before they were ready for sale." Instead, these days he bought up to a thousand birds at a time from one of the larger farms, fifty miles north—more when there were festivals that his customers would be catering for—and kept them for the shortest time possible in his own, relatively small sheds until they were ready for sale. He explained the process as follows:

When we started, we tried to buy and raise chickens from closer by from the smaller farms, but they couldn't compete on price. The bigger farms can take big loans and buy chicks in bulk: they'll do it in a big way, a hundred sheds or more, and they'll buy lakhs of birds along with large quantities of feed, so they will get a good rate.[4] The breeders will give the best birds to the biggest farms—it's easier for them to sell everything to one place. Smaller farms can only get lower-quality birds, the ones that the bigger farms don't want, and because they can't buy so many, they won't get a good rate either. The really big farms can also buy when the rates are low and hold out until the selling price is high, but the smaller farms can't afford to do that; they can't wait. It has meant that a lot of the smaller farms closed, and the larger ones became even bigger. They even made multistory farms, on the outskirts of villages and in the business center of [the nearest city]. Nowadays we buy them in cages and bring them back by truck; you can get up to two thousand in one lorry. The whole lorry, with the chickens inside it, gets weighed on a special weighing bridge.

The birds would then be transported, twenty or so at a time (more ahead of the Sunday rush), to Ramaswamy's shop in the market, where they would be displayed in wire cages and slaughtered by one of the two cutters he employed, more or less to order. Refrigerated storage was limited on-site, and most customers did not have fridges at home either, so they were keen to ensure that the meat they were buying was fresh.

Promoting the Broiler

In the early days, Ramaswamy conceded, the broilers were less popular among customers than the country chickens. As my own informants attested, they liked the chewiness and the stronger flavor of the home-reared breeds. "But then came the advertising, on billboards, in the newspapers, on the radio, and later on TV," he said. "The message was: come and try it! People started to learn that it took less fuel to cook the broilers and less cooking time, and it had a better taste and was also good to fry. The country birds, they are older, so they can be very tough: okay for boiling in a gravy-based curry, but not so good for chicken fry. And within three years, everyone came around to it; the rate was much lower, and the chicken was good."

With it taking only six to eight weeks from hatching for the broiler birds to be ready for sale as meat, as opposed to up to six months for the local varieties, the latter simply could not compete, either on price or in terms of meeting growing demand. Chicken, even at its most expensive, was no costlier than the once-cheap option of beef and, during the hot season, was often considerably cheaper. With inflation hitting the prices of vegetables and other foods, chicken could also, according to an advertising campaign launched to market the Godrej-branded "Real Good Chicken" (RGC) in major cities, even compete on price with vegetables; "Ab chicken sabzi se bhi sasta!" (Chicken is now cheaper than vegetables!) rang out the company's message from urban bus stands and billboards in 2014, imploring even the poorer residents of Mumbai and Bengaluru to buy their chilled, prepackaged 400-gram packs of chicken (Menon 2014).

Global Chickens: The US Influence

The anthropologist Steve Striffler documents a similar process that had occurred a few decades earlier in America:

> The amount of time required to turn a day-old chick into a full-grown broiler decreased by almost 20 percent between 1947 and 1951 alone. At the same time, the bird required less feed. In 1940, chickens required more than four pounds of feed for every pound of weight gained. By the late 1980s, this figure was down to around two pounds. As a result, from the 1920s to the mid-1950s the price of chicken declined steadily (and faster than the prices of its main competitors). In the late 1980s, the real price of chicken was less than one-third of its cost in 1955. (2005, 16)

Indians ate chicken differently from their American counterparts, in different dishes and at different frequencies, but the birds consumed in each case have followed remarkably similar trajectories, helped along by the economic liberalization that transformed India in the 1990s and the rise of "the global chicken" (Dixon 2002). Indeed, the story of chicken in both locations has become increasingly intertwined in recent years. The American chicken giant Tyson—a company frequently referenced by Striffler (2005) in narrating the history of chicken in the US, and originally built up in the 1940s and 1950s by its founder John Tyson (Schwartz 1991)—has been working with the Indian company Godrej since 2008 in order, in the words of Godrej's own website, to "cater to India's expanding food service industry, quick-service restaurants and the universe of modern retailers, with innovative food solutions, at world-class standards, customized to local tastes. We even offer some iconic Indian food items and bring restaurant-like experience to your home, at affordable prices."[5]

While the smaller-scale or more transient stalls that sold chicken *pakora*s and the like relied on sellers like Ramaswamy for their stock, Rock Starz and the other self-styled fast-food centers in Bhavanipur purchased their stocks already processed from Godrej or its competitors. One might also compare the rise in US chicken consumption and decline in sales of beef, about which there have been health concerns (Striffler 2005, 17), with how the two kinds of meat have fared in the Indian context. Indeed, one might suggest that this pattern represents a global trend. The Dutch Rabobank, which carried out an assessment of the poultry industry globally over fifteen years ago, found that, even then, "worldwide demand for poultry products had increased substantially in both developed and developing countries at the expense of beef and pork consumption" (Rabobank International 1993, 21, cited in Dixon 2002, 169). The forces of *Hindutva* were clearly not alone in shaping the relative popularity, in terms of consumption, of chicken over beef.

In both America and India, the meat from broilers also proved more versatile than that of other breeds, opening up the possibilities for different preparations than in the past. In India, the more tender meat was better for dry fries, *pakora*s, and Chinese-style recipes than its country counterpart, and, according to Ramaswamy, these days "higher-class people also buy boneless chicken to cook and eat in a sandwich." Certainly, meat sellers had risen to the challenge of providing what buyers, domestic and wholesale, appeared to want (or, viewed from the other direction, consumers had warmly responded to what was being offered). In the early 1980s, if one wanted to buy chicken it was usual to buy a whole bird, which was slaughtered and cut at the point of sale into bite-sized pieces, bones included, that would then be rendered into a *pulusu*. Nowadays it was increasingly possible to choose to buy chicken with or without skin, boneless and, in the cities (no doubt helped by the likes of Tyson and Godrej), by cut rather than bird. The anthropologist Henrike Donner told me, for example, that in Kolkata—where she worked with middle-class women in domestic contexts (2008)—shops had begun offering frozen packs of chicken breasts, thighs, or drumsticks rather than simply chicken as a whole bird. This had upped chicken's status as a cheap meat to a product through which one could showcase one's class credentials and high levels of sophistication. A pack of chicken breasts, for example, made it possible for middle-class buyers to prepare European-inspired recipes like "chicken Neapolitan," dishes that in the past would have been unachievable.

Sanitizing the Chicken

Most of my own informants, whether in the countryside or the city, still bought their chickens freshly slaughtered from the market. In common with the Moroccan women in whose homes Katharina Graf learned to shop and cook, they tended to "rely on their own bodily and knowledgeable practices of self-certification to identify and name what they consider proper food" (2016, 73). Quality and safety were likewise generally identified not by smart packaging and labeling but by "familiarity, traceability or proximity of food products" (75), as well as by "consumer competence" (Jung 2014, 109). Nevertheless, for the middle-class city dwellers who could afford it and who were arguably more distanced from the everyday sourcing and preparation of the food consumed, processed chicken had its attractions. Buying the meat chilled, safely contained in plastic packaging rather than warm and bloody from the butcher's block, even enabled customers to delegate chicken purchasing to their children, who would not otherwise have been exposed to the excesses of the meat market (Menon 2014). In the same way that the disassociation of slaughtering and butchery had begun to sanitize meat in eighteenth-century Europe (Vailles 1994, 15–17), such moves in India also helped to distance chicken from its origins as meat, rendering it less of an overt threat than that posed by the raw flesh, chicken or otherwise, sold amid the animal stench of the market.

Packaging also embellished the products with what Harris Solomon calls "invitational qualities," simultaneously "filtering out public scandals of adulterated, open-market foods while retaining the nutritional, healthy goodness connecting bodies to companies" (2016, 119). The potential for such shifts were not lost on companies such as the American fast-food chain McDonald's, which had pulled off the feat of running restaurants in Ahmedabad that served nonvegetarian fare in which vegetarians were still prepared to dine. Most strict vegetarians would not consent to eating food that had been produced in a kitchen where the cook had touched meat. McDonald's had managed to attract them both through clever advertising and by offering their food, in contrast to the darkened nonvegetarian eateries with private booths where meat could be eaten surreptitiously, in the full glare of brightly lit visibility. Vegetarian food, color-coded green, was observably kept fully separated from the orange-coded meat products: "Employees use separate equipment and machines to prepare vegetarian and nonvegetarian items, which is advertised on every menu card. The assembly lines of the restaurant, as well as the menu, are clearly separated into orange and green sections, and all cooks who prepare vegetarian items wear green aprons and are theoretically forbidden to cross into the orange section" (Ghassem-Fachandi 2012, 160–61).

Like the chilled and packaged meat offered by Godrej, McDonald's chicken burgers were also sanitized, scarcely distinguishable from the vegetable-based alternatives: "'Meat' is a euphemism for the bland substance of the McChicken sandwich.... [It has] the same consistency and color as the vegetable mix in the McVeggie or McAloo Tikki burger" (Ghassem-Fachandi 2012, 160). As is the case elsewhere in the world, no other animal, at least to date, had shown quite the versatility to adapt to the various contexts of contemporary India as the broiler chicken. To quote Jane Dixon, whose focus is on the Australian chicken market, "Chicken is one of the few traditional foods that has not attracted religious, economic or social taboos." The point she goes on to make—that chicken in some cases might even be acceptable to those who identified themselves as "vegetarians" (2002, 171)—no doubt also contributed to McDonald's success in India, where chicken is the only meat served.

In the Indian context, chicken has never quite achieved the nonmeat or nonanimal status that it has elsewhere (Dixon 2002, 171), but the versatility attributed to it was possible, at least in part, because chicken—unlike beef or, for that matter, pork—was also acceptable to everyone who ate meat. In Bhavanipur, a town with around 20,000 households, Ramaswamy's shop sold around five hundred kilograms on Sundays—about half of his total weekly sales—mostly to domestic customers, the majority of it freshly slaughtered and chopped and sold by the kilogram. He estimated that around two-thirds of his customers were men but that they came from across castes, social classes, and communities: "Laborers will sometimes buy meat on the way to work. The higher classes, they will come out and buy on Sundays. Christians—there are lots in Bhavanipur—will often buy on Sundays too. Hindus only eat on Sundays and on holidays, but Christians like to eat it more often if they can. Hindus may be prevented from eating it because of pujas and festivals, and over the summer months, when people's bodies are already too heated, no one will take it as often. September, October, and November are the best months of all." Although a few of Ramaswamy's customers might have consumed the meat in what they identified as "continental styles"—such as the more tender, deboned meat in a sandwich—nearly all of them, he predicted, would serve the chicken they purchased in a spicy *pulusu* and/or coated in spices and fried, alongside mounds of white rice.

MEAT AND HEALTH

Changing health concerns, themselves informed by multiple discourses, also had important implications for what people ate, how often, and in what forms. The people I knew read internationally syndicated stories about health scares—sometimes sensationalist, mostly decontextualized—in the newspapers, heard about them on television or, among the younger generation, picked up information from the internet. They were also exposed to the might of the advertising industry (Mazzarella 2003), which increasingly countered food-adulteration scandals and news stories of food-induced health crises with processed foods marketed as curative in themselves (Solomon 2016, 129–33). In addition, people learned things from their doctors and other healers, shared their own stories with peers, and drew on folk medical theories passed down through their kin and friendship networks. Although knowledge was unevenly spread and partial, the dominant emic medical categories deployed by my informants in relation to diet—as elsewhere in India—were consistent. People talked about "sugar" or being a "sugar patient" (referring both to diagnoses of diabetes and diabetes-like symptoms); "BP" (referring to high blood pressure, but also used as a shorthand to describe feelings of "tension"); and, more transiently, "gastric troubles" (to encompass indigestion, wind, and stomachaches).

Causation of these conditions, which themselves drew firmly on biomedical categories, was expressed in more humoral terms, particularly in relation to notions of heating or cooling substances. Although people I knew did not allude specifically to the humors—wind, bile, and phlegm—to which Ayurveda and other medical systems make reference,[6] and there was also significant variation in how foods were classified,[7] there were certainly parallels between their emic categories—organized around ideas of hot and cold—and those of the classical Ayurveda in which these ideas were rooted. Meat in general, for example, was universally categorized—both by my interlocutors and in Ayurvedic texts—as heating. This helped to explain its relative suitability to particular kinds of bodies. "Too much meat will be heating," as one man put it. "Then you'll need to buy Limca to cool your body, and that just adds to the overall cost!"

Health concerns around meat, it is important to note, were not entirely separable from the discourses that informed Hindu nationalist perspectives on meat eating. It was widely supposed that Dalit bodies, for example, had less delicate constitutions than their higher-caste peers, and that the heavy labor they had traditionally undertaken required the consumption of food, including meat, that gave them strength. Muslim bodies were likewise categorized as constitutionally different. Such beliefs not only fed into the negative stereotypes of caste and community that maintained discrimination against particular groups of people; they were also played upon by Dalit activists in their demands for beef as the food of their "toiling Dalit brethren."[8] As E. Valentine Daniel put it—in what probably still remains the most thoroughly ethnographically grounded exemplar of the ethnosociological approach in the regional literature—different castes maintained their "substance-codes" through the *kinds* of food they consumed.[9] His analysis resonates with what my own interlocutors had to say. Daniel explains that "the hot castes"—which would include Dalits—"more readily, willingly and customarily eat hot foods than do the cool castes." (1987, 186). Foodstuffs recognized to be heating, such as meat, onions, and garlic, should, Daniel's informants made clear to him, be avoided by cool castes— which would include Brahmins—as well as by particular categories of people, such as widows, in whom they might inappropriately inflame passions (see, for example, Lamb 2000). Conversely, consumed by the right people—those whose bodily substance is compatible with them—heating foods such as meat and alcohol might positively be transformed "into outputs of greater gifts, payments, sexual power and violence" (Marriott 1976, 123).[10] Children's bodies might also be less susceptible to the health risks associated with meat and, consequently, their desire for it more easily pandered to than that, for example, of an adult woman on whose gustatory conduct a family's reputation might rest.[11]

Health benefits or risks from meat were, then, to some extent relative to the diner, although among those I spoke to in Anandapuram and Bhavanipur, there was a general consensus on the overall health concerns attributed to meat in general—"Too much of it will lead to digestion problems, sickness, and loose motions, and the masalas [the mixtures of spices and alliums within which it is cooked] can cause gas"—as well as between different types of meat. For example, goat—although it attracted less comment because it had become so rarely eaten—was widely seen as difficult to digest (so could create "gastric troubles" or cause "gas"), particularly if those eating it were not engaged in the kind of physical work that could easily burn it off. There was also one "heart patient" who told me his doctor had advised him against eating it. Overall, however, it was viewed as "less heating than some of the other varieties of meat," and the risks associated it with were transitory and mostly related, as one friend put it, "to the masalas and the oil it's cooked with, not the meat itself."

It was beef, unsurprisingly, given the divisions between those who ate it and those who did not, that evoked the most comments from my informants.

One man, himself a Mala but one who claimed not to eat beef, told me that someone had once told him that "beef can make you sluggish and more dim-witted. In children it can also cause the tongue to become fat and impede their speech." More common was the assertion that "beef can lead to laziness and to memory decline" or "a loss of memory power," suggesting that consumption of an animal could lead to its human consumer taking on some of the characteristics attributed to the animal itself. The bovine, despite its sacred qualities, was also recognized as slow and languid. Others, like Sambrajamma, my first cook in Anandapuram, a Madiga who was known at the time in the village as a trader in dried beef, distinguished between the meat of the cow and that of the buffalo in health terms. "Cow meat is good for health, better than buffalo," she asserted, "so we should eat it." But there were caveats: "Those with health problems shouldn't eat too much. I've got sugar and BP, so I need to control my diet. But it's very good for you otherwise. They say that after delivering a baby, you should eat beef. Now I only eat chicken and goat though." Associations between high blood pressure and beef were particularly strong. Comments like the two below were fairly widespread:

> Eating too much beef can give you a heart attack, and higher BP as well.

> BP people shouldn't take beef, and if you eat more, it will also be the cause of BP.

As with meat in general, then, the health implications of beef were contingent on the diner. As Sambrajamma's double-edged response suggests, beef was neither unequivocally portrayed as unhealthy nor, for that matter, of exclusive benefit only to the putatively lowest castes. "I was very anemic, and the doctor told me to eat beef," one woman, from a non-beef-eating caste told me. "I didn't want to, but what could I do? I ate it as medicine. Anyway, nowadays even Vaisyas and Brahmins are eating beef!" Reference back to advice from doctors and of beef as medicinal was an extremely common trope, for Dalit diners looking for neutralizing logics beyond caste identity for eating it, as well as for higher-caste consumers who felt a need to justify their culinary decision. "I have always eaten beef, since I was a child," one Madiga man explained it, "but cow beef is anyway the best for health—doctors say so! It's good as a guard against tuberculosis, good for blood, and it makes you strong. There are good *medical* reasons for eating beef." Another told me that it was even served in some of the area's best-known mission hospitals, whose clinicians had recognized that "beef will help build up resistance to infections like tuberculosis and AIDS. Patients with those conditions should be eating it daily." Mariamma, another friend who drew a link between beef and tuberculosis prevention and cure, told me that is was her family's regular consumption of it when she was a girl that meant, despite them being poor, she and her siblings never had bronchial-related problems, and all grew up to be physically strong.

For Aziz, one of the Hyderabad butchers I worked with, the benefits of beef were, unsurprisingly, manifold. "Let's stop talking about the problems," he said finally, after a long, depressing discussion about the difficulties he had been facing from antibeef vigilantes. "Let me tell you instead about the benefits. This meat is the cheapest and best. It can cure cancer—ask any doctor! Eighty percent of all medicines come from this meat. You can even make shirt buttons from the bones." In common with many others I spoke to, he also referenced Ayurvedic medicine to back his claims about the curative properties of beef, the inference being that if *even* classical Hindu sources—the very texts on whose authority the Hindu right claimed to draw—recommended beef, who could argue against it?[12]

While one of the arguments sometimes used in favor of chicken was that it was a healthier, less fatty meat than the alternatives, it was not unambiguously pitched against beef and other meat by those I worked with. Even those who agreed with the dominant global view that chicken was a low-fat, cholesterol-fighting meat that could be more safely consumed by those with high blood pressure, diabetes, or gastric problems (see, for example, Dixon 2002, 168–72), there was little fervor in the ways they reeled off those qualities. They knew it intellectually—had seen it reported on the television or on the advertisers' billboards—but in their mouths, the cooked flesh of a broiler chicken was too soft and too bland to evoke much enthusiasm. It did the job of marking a change from the dal and vegetables of everyday consumption, and on price and availability it was unassailable, but my friends talked about the ubiquity of chicken as a fait accompli rather than something to be celebrated.

Chicken was also associated with some of the health problems of other meat. Rajiv, a graduate in his early twenties living in Anandapuram, told me,

> Chicken is heating—and sometimes it helps to cause seasonal or viral diseases like chikungunya or malaria. Chicken farms use medicines in feeding the birds—they give them antibiotics and other things—so if someone is affected by disease, they should avoid chicken for six months, because they may have already

been treated for that, and if they eat the medicines again in their meat, it will cause a relapse. House chickens are OK though. They are good for muscle development, but you should eat the hens only, not the cocks. Cocks are not okay because they go around and eat anything at all, unlike the female birds, who stay close to the house. There's also something in their bones that's not good for our human bones.

The mosquito-spread chikungunya virus, which had hit Anandapuram and Bhavanipur as well as parts of Hyderabad during my visits in 2005–2006 and again in 2010, is not, despite the unfortunate phonetic similarity, related to chickens (Lahariya and Pradhan 2006). However, many of my informants, Rajiv among them, made that connection, which fitted with a longer-held view that broiler chickens were suspect because they had been produced in laboratories through crossbreeding rather than being a naturally occurring species. They were then "fed chemicals" to make them grow, processes that, many people thought, might lead to what they glossed as "side effects." Although my informants were generally sketchy when I pressed them on what those side effects might be (although there were newspaper articles documenting more specifically some of the possible risks[13]), it was clear that the dichotomy they drew was not necessarily between chicken as pure and beef as tainted. Rather, in everyday discourse, the split was between what were thought of as unnatural, soft, and bland broilers on the one hand and natural, tough, and tasty home-reared birds on the other: broiler versus country chicken. Johan expressed the collective view as well as any when he told me, "Broiler farm chickens are fed all kinds of 'medicine' that may have different side effects. So that might not be good."

The real concern with chicken, however, was not so much the health implications of eating its meat but the wider effects of farming it on the neighboring environment in which people lived.

MEAT AND THE ENVIRONMENT

Fears concerning the detrimental environmental impact of rearing different kinds of animals in particular ways, as well as the impact on health of eating their meat, contributed in complex ways to the decisions my informants made about what meat to purchase and when, and also shaped the landscape within which those choices could be made. The changing ecology, for example, had also changed the range of what was available to eat. My interlocutors did not talk directly about environmental movements, nor were they overtly concerned with animal rights activism, so one might argue that the influences of either were relatively insignificant in molding their culinary choices. Environmentalism might be seen as "a full-stomach phenomenon" (Guha 2006, 1), the concern of educated and economically secure elites, liberal or otherwise, who were less preoccupied with the day-to-day struggles of survival than the majority of my research participants were.

Certainly, on the face of it, activists working to protect the environment appeared to be ideologically most aligned with the university-based Dalit activists lobbying for subaltern rights, from whom many of my interlocutors, as discussed in the previous chapters, distanced themselves. Organizations like, for example, the Society for Environmental Communications—publisher of the environmental magazine *Down to Earth*[14]—focused on the sustainability of meat production rather than ideological arguments about its consumption.[15] Similarly, well-known environmental activists such as Vandana Shiva, director of the Research Foundation for Science, Technology and Natural Resource Policy, have often explicitly positioned their arguments within ecofeminist, antidevelopment, or anticapitalist frameworks. Such arguments resonate more with what some on the right have disparaged as "Lutyens' ecosystem" or "the chattering classes"—liberal intellectuals and media engaged in setting the agendas of public debate—than the also powerful forces of conservative nationalism against which minority groups in India were pitted. Nevertheless, some of Shiva's arguments also risked appropriation by those who make the case for a nation shaped by particular Hindu values (Mawdsley 2006, 2010).[16] Furthermore, Shiva's claims in respect to cows and buffaloes, which include an assertion that billions could be saved by ceasing to slaughter cattle because of the value of their labor and products (Shiva 1999, 60), have been referenced positively by *The Organiser*, an official journal of the RSS (Nanda 2002, 30).

O. P. Dwivedi (1990, 1997), likewise, is criticized by Mawdsley for using selective quotations from the Vedic texts to make romanticized claims about the ecological balance of ancient India. Taking the stance that Hindus, Muslims, and Christians each formed discrete, homogenous, and oppositional groups with radically different value systems—among which only Hinduism was truly ecologically sensitive—Dwivedi posits that the environmental problems of the present are a consequence of the evils of colonialism, science, and development (Mawdsley 2006, 384). It is a compelling argument for a postcolonial age, and Dwivedi's sentiments are liberal. But they are also historically wrong: "Although almost certainly unintentionally, Dwivedi's assertions provide fuel for Hindu nationalism by projecting a historically inaccurate past environmental harmony, and an equally inaccurate past social harmony, both of which have been contaminated and degraded by 'foreign cultural domination'" (Mawdsley 2006, 384).

Colonialism might well have accelerated environmental degradation, but, as archaeological and historical evidence testifies, it did not start it.[17] Neo-traditionalist accounts of the environment, Mawdsley concludes, "must be understood as a political project for the present, as well as an analysis of the past" (2006, 387; see also Sinha, Gururani, and Greenberg 1997).

Direct evidence of the potential link between what appear to be liberal projects of environmental protection and Hindu fundamentalism in contemporary India is perhaps most visibly embodied in the politician Maneka Gandhi, arguably the most famous figure openly associated with both environmental activist and right-wing Hindu groups. Her stance also transports us directly back to the issue of cattle slaughter. The widowed daughter-in-law of the former Congress leader and prime minister Indira Gandhi, from whom she later became estranged, Maneka Gandhi had subsequently served as a minister in the BJP-led government of the late 1990s and again, as the BJP's Minister for Women and Child Development, following its victory in the 2014 general election. She was also well known as a provegan, environmentalist, and animal rights activist; vocal in campaigns to close down abattoirs; and founder of the organization People for Animals (PFA) in 1992.[18] The PFA's home page on its website extols the particular virtues of the cow as "a symbol of grace and abundance" and invites visitors to the site to click on a link to pledge their support to saving cows in India. The PFA sets out to distance itself from the anti-Muslim stance associated with *Hindutva* by designating the cow an *Indian* symbol, "revered and protected down the ages by Hindu and Mughal rulers alike." Nevertheless, those who trade in or consume beef were clearly among the PFA's key targets. "Every day brave People for Animals raiding team seize over trucks that are taking cattles for illegal slaughtering," the website elaborates. "With a courage in heart and passion in their souls, they try and rescue these cattles *by any means possible*" (my emphasis, although the wording is verbatim).[19]

My friends in Anandapuram and Bhavanipur, neither fitting into the liberal activist mode nor, for the most part, overt supporters of Hindu nationalism, tended to be dismissive of the suggestion that their meat consumption might be harmful to the environment. Not unreasonably, they argued that their modest meat-eating habits, rarely more often than once a week, had relatively little impact on the world around them. They did, however, share concerns about risks posed by meat farming methods in relation to their own consumption. Rajiv's comment in the previous section resonates with the opinion offered by a doctor in Mayank Jain's 2017 documentary film *The*

Evidence: Meat Kills, which Maneka Gandhi helped to launch[20]—linking it, intentionally or otherwise, to nationalist projects of the state. In the film, Ramesh Bijlani, previously head of the physiology department of the All India Institute of Medical Science (AIIMS), makes the claim that "[the] use of antibiotics and hormones has become almost routine in not only poultry but also in the meat industry in general, and the types of antibiotics that are used are very often those which are not fit for human consumption. They are not approved for human use but these are given to these animals, [so] indirectly, the same antibiotics get into human beings when we consume meat."

Beyond a sense that the birds were consuming things that heightened the risks of eating their flesh, those I interviewed about the issues in Anandapuram were more concerned with the dangers that the farms themselves—and, by extension, intensive meat production—presented. Nearly all of them, in talking about the issues, referenced the chicken farm that butted up to Anandapuram's border. It was small by the standards of contemporary broiler farms, used mainly, like Ramaswamy's farm, for the holding of pre-hatched birds that were almost ready for sale. Nevertheless, during the monsoon rains or when the cages were being cleaned, the stench that enveloped streets on the edge of the village was not only unpleasant but feared to be potentially dangerous. "If you live close to chicken farms," one man told me, "inhaling the fumes can create diseases, especially in children: heart disease, respiratory disease, allergies, TB. Farms are necessary, but they should be located far away from where people live. The local farm is too close."

Such perceptions, informed as they were by existing knowledge, were also strengthened by subsequent news stories. Swine flu (the H1N1 virus), for example, had featured prominently in the media when I was in Anandapuram in 2009, and in Hyderabad and other urban centers, face masks had been a common sight. Such viruses, people said, could be carried via air from the farm into the village. "There's lots of risk from that farm," said Chandrasekhar, whose compound gate opened out to a view of chicken sheds, separated only by a dirt track and a barbed wire fence. "When they clean the shed, they dig up the feces from the ground, and a horrible smell comes from that. From the dust of their feces going into the air, we breathe it in, and that can cause diseases. They also feed them with medicines, which is not so good. House-reared are better—they only eat paddy and plants . . . but in farms they get injections and medicines."

The other environmental danger people mentioned was the "medicines"—agrochemicals such as fertilizers and pesticides—that were used on crops. Villagers were well aware of the strength of these and the potential harm they could do: drinking pesticide was the most common cause of male suicide within the community (Staples 2012a, 2012b, 2015). Commonplace since the Green Revolution, their increasing use to enhance crop yields was cited as one of the key reasons that people were less willing than in the past to rear chickens domestically. "Apart from the fights that chickens cause with neighbors, eating the plants, digging holes, and defecating near their houses," said one previous keeper of chickens, "if they eat plants that have been treated with 'medicine,' they can get sick and sometimes die. It's much harder than it used to be." The same logic was applied to the decreasing number of households in Anandapuram that kept goats or buffalo. Whereas a decade earlier it had been commonplace for households to keep a buffalo or two tethered up outside, nowadays they were only kept, and in larger numbers (usually between six and a dozen), by a few families with sufficiently large plots to house them.

"In the old days, everything was grown more naturally," an elderly man told me wistfully. "If chickens ate plants, no harm came to them, but now there are pesticides. There's a risk that they will die or, if they don't, that we'll become ill when we eat their meat." In addition, increasing pressures on space meant there was less common ground available for grazing of any domestically reared animals, and feed, my interlocutors complained, had become more expensive. Chicken farms were more than able to counter the decline in domestically reared chicken numbers, and the overall increase in their production vis-à-vis goats and, to some extent, cattle also accounted for the price shifts I have described. Nevertheless, the ubiquity of the broiler chicken had not made it unambiguously desirable to my research participants. The current centrality of its place in the Sunday cooking pot was one that was slightly grudgingly accepted rather than celebrated, suggesting possible grounds on which other types of meat—even those most thoroughly tarnished by the forces of Hindu nationalism—remained an option.

CONCLUSION: CHANGING MEAT-EATING PRACTICES

There were many forces besides those of Hindu nationalism that helped to determine what meat, if any, the South Indians I worked with consumed, as well as how and when they ate it. Health concerns, environmental issues, marketing, and the industrialization of some production processes and not others that, in turn, had led to shifts in the relative price of the meat of different animals all rubbed up against one another to shape the purchasing decisions taken early on Sunday mornings in Bhavanipur's market. The changes in taste and texture that index those shifts in industrial production, as well as possibilities for new meat products—from the McChicken sandwich (Ghassem-Fachandi 2012, 160) to chicken Manchurian—also have a clear impact on what is consumed. Such changes might, for example, see chicken entering the diet at other times of the week through stealth: small pieces strewn through a snack of stir-fried noodles hastily consumed by the man of the house on the way back from a midweek grocery shopping excursion, for example, or predinner chicken *pakora*s guzzled down with a small bottle of brandy in the alleyways outside Bhavanipur's bar.

Nevertheless, although all these factors, themselves shaped by the forces of global capitalism and international campaigns by environmentalists, might be seen as occurring in different realms than those occupied by Hindu nationalism, my explorations have made it clear that they cannot be seen as entirely separate from them either. They are liable to both crossover with or inflect political debates *and* to be appropriated by politicians. Whatever Shiva's or Dwivedi's intentions in presenting a particular history of environmental degradation in India, for example, there is no doubt that their arguments have been mobilized in support of Hindu nationalism, used to bolster arguments in ways that would appeal beyond a particular vote bank. What this also alerts us to is the danger of thinking through universal binary oppositions, such that environmentalism and vegetarianism are assumed allies of liberalism, inevitably opposed to nationalist conservatism. Such assumptions blinker us from the appropriation that goes on in plain sight, blurring the categories we use to make judgments between what is acceptable and unacceptable, between the colonial and the postcolonial, the democratic and the autocratic, or the liberal and the conservative. However, the very blurring that enables nationalist projects to commandeer apparently scientific discourses about health or the environment to their own ends also opens up potentials for meat eaters in India themselves to reframe their practices in new, more positive ways.

CHAPTER SIX

From Caste to Class in Food

DESPITE what appeared to be the spread of a vegetarian, anti–cattle slaughter hegemony in India—one endorsed by Modi's BJP and its followers—meat eating has been simultaneously presented and experienced in alternative, and sometimes more positive, ways. Meat could, for example, serve as a source of communal pride, with Christians like my Telugu teacher Victoria-Rani binding themselves together, in contradistinction to high-caste Hindus, through a mutual appreciation of beef. Meat could also be framed as medicinal; as special or celebratory, vis-à-vis other foods; and more generally as nourishing, tasty, and enjoyable. In short, despite antimeat arguments self-consciously rooted either in Mahatma Gandhi's promotion of vegetarianism as a counter to colonial oppression or, alternatively, in Vandana Shiva–style neotraditionalist environmentalist perspectives, attitudes toward meat in India were actually characterized more by ambivalence and contradiction than by an unequivocal rejection of it. Meat invoked desire as much as disgust (and sometimes both at the same time). It was in this ambivalence, in this blurring of categories that had been exploited by the Hindu right to widen arguments against cattle slaughter, that meat eaters might themselves find justifications for their own practices.

To be sure, meat as a weapon of the subaltern had its limitations. Victoria-Rani's appropriation of beef as a positive symbol of her Christianity—and a tasty one at that—was (a) necessarily inward-looking, and thus limited, in that non-Christians were unlikely to buy into such a categorization; and (b) required, a priori, a certain level of sociocultural and economic capital to be carried off effectively, even within limited contexts. As will by now have become clear, the most vocal pro-beef advocates I met in 2000 lived in self-established housing colonies, often in brick-built houses that they owned, with other Christians from similar caste backgrounds as their neighbors. They had strong bonds with local churches and had jobs—often with Christian NGOs, nursing homes, or schools—that did not require them to engage intimately with Hindu caste society in their everyday lives. There was no one to complain if cooking smells revealed that they were cooking beef, nor immediate neighbors who might refuse their hospitality and reinforce their social inferiority. For men like my friend Prakash, by contrast, cooking and eating beef in his family's rented rooms in Hyderabad could have meant eviction, while beef eating also made it difficult to find respectable accommodation in the first place.

Working outside the bubble of Christian NGOs also exposed one to others' prejudices on a daily basis.[1] Meat eating was often glossed not as a celebration of identity but as a potential cause of offense to others' cultural sensitivities. Elsewhere in India, in Gujarat and Uttar Pradesh, the situation was harder still. Reports of police raids on meat shops and of criminal charges brought against those serving beef to their wedding guests, for example, demonstrated that mobilizing beef as a marker of communal pride was not plausible in the ways that it still was in the southern or northeastern states.[2] Other positive claims likewise brought with them limitations, the putative medicinal qualities of beef might provide cover for limited consumption, for example, but only in certain contexts. And contrary claims about the risks it presented to those with high blood pressure or heart problems might also prevent its consumption by those who would otherwise relish it.

In short, positive claims about meat framed within existing discourses about identity and community, and even within the more apparently secular realms of health, all depended on context and preexisting capital (in the broad senses that Bourdieu [1986] used the term) to be successful, and even then were subject to counterattack from those espousing a vegetarian or pro–cow protection worldview. One important way of countering such jostling on the ground was to situate the debates *outside* the constraints of caste and community altogether, and to attempt to locate them instead within the more transnational framework of class, where caste or religious affiliation, it could be claimed, carried less salience. However, class can never fully accommodate caste. Other than for the exceptionally wealthy, the cosmopolitan, progressive meat eating associated with the upper echelons of the middle classes was, paradoxically, usually only an option for those already demarcated as high-caste.

Many of the urban-based Indian academics I knew, for example—some of whom lived in Indian cities but who moved relatively seamlessly across national borders and, by their own admission, often had more in common with their counterparts in US or European universities than with less educated villagers in India—appeared to have few qualms about eating beef. A Brahmin engineer I knew in Kolkata with daughters working in Europe told me that he "would eat anything—*anything!*"—beef included. By way of evidence, in taking me through his family albums, he pointed out photographs of himself and his wife enjoying burgers at a McDonald's restaurant in London, being reminded, in doing so, of a particularly delicious beef dish he had eaten with noodles in a Chinese restaurant in his home city. They did not, he conceded, eat beef at home; he said it might have offended their Brahmin cook, who would anyway not have been willing to prepare it. The cook was uneducated and, by implication, more conservative. But in the course of my engineer friend's everyday social life, oriented outward from India and not subject to the ideological conundrums that affected those more embedded in their immediate surroundings, he would enjoy beef, not as a transgression in the darkened booths of a restaurant but unselfconsciously as a visible marker of cosmopolitan sophistication.

It also marked him, as literature scholar Kalyan Das (2015) explores, firmly as a contemporary *bhadralok*, someone both high-caste and high-class, educated and urban. Indeed, Das's recent description of the perfect *bhadralok* family strongly resonates here:

> A progressive father who belongs to a professional class and takes pride in not having any taboo about alcohol or beef; a pious god-fearing mother who does not enjoy this life directly, but shares the pride of belonging to a progressive household and basks in that reflected glory; a son who studies in a city college or a university and enjoys beef and alcohol with friends; the mother politely and affectionately tells him not to overindulge himself; the son loves his accommodating mother and nurtures a strange ambivalent relationship vis-à-vis his claim of being progressive, which gets bifurcated into beef/alcohol consumption and a secret (but deep-seated) admiration for his mother. (2015, 110)

Gender distinctions were clearly significant in enabling such an outward-looking perspective on meat eating among upper-middle-class men. In my own breaks from fieldwork—on weekends away to tourist beach resorts or for lunch in five-star international hotels in Hyderabad and Delhi, for example—I witnessed similar occurrences. I encountered plenty of men from high Hindu castes—identifiable by the sacred threads they still wore across their torsos and markings on their foreheads—bathing in the swimming pool of a resort I stayed in, who could later be spotted having dinner in the restaurant with their families where beef dishes, as well as other meat options, were on the menu. Those diners might not have selected such dishes, but—as in the McDonald's restaurant in Ahmedabad that Ghassem-Fachandi (2012) described—they seemed undisturbed to be eating alongside those who were. Unlike McDonald's, however, where the lines between vegetarian and nonvegetarian were visibly demarcated, and where the processing of the meat itself appeared to sanitize it, here there was no obvious separation of cooking spaces or preparation and serving staff. Nor was there any color-coding of the menu. The offering of beef, rather than just the processed chicken of McDonald's burgers or Rock Starz's chicken lollipops, similarly marked these menus as different. But the space in the resort also stood out from the darkened city restaurants, eating houses that offered further seclusion through discreet seating booths where one might surreptitiously eat meat, often accompanied with alcohol. The restaurant in the coastal resort was light and spacious, open to the gardens that surrounded it, and with all the tables visible to anyone who came in to eat.

This, I suggest, was because the restaurant was successfully imagined as a cosmopolitan, transnational kind of space, one that existed within different moral parameters than either the home or the local restaurant. Here, to object to the serving of meat in the same space as vegetarian fare would have been seemed parochial, lacking the imagination to think beyond the confines of one's inherited cultural boundaries, in the same way that eating the food quickly with one's fingers rather than the cutlery provided might have identified one to others as unsophisticated. Similar mixing of vegetarian and nonvegetarian cuisine was also observable in costly urban bars and restaurants that, aesthetically at least, were often indistinguishable from comparable bars in, say, New York or London.[3] A manager of an international hotel I knew in Delhi told me in 2017 that beef dishes had recently been removed from the menus of his restaurants, a preemptive move to placate the government, but comparable hotels I visited at that time outside the northern "cow belt" were still listing beef on their own menus.

A relaxed attitude toward the eating of meat, then, at least in specifically demarcated spaces, was a marker of belonging to a particular, higher stratum of the middle class. Members of this elite successfully positioned themselves neither in relation to Hindu nationalism (even if some of them celebrated the economic achievements those political parties were alleged to have made) nor in relation to an index of purity and pollution that would have ruled out eating certain things or eating them alongside, and from the same crockery and utensils, as people from different castes and communities, even if the kind of expensive restaurants in which they ate them created new "regimes of exclusion" (Dewey 2012, 129). These urban, cosmopolitan elites, as anthropologist Paolo Favero explained on the basis of his fieldwork with young upper-middle-class men in New Delhi after economic liberalization, are characterized more by their capacity to switch between frames of identity than through any single fixed way of being. "One moment they would appear as the ideal heirs of the Gandhi-Nehru legacy, another moment as 'crypto' Hindu nationalists and yet a moment later as hard-core 'Westoxicated' (Gupta 2000) youths," as he put it (Favero 2005, 5–6)—frameworks within which meat could be celebrated or disavowed according to context.

The bulk of my informants were not members of an elite class or even close to its outer peripheries. Most of them were not urban, and those who did live in the city were decidedly marginalized or subaltern. Their recognition of elite attitudes toward the consumption of meat, however, could in itself have a subtle impact on their status. To be aware, as cultural anthropologist Susan Dewey (2012) argues in relation to Mumbai's elites, was a key component of class membership. First, for my associates in coastal Andhra, it illustrated an alternative way of framing meat beyond the split between Hindu fundamentalists and Dalit/Muslim activists that dominated media representations. Second, it was also useful as a way in to understanding how the people I worked with—very few of whom could convincingly be identified even as "middle-class"—came to position themselves, some of the time, in relation to meat. Claims to modernity, bolstered by other actions that simulated those of a more affluent upper middle class, were an essential part of building and maintaining a positive self-identity that could resonate beyond their class or community and that, crucially, improved their status within it.

CLASS IN SOUTH INDIA

The interest in class currently being taken by anthropologists of South Asia is driven by at least two overlapping concerns. For one, attending to class distinctions addresses what has been criticized as an overemphasis on caste as *the* defining feature of Indian social life in ethnographies from the "village studies" era onward. If we could understand caste, it was previously implied, we could understand India.[4] This was a viewpoint associated in particular with Louis Dumont, whose influential work on caste in *Homo*

Hierarchicus (1980) led to other significant forms of social division—including gender, sect affiliation, or position in the life cycle (Appadurai 1981, 495)—being overshadowed. Such a focus has subsequently come under sustained critique. Historical evidence has been used to challenge Dumont's central argument that caste was a distinctively Hindu, ideologically based system that could not be compared, for example, to Marxist notions of class (Dirks 1997, 2001). By contrast, caste was at least shaped—if not actually invented in its current form—during the colonial period. "It was under the British," as Nicholas Dirks phrased it, "that 'caste' became a single term capable of expressing, organizing, and above all 'systematizing' India's diverse forms of social identity, community, and organization" (2001, 5).[5] For others, caste ideology needed also to be read in terms of class struggle, or as a mystification by Brahmins that the putatively lower castes in reality saw through.[6] In short, then, the beginnings of a turn from caste to class was in some ways a corrective to the Orientalist tendency to imagine India in radical opposition to the West.

The second impetus toward a shift from caste to class can be found in actual changes that were taking place after the economic liberal reforms that began in India in the early 1990s. André Béteille (1997), for instance, has argued that the growth of a "new middle-class" (Säävälä 2003), or what some have dubbed a "consuming class" (Corbridge and Harriss 2000, 123–24, cited in Fuller and Narasimhan 2007, 125) over that period has significantly changed the ways in which people in India identify themselves. Empirical evidence of such change is offered in research with workers from the Bhilai Steel Plant in Madhya Pradesh, where caste distinctions have been diminished for some groups of workers through the bonding nature of shared working conditions (Parry 1999). Even in Nepal—until 2006 a Hindu kingdom, and so spared the Mughal and colonial influences that prevailed in India—a shift from a caste-based logic of interaction to one based on class has been noted (Liechty 2005, 21). Caste alone was no longer adequate, if ever it was, to explain the realities of on-the-ground social distinctions.

Whether "class" was any better equipped to fill the void left by the move away from caste is, of course, open to debate, particularly since the term came heavily laden with baggage from its use in primarily Western discourses (Favero 2005). However, in being appropriated into discussions about Indian social categorizations, ideas about "class" have also been remolded to speak to the specificities of life in the subcontinent. Describing people in terms of class is less to imply a Westernization of India than to note the complex social effects of globalization on how people identify themselves and others, particularly in urban contexts such as Delhi, where many do not think of themselves as Western; rather, they reimagine urban "Indianness" itself as global, cosmopolitan, and sophisticated (12).

What, then, does this tell us about "class" in a South Asian context? Although the differences between caste and class are often blurred—a large number of newly middle-class IT professionals in Chennai, for example, are also Brahmins (Fuller and Narasimhan 2007), suggesting that the two are not mutually exclusive categories—class is generally understood as less immutable than caste, an identity performed as much as it is ascribed. Used as an index of self-identity, class might also allow ritually lower castes to claim elevated status on the basis of their economic power or other attributes. Where I conducted my research in rural Andhra Pradesh, for example, my informants recognized members of Kapu and Reddi castes—both from the Sudra, or lowest, *varna*—as socially important ("almost like Brahmins," was the shorthand often deployed) because they owned a disproportionate amount of farming land compared to other castes and were well represented in the state-level political scene. In Dumontian terms of ritual purity, they ranked low; in terms of economic, political, and social power—what some might think of as class, in other words—they ranked much higher.

The existence of a "middle class" is not, as the above reference to Kapus and Reddis implies, new in India. For example, the Bengali notion of the *bhadralok* invoked above—literally "the respectable people," so implying class as well as caste—has been in circulation at least since colonial times. Broomfield (2016, 218) prefers to think of the *bhadralok* as a status group rather than "middle class," not least because they occupy the higher echelons of society rather than the middle. His much earlier description of them, however, certainly resonates with more contemporary definitions of the middle class in India: "A socially privileged and consciously superior group, economically dependent upon landed rents and professional and clerical employment; keeping its distance from the masses by its acceptance of high-caste proscriptions and its command of education; sharing a pride in its language, its literate culture and its history; and maintaining its communal integration through a fairly complex institutional structure that it had proved remarkably ready to adapt and augment to extend its social power and political opportunities" (1968, 5–6).

There has, then, long been what its own members and others might describe loosely as a "middle class" in India, including those, for example, who from the colonial period on were employed in clerical government jobs, as doctors and bank managers, as teachers and lecturers, and others in relatively high-status, if not necessarily high-salary, occupations. What has changed in the years since liberalization, in addition to a significant expansion in numbers (see Favero 2005, 18), is the increased transnational traffic in people, ideas, and images that has come with globalization (Reddy 2005, 217). It also enabled forms of conspicuous consumption that were simply not achievable in the past.

By way of an example, a local doctor in Bhavanipur, whom I have known since the 1980s, was much harder to distinguish from his peers when I first knew him than when I visited him again in the late 1990s and early 2000s. In the early days, the rooms he and his family occupied above his small surgery, while brick-built rather than mud and thatch, were furnished with the same traditional beds as people I knew in the village, with the family's clothing likewise hung over a wire that crossed the room or housed in a slightly dented steel cabinet. The roughly whitewashed walls were scuffed and grimy, adding to the austere gloom that was cast by the naked tube lights. There were, though, always small markers of distinction to be found if one searched for them. He insisted, for example, on taking an upright, covered rickshaw to the clinic he attended a few times a week in Anandapuram rather than one of the more commonly used flat ones, which he considered beneath his dignity. But the substantial difference between his own wealth and that of the villagers I knew was not otherwise immediately obvious. His wealth was stored in gold, kept in the bank (some of it in anticipation of his daughter's dowry), and found in acres of paddy fields back in his natal village, which both provided ample rice and rental income. In the postliberalization years, however, I watched his apartment gradually become upgraded and filled with consumer goods, from sofas and dining tables to televisions and refrigerators, that marked out much more clearly his economic and social status.

Contemporary members of the middle class, then, might be more readily identifiable than they once were. According to the literature, its newer members also tended to be broadly defined by their educational attainments and their professional and technical skills, including use of English, as well as by their capacities to use and embody those attributes in socially acceptable ways.[7] Favero offers an even broader definition: "that part of Indian society that has received schooling, speaks English, has a house made of bricks and possesses some kind of transportation vehicle" (2005, 18). Unlike the older, more established middle class, the "emerging middle-classes" have been characterized as vulnerable and anxious, an existential state befitting the employment instabilities of a market-driven economy, rather than the secure, if less immediately financially rewarding, public-sector posts of the past (Mankekar 1999, 97; Säävälä 2003).[8]

Contemporary analyses also tend to frame class in India as performative or behavioral, something learned, shaped, and expressed through embodied action, rather than determined, as more strictly Marxist or Weberian interpretations might have it, by access to economic resources and wealth. According to Sara Dickey, for example, attributes of a middle-class identity include moderation, control, and self-discipline (2016, 5), suggesting, as Sherry Ortner does, that class is "a project ... something that is always being made or kept or defended, feared or desired" (2003, 13–14). Class is also something that anyone, whatever their caste background, can actively work on (even though levels of success might vary considerably, and might be at least partially determined by caste status). It is in this performative context that there has been a focus on the relationship between class, taste, and consumption. As Mark Liechty notes, class "is not prior to or outside of discourse and performance but an emergent cultural project wherein people attempt to speak and act themselves ... into cultural 'reality' or 'coherence'" (2005, 3; see also Dickey 2010; Säävälä 2003). Although much of this work centers on public consumption in general, there has also been attention given to contemporary restaurant culture and public dining, as well as to changes in domestic cuisine and commensality.[9]

In common with Dickey, I am drawn to an understanding of class that focuses not only on the tangible, objectively observable markers of status, important though those are, but also on its subjective, more ephemeral aspects. "An intangible good such as honor or respect," she tells us, "can affect ... access to credit and the terms of repayment ... or marriage prospects for children" (2016, 17). Documenting the subjective *experience* of class, in other words, is not just a record of how it makes people feel; the projection of that experience is potentially productive in more objectively observable ways. In making this case, Dickey draws on Bourdieu (1986) and his expansion of capital beyond the economic to encompass also the cultural, the social, and the symbolic, with a particular focus on cultural capital. The latter might be objectified in the form of cultural goods—including food and the paraphernalia that goes with it—but also, crucially, in knowledge about how to use those particular goods.

Where Dickey differs from Bourdieu, however—and, again, I agree with her position—is over his suggestion that in order to be viewed positively, capital must be viewed as legitimate by the ruling class. She argues, contra Bourdieu, that the concept of capital is "more useful when it is understood as providing either positive or negative value within a *relevant social group*." (2016, 20, original emphasis). Class-related behaviors are not only a matter of trying to attain the approval of those much higher up the scale or of moving upward—which many of my own informants, however much they might have liked such outcomes, had no allusions that they could achieve—but of gaining the respect of (and other potential advantages from) their peers. Cultural capital in this sense is an instrument by which class is determined, while *dignity*—that which makes one count—is determined by it (Dickey 2016, 23).

Before moving on to consider how class might be implicated in food and, especially, in relation to meat, I want finally to consider the question of how relevant or useful the notion of class is beyond the urban contexts in which it has been most widely discussed. Nearly all accounts of India's contemporary middle class that I have alluded to above, after all, focus on urban cosmopolitans. The people I worked with, even if some of them might just meet Favero's (2005) minimal criteria for membership in the middle class, did not generally consider themselves—nor would they have been considered by others—as part of such of a grouping. In the same way that Dickey's poorer informants described themselves in contradistinction to "big people" or "moneyed people" (2016, 5), my friends in Anandapuram, Bhavanipur, and Hyderabad often alluded to themselves as "ordinary people," the kind of people who got on with the business of everyday life, leaving decision-making or activism to "bigger people" or, referencing those they considered more important than them, "people with bigger heads than ours." Many of them, for example, had relied on begging or other marginalized occupations for income (see Staples 2007), and very few had the added security of agricultural land or property.

Nevertheless, my friends also, at times, disassociated themselves from those they considered lower, and not only on the basis of caste distinctions. Unsatisfactory food at a feast, for example, might be dismissed as "the kind of food they eat in very poor villages," and my research assistant Das often explained away mystifying behavior on the part of others with the phrase, "What can you expect from *those* kinds of people?" And while in the latter case, Das, as a Brahmin, was sometimes also referring to people of lower-caste status, it was also (as our many discussions around the topic made clear) a shorthand description of people without the kinds of knowledge, education, or exposure that might define them as higher class. What became clear to me, then, was that even if my informants did not belong to this elusive middle class—new, emergent, or otherwise—they (a) still defined themselves and related to others in terms of class as well as caste; and (b) used the very same tropes that urban middle-class people used (albeit in their own distinctive ways, not simply a matter of copying or mirroring) to distinguish their own behavior.

FEEDING GUESTS IN ANANDAPURAM

As the above makes clear, what urban middle-class people did was also relevant to social organization in Anandapuram. The people I worked with, as the following vignettes illustrate, did this through the medium of food.

Lunch at Babu's

The week Babu called me to his mother's house for lunch in 2017 was one in which I had eaten out sometimes twice daily: my time in Anandapuram was coming to an end, and there were lots of social obligations to fulfill before I left. For Babu, in his early twenties, the meal was to thank me and—in his words to Das, my research assistant, through whom he made the invitation—"to show respect." On a previous visit to the village, I had briefly helped him to complete some paperwork that, in turn, had led to a funded place—to which, as a Dalit, he was entitled under a government scheme—in a postgraduate degree course. Although I am sure he could have achieved much the same result without my intervention, as far he was concerned, it was "through you only, sir, that I got that MBA place," through me, he insisted, that his future now seemed much more secure. His own father had been a heavy drinker who went begging and who had died of an alcohol-related disease several years previously. His mother had subsequently found work as a maid in Saudi Arabia, sending home remittances to support him and his older brother and sister. His sister was now married to a local NGO worker from the same caste and lived in a neighboring hamlet. He had, then, the English language skills, the education and, through his mother's remittances, almost the income to qualify as emergent middle-class, yet his background and his continued residence in a small village continued to set him apart from the urban cosmopolitans described by the authors cited in the previous section.

On the day that Das and I visited, only Babu was at home. In the main room of the family's two-roomed, brick-built house, now enclosed within a small compound and accessed through an elaborately carved teak front door, he had erected a folding table, neatly covered with a checked cotton table cloth, with a chair placed at either side. Fulfilling the most basic material requirements that Favero (2005) suggested were prerequisite for a middle-class life, he also had a two-wheeled scooter parked outside. Once he had seated us, Das and I were each given our own plastic bottle of chilled mineral water and a crystal-effect plastic glass from which to drink it, and then flowery melamine plates on which our food was to be served. The serving dishes came out next: a fillet of white fish that had been gently fried with

6.1   Fancy domestic dining in Anandapuram. Clockwise from top left: raita, Kinley bottled water, dal, basmati rice with cashews and sultanas, *gongura patchidi*, and spicy fried prawns.

just salt and a little turmeric, the bones carefully removed and the flesh cut into portions; prawns encased in a light, mildly spicy batter; and dal with mixed vegetables. There was also a small glass dish of *gongura patchidi*— the green-leaf chutney without which no celebratory meal was complete— and a raita, in place of plain curd, flavored with grated carrot, finely sliced red onion, and chopped green chilies. The rice, which I saw him decant from the cooking pot into a thermal serving dish in the back room, was top-quality basmati, some of the grains almost an inch long, and it came lightly fried along with plump sultanas and cashew nuts (figure 6.1). Dessert was *semiya payasam*, a sweet vermicelli-and-milk pudding, also mixed with nuts and dried fruit. It was served to us in fancy glass bowls with teaspoons rather than, as had previously been the fashion, in stainless-steel tumblers from which a runnier version of the same pudding would necessarily have been slurped.

Structurally, the meal was familiar: like everyday meals, it was based around a core (rice) and peripheral items (the two seafood dishes and the dal), the dryness of the prawns and the fried fish offset by the wetness of the dal. And in place of the plain curd or buttermilk that would have marked the end of the savory part of the meal, we were given a more complex raita. The dessert, too, was a variation on what was always served, but the *payasam* in this case was firmer than that usually offered in a steel tumbler and, displayed in glass bowls with chopped nuts as a garnish, was more artfully presented than would usually have been the case. What was different, then, was the quality of the ingredients and the delicacy with which they had been prepared: the rarely eaten basmati rice, the expensive addition of cashew nuts and sultanas, the deboned fish fillet, and the Kinley bottled mineral water rather than the offer of municipal drinking water in a steel or brass *chumbu* (pot). The food demonstrated both Babu's skills and his knowledge. The presentation also demarcated difference: all of the main savory dishes were adorned with chopped coriander leaves; the spices were finally pounded and subtly applied rather than whole or coarsely sliced; and a table, tablecloth, melamine plates, and special serving dishes, separate from those in which the food had been cooked, had all been deployed.

Babu had stayed true to the *structure* of a South Indian meal, but he had utilized the cultural capital at his disposal to play with the elements and the background against which it was set to transform it into something particular. Although the house in which it was offered was modest—two rooms, not more than two hundred square feet of floor space between them, and originally constructed under a government housing scheme for the rural poor—its interior was both scrupulously neat and clean, and it contained several indicators of a middle-class aesthetic and lifestyle. There was a small, flat-screen television and a tall refrigerator; a bed with a carved, polished wooden headboard, rather than the more usual simple cot strung with cotton tape; a dining table (as already described); and floors that had been laid with shiny, marble-effect tiles. As I also noticed in other people's houses, it seemed that there was a subtle shift away from what has been described as the "bazaar kitsch" (Pinney 1995) aesthetic of provincial India's recent postliberalization past to one that emulated more closely that of an urban elite.[10] Cake-like houses of lurid pink complete with orange or turquoise piping, for example—dramatically different from the subdued mud and thatch dwellings of the less affluent alongside them, but equally different from the more muted tones of elite city apartment blocks—were noticeably less common among the rising affluent of Bhavanipur than they had been fifteen or twenty years earlier.

Some of Babu's adoption of contemporary middle-class symbols was achievable, at least in part, because, in the same way that single-serving packets—of coffee, of cool drinks, and so on—increased the array of consumer products to which poorer aspirants could occasionally gain access, so too were better copies of the *things* that marked out a middle-class life within reach. New patterned melamine dinner plates or plastic dessert bowls and crystal-effect glasses, for example, communicated at least the idea of the china or cut-glass versions and, crucially, demonstrated that their owners were knowledgeable about how those wealthier or more educated than they were conducted themselves. They may not have been able to access the real thing, but they showed that they would know what to do with it if they could.

Dinner at Sarojini's

In the houses of those younger than I am, although women remained nearly exclusively responsible for the preparation and cooking of food, some of those women had also begun to break away from the practice of learning to cook as apprentices, first of their mothers and then of their mothers-in-law, simply replicating or slightly amending the same dishes for another generation. In Anandapuram—and this was also evident in the houses I visited in Bhavanipur and in Hyderabad—many women now also learned to cook from recipes they picked up from newspapers, magazines, or YouTube recipe channels, generally accessed via smartphones.

Sarojini, for example, was married to Paul, a rickshaw driver in his mid-forties, and the couple lived with Paul's widowed mother and their own unmarried children. Although they were economically poorer and less educated than Babu, so could not compete in offering dishes artfully fashioned from the most expensive ingredients, they did offer me a wide range of dishes when I went for dinner, including what Paul described as several "modern" preparations that Sarojini had learned from cookery television programs and other media. Her *gutti kakarakaya* (stuffed bitter gourd), for example, which involved the careful tying back together of the vegetables once they had been filled with a mixture of spices and alliums, while no doubt based on recipes that had been circulating in Andhra for a long time, was new to her and, as Paul told me proudly, was not something many households in the village would have known how to prepare. In their house we still ate on the floor, but Paul and his son ate alongside me—an act indicative of egalitarianism

and friendship rather than hierarchy, mirroring more elite eating styles—
and the flowery plates and dessert bowls that added class to Babu's meal were
again in evidence.

Remembering Past Repasts

To offer some historical context, thirty years previously, such dining was
very different. I was almost always left alone in a room to eat on a mat on
the floor, where a much smaller repertoire of side dishes would be served to
me on a steel or aluminum plate, often directly from the aluminum cooking pots in which they had been cooked, rather than individual serving
dishes. It may be that my capacity for rice had increased over the years, but
it seemed to me that the quantity (although not the quality) of rice pressed
upon me was significantly larger in the past and would have been followed,
almost without exception, by runny *semiya payasam* in a steel tumbler. There
was very little variation; respect was shown then by the *quantity* of food
offered, and by the provision of meat, usually goat or chicken.

Vegetarian diners presented something of a conundrum, at least in
households where meat was eaten, not because they did not have a range of
vegetable-based dishes to choose from—those were, after all, what they ate
six days a week—but because it was much harder to make a distinction
between the special and the ordinary. Knowledge about how to do so properly, however, was in itself a mark of distinction. Das, my research assistant,
was a Brahmin who, despite an intercaste marriage to a meat eater, maintained a vegetarian diet as a marker of his own identity, one that he related
to caste but that had little to do with ritual purity and much more to do with
acquiring the cultural capital through which claims to class could be asserted
(see Staples 2014). For example, he would often turn his nose up at dishes
that, although vegetarian, to him lacked refinement. Preparations that were
too heavy-handed with the masala or where the spices were not properly
ground, that had an excess of onion or garlic, or too much oil or chili did
not only taste less delectable; they were, in his view, less than fully respectable. Vegetables, as he saw it, should be simply prepared with mustard seeds,
turmeric, chili powder, salt, and just the right amounts of onion, garlic, ginger, and coriander leaf.

Interpreting Anandapuram Dining

What, then, was going on here? What, if anything, was it that my hosts were
signaling through their different uses of food, the objects through which it
was conveyed, and the contexts in which it was served? Certainly, meals of
the kind described involved the use and generation of cultural capital:

unevenly distributed, even within families or between genders and generations, although often pooled collectively within a household to maximum effect. This capital, in turn, generated dignity or, unpacked still further, made them count in the eyes of those around them (Dickey 2016, 21). In each of the cases I have described, the hosts conveyed specialist knowledge that their education (whether formal or not) had given them access to: of recipes, in Sarojini's case, or of artful presentation, "like that of a five-star hotel!" as Das expressed it, in the case of Babu, much to the latter's satisfaction. Interior décor, furniture, plates, and the fine-grained qualities of the food all depended on knowledge and skills that, in turn, could confer status.

These accoutrements and the knowledge of how to use them also demonstrated ways of doing hospitality that were not grounded in the logics of caste. Such logics would, in theory at least, have excluded anyone not born from similar Dalit backgrounds from taking food at either Babu's or Paul and Sarojini's houses. There might well have been local higher-caste diners who would have avoided eating in either of their houses for precisely that reason—and the tacit knowledge of the hosts would no doubt have prevented such invitations being sent out—but at least in that case, their avoidance would have identified the invitees as parochial rather than, as a conventional reading based on caste would have it, of higher status. In avoiding such contexts, a benign reading would cast those who avoided dining with them as quaint, lacking the skills and knowledge to reconcile their traditions with the changing demands of the modern.

In addition, my interactions demonstrated that it was not just that my hosts in Anandapuram and Bhavanipur had learned how to perform middle-classness but, like the elite Delhi-based young men Favero (2005) describes, they also embodied the capacity to switch between modes of being according to different audiences. So, while displays of sophistication to a visiting foreigner enhanced their status among less knowledgeable neighbors and thus helped to achieve the dignity inferred by class, when they used food to lobby the village elders for support over, say, an internal village land dispute or for finding a marriage partner, decorative plates or fancy tablecloths were irrelevant. In such cases it was the quantity and type of food offered that mattered: the elders expected meat and biryani rice, but they were quite happy to have it ladled out to them in their own stainless-steel food carriers to be shared and eaten back at home.

Food, then, because of its relative accessibility—compared to the costlier trappings of a middle-class life, from fridges to motorcycles—was a particularly important medium through which identities *beyond* caste could be performed and negotiated. Using their knowledge of urban, transnational dining styles to impress a foreigner and, in doing so, their neighbors, did not in itself render my dinner hosts middle-class. In addition to being realistic about their social aspirations, they were also discerning about which elite styles they emulated. For example, offering alcohol with a meal—which, among the hip of Mumbai "had emerged as a fetish that announced social status" (Dewey 2012, 139)—would have been a step too far. Despite alcohol consumption being common among men, it was still afforded negative social status in Anandapuram, a community where the demonstration of putative Christian values, avoidance of alcohol among them, remained important. Nevertheless, hosting the kind of culinary events to which I was invited did enable my friends to showcase (and, through practice, to fine-tune) the particular cultural capital they had at their disposal. In doing so, they achieved the dignity they strove for.

But what happens when meat—and, more specifically, beef—is entered into the equation? Can offering meat similarly confer class, or, in common with alcohol, does its close associations with caste undermine its usefulness to those low down on the social scale?

MEAT, CLASS, AND CASTE

Meat was used in the various places in which I conducted fieldwork to denote class at a number of different registers. Offering meat, as discussed throughout this book, communicated both respect and specialness and, as for people like Victoria-Rani, celebrated an alternative, Dalit Christian identity, in opposition to the caste-Hindu one. At a New Year's "Love Feast" held in Anandapuram in 2017, for example—provided for everyone in the village by Solomon Raju, a wealthy Dalit Christian philanthropist from Bhavanipur—meat featured heavily. It demonstrated both his wealth—because meat was more expensive than vegetarian alternatives—and his refusal to buy in to a Brahmincentric perspective on the world. In addition to two types of chicken dishes—a dry fry and a *pulusu*—there was also an offering of chicken kidneys to honor the most distinguished guests (mostly dignitaries invited from outside the village, who were seated along the first long table), small pieces of meat mixed into the *gongura patchidi*, and what was billed as a mutton pilaf. A similar focus on meat was evident in the mass public wedding feast hosted by Chellasamy, a Madurai industrialist, described by Dickey. The feast included "soup with 'a large piece of meat,' a chicken leg and thigh . . . mutton curry, mutton biryani with a boiled egg and condiments, chicken biryani . . . another mutton curry (this one with bone sauce), goat intestine sauce, rasam, buttermilk, and sambar" (2016, 196).

Such feasts of potlatch-style proportions might be seen, at least in part, as demonstrations of capital turned into prestige writ large:[11] exaggerated but structurally consistent versions of the standard non-Brahmin wedding feast fare in Andhra of chicken curry, biryani rice, *sambar*, raita, and *gongura patchidi*. Solomon Raju, sponsor of the Love Feast, was a Dalit convert to Christianity, and through such events he clearly gained the awe and respect of the much poorer diners who attended them, as well as demanding the attention of local politicians, whose support he clearly valued. Inviting the local press and a selection of VIPs ensured that his generosity did not go unnoticed, in turn helping to reinforce his status as a local "big man."[12]

Such demonstrations of status through the extravagant provision of meat, however, were different from the lower-key, domestic celebrations I described in the previous section, as well as different from elite, urban meat consumption. In Solomon Raju's case—and also, I would hazard a guess, in that of Chellasamy, whom Dickey describes—the focus on a "rag to riches" story also drew attention to his low-caste origins. Meat eating, for him, was a direct celebration of his identity in much the same way that university beef festivals celebrated Dalit or Muslim identities. The social success of smaller-scale dinners modeled on a modern, middle-class aesthetic, however—whether they contained meat or not—depended instead on side-stepping the question of caste altogether. Other, meat-specific examples of this latter kind of consumption might include the young, college-educated men who told me proudly about ordering a beef or even pork dish when they had been taken to a Chinese restaurant in a city during a training course. To do so did not just indicate a sense of adventure, inquiry, or "awareness," attributes valued among the educated; it was also a way of revealing that they had more sophistication than, in many cases, their forefathers or even their peers. Attaining such "awareness" (Dewey 2012) of how to order or to eat such items could be bundled together with other knowledge of the contemporary in ways that also had tangible value for the men concerned. Samuel, for instance, who knew how to get the flesh out of a crab claw or how to eat Chinese pork balls, was often summonsed by the elders to advise on the best way of approaching, say, an NGO from which they hoped to get support. Perceived sophistication enhanced one's status in tangible ways.

In short, then, when meat was served in particular contexts—in international hotels or restaurants or even in the home, amid the other paraphernalia of middle-classness—it denoted not only the specialness attributed to it by nonvegetarian Indians in general but, at a register beyond the immediate, a kind of refinement that those *not* in the know were unable to attain. However, knowledge alone, while vital, was insufficient to emulate unproblematically a transnational class. Let me compare the cases of two men I knew fairly well to explore what else was at stake.

Kotaiah: High-Caste Meat Eating and Urban Success

Kotaiah, first, was a twenty-eight-year-old Anandapuram man I knew from a Kamma-caste family (a relatively high-ranking, Sudra subcaste that, like Kapus and Reddis, traditionally ate meat but not beef). His parents, both of whom had converted to Christianity before Kotaiah was born, worked as tailors and sometime moneylenders. With their support he had attended an English-medium school and obtained a law degree at a local college and, through judicious networking over a period of several years, a job with a large private insurance company in Hyderabad, where he now lived. Clearly successful at his job, he had been promoted several times in a relatively short period, and he had subsequently managed to borrow money from the bank to buy an apartment that, although a two-hour commute on his motorbike from the office, was in a relatively high-status, newly constructed block. He had recently married, and, the last time I saw him, his wife was due to give birth to their first child.

In his new life, Kotaiah had continued not only to eat meat but, on particular occasions, also to consume beef. He did so, however, not on the basis of preferences associated with the caste into which he had been born but as a highly educated, newly urban, middle-class man. If he took clients to a restaurant, he told me, he was at ease eating what they ate, as happy to use cutlery or chopsticks, if called for, as the fingers of his right hand. His education, and his particularly confident grasp of English not only enabled him to pass in that role but also, as he saw it, meant that among his similarly educated colleagues in the city he was judged on his own merits rather than on his background. What was particularly striking in Kotaiah's case, then, was that it was his caste and community status, as non-Dalit and non-Muslim, that enabled him, ironically, to get away with eating beef on the basis of his newfound, cosmopolitan social class.

Prakash: Lower-Caste Beef Avoidance

My friend Prakash, by contrast—whose story began chapter 4—had advanced socially by doing the precise opposite: by giving up beef, which his own Dalit caste status permitted him to eat. The reasons for this difference were complex. First, he lacked the levels of economic, social, and cultural capital that Kotaiah enjoyed. He was educated, but in a less lucrative field, and his work at an NGO was less secure and less well remunerated and, crucially, brought him less into contact than Kotaiah with those who modeled themselves as young, sophisticated, and modern. Nor did he have the access to the kind of credit that Kotaiah had been able to obtain, so he was constrained by the vagaries of the housing rental market.

Second, for him, eating beef—even, should he have been able to afford it, in the more expensive, international restaurants that Kotaiah sometimes dined in with clients—always ran the danger of exposing him as a Dalit. This, in turn, would put at risk the social advantages he had carefully accrued for his family, including their accommodation, albeit rented, in a middle-class area, which in turn enabled his children to pass as middle-class in the best schools he could afford to send them to. Although his situation was always precarious, by *not* eating beef and by regulating his family's habits in other ways, he made it less likely, he felt, that his children would be identified as Malas. He could perform respectability, but being cutting-edge—as he would have been the first to admit—was beyond his skills. While another Mala in Prakash's position might have been bolder about eating meat, he was also a reserved, quiet man who, as he told me, liked to avoid unnecessary fuss. Prakash's situation, then, was not only different from that of Kotaiah but also that of men like Solomon Raju, whose *economic* status—and the other forms of capital he had been able to extrapolate from that—meant that he no longer needed to concern himself with what high-caste Hindus thought of him. Solomon Raju's financial security meant he had no use for the symbols of transnational elites.

Chic Meat versus Dalit Consumption

The perverse importance of caste in enabling those of higher-status elites to claim beef eating as chic is well brought out in Kalyan Das's forensic examination of a university beef festival held in 2014 at the Centre for Studies in Social Sciences, Calcutta (CSSSC). Organized by Dalit research scholars, the festival was intended to celebrate the April 14 birthday of Bhimrao Ramji Ambedkar, a social reformer who campaigned against discrimination against Dalits. Das draws on an article by Drishadwati Bargi (2014), a Dalit researcher at Jadavpur University, which he described as "a scathing critique of the uber cool Bengali *bhadralok* who flaunts his 'progressivism' by consuming beef and, yet, chose to be almost absent from this event" (2015, 107). In short, although—as already noted—the *bhadralok* was prepared to relish beef as a modern, iconoclastic act, he (and gender was significant here) had no desire to eat it as an act of solidarity with Dalits and Muslims. Context, when it came to understanding meat consumption, was everything.

Indeed, as Das goes on to suggest (and this resonates with Donner's work among middle-class families in Kolkata), the *bhadralok*'s progressive consumption also relied on their womenfolk, as "the torchbearers of the great traditions of our society" (110), *not* eating beef. Understanding gender distinctions is always a vital part of understanding the politics of food and eating. *The bhaldralok*s also drew a distinction—in common with a distinction drawn between many of my own informants—between killing animals and eating them. As Das summarizes their position, "the violent Muslim butcher kills the animals and the caste-Hindu *bhadralok* simply eats it" (111). Meat eating, in relation to negotiating social status, was particularly fraught.

CONCLUSION: SOCIAL DIFFERENTIATION THROUGH FOOD

Social differentiation shaped the dietary and commensal choices made by those I encountered during my fieldwork in coastal Andhra and Hyderabad in all kinds of ways. Those food-related choices might also be made more or less self-consciously in ways that can help shape one's social identity. In line with my own informants' perspectives, I have taken "class" to refer to mutable aspects of one's overall social standing in relation to one's peers, those through which one, or one's family, might come to count in the eyes of those around them. But the material and cultural symbols through which class standing in those terms is negotiated draw, in turn, on the much wider practices of those already established as middle- or upper-middle-class elites. Those practices are ripe for appropriation by some economically poorer people in ways that they were not in the past. First, even the bazaar of a provincial town like Bhavanipur now offers affordable copies of some of the material symbols of middle-class dining, including the plates, glasses, tables, and tablecloths that had begun to greet me in the homes to which I was invited to eat. Second, education and the ever-extending tendrils of media, including the internet as well as television and newspapers, bring knowledge of how to prepare and serve food in ways that appeal to middle-class sensibilities: dishes that use familiar ingredients, for example, but that involve culinary techniques that were not part of the immediate family's repertoire of recipes, or that are served in fancy serving dishes and garnished with chopped coriander leaves. The point is not that these dinners transformed those who host them into members of an elite social class; rather, it is that they enable them to use food in the same ways that elites do: to negotiate status in their immediate milieu and outside the more immutable constraints of caste.

Expressed in these terms, the food-related actions of those I spent time with appear particularly self-conscious and performative, not least because

I was documenting them and asking questions about them in a way that demanded reflexivity on the part of my interlocutors. In reality, of course, a great deal of their food practices were embodied and habitual, changing gradually and over time without a great deal of conscious thought. While my hosts were no doubt aware that it was desirable to have certain props or to display certain manners when entertaining guests they wanted to impress, in most cases they were not actively aware that they were working on their social status in doing so. Often, unsure how best to show a guest respect—especially one from abroad for whom the usual rules might not apply—they were simply mirroring aspects of behavior they had observed in their peers.

This capacity to negotiate status might be read as a positive move for those young, educated people I knew like Babu, for whom it offered an alternative route to social mobility not inhibited by their Dalit or otherwise "other" identity. Even putting aside the fact that such status is relational (in that it requires others to be of lower social status), the precarity of such class-based identities is thrown into sharp relief when meat—and especially beef—is entered into the culinary equation. While the highly prosperous, politically powerful Dalit can be seen to flaunt meat-rich feasts as a show of wealth and as an alternative, non-Brahminical mode of celebration, for those with smaller banks of capital, caste and community remain important issues. Beef eating by the elites—whose styles some of my informants cultivated—was, it became clear, more often a "progressive" act shared with one's own high-caste and high-class fellows, not those outwardly identifying as Dalits and Muslims. The very elites whose styles offered alternative routes to dignity paradoxically also reinscribed them, at least implicitly, with caste and community. And here lies the problem of thinking of "class" as an alternative to "caste" in considering social differentiation in the Indian context. An understanding of the former was long overdue—and does indeed offer people on the ground something new to think with—but caste continues to remain of central importance in understanding Indian foodways.

Conclusion

Taking on Sacred Cows

THIS has in part been a book about cattle, beef eating, and foodways in a more general sense, but it has also been an exploration of how competing discourses about each are deployed by, for, or against various groups of people in South India to define or mobilize them socially. Animals, meat, and other foodstuffs all carry significant, if changing and contingent, symbolic meanings. At the same time, the very *materiality* of bovines and beef—how they feel, smell, look, and taste at different times and across different contexts—shape the ways in which they can be used symbolically against a rapidly shifting political landscape. Meanings are not fixed but are continually wrestled over.

The questions that shaped the research on which this book draws included ones about how and why cattle achieved such iconic status in India, as well as how and why—in the light of historical evidence that challenges the dominant narratives on which bovine politics are based—that status has been maintained and effectively utilized by Hindu fundamentalists in contemporary India. In responding to those questions, the book draws not only on the historical record but also, more significantly, on ethnographic evidence collected during multiple field trips both to coastal Andhra Pradesh and the urban center of Hyderabad. Documentation of the everyday practices of ordinary meat eaters enables us to challenge the rhetoric of the far right and, indeed, to add nuance to that deployed by activists in opposition to it. Such fine-grained data illustrate the gap between on-the-ground realities and dominant ideas associated with cattle, beef, and those involved in its production and consumption. In drawing the book to a close, I also consider some of the wider lessons that the material might offer, both for anthropology in general and the anthropology of food in particular, as well as to the regional ethnographic record.

BOVINE ASSUMPTIONS

Obvious though it might appear, to suggest that cows might mean different things to different people in the Indian context is, in itself, to take on a figurative "sacred cow." Assumed Indian attitudes toward the bovine are, after all, the original source of the expression "sacred cow," an idiom in common use in English for well over a century to denote anything that cannot be questioned (Ammer 2013, 387). So embedded is the assumption of the cow's unambiguous holy repute in our imaginaries of India that any moves to afford it further protection—such as BJP leader Narendra Modi's calls for an end to tax breaks for slaughterhouses in the run-up to the 2014 election, or subsequent moves to ban the sale of cattle for meat at markets—risk being interpreted straightforwardly only in that light, the politics behind such moves stripped out. Even vigilante violence, shocking to read about in the press as it may be, at least seems *explicable* in terms of what people think they know about India.

Various acts euphemized as "cow protection" can be read simply as facets of Indian "culture" or "heritage." Indeed, the Hindu right plays specifically on that notion of "heritage" when it calls for beef bans and, more generally, celebrates vegetarianism. Excluding nonvegetarian food from public and institutional space appears in this context as little more than reasonable sensitivity to Hindu cultural values (Bhushi 2018, 12). Omission of meat altogether from the government's midday school meals program or from the public distribution system for subsidized foodstuffs, for example, or the ban on beef during the Commonwealth Games in Delhi in 2010, all appear as normal against a background of holy cows and apparently widespread adherence to the doctrine of *ahimsa* (respect for all living things).[1] The upshot of such normalization is uncritical acceptance and a lack of further scrutiny.

CONTESTED HISTORIES

How and why did cattle come to achieve such iconic status in the Indian context? A common narrative, reinforced by politicians and perpetuated through everyday discourses, is that contemporary bovine ideologies are rooted in the ancient Vedic texts, with cattle slaughter, imagined as a foreign practice, emerging *only* under the Mughals and later the British. Such stories fit comfortably with the notion that only Muslims, Christians, and Dalits—the latter sometimes cast as descendants of the Harrapans, whose civilization the Aryans replaced in the Vedic era (Achaya 1994, 34)—slaughter and consume beef, while caste Hindus do not.

As Modi has himself alluded to in speeches, however, it was Mahatma Gandhi—himself a "sacred cow" in official narratives of Indian nationalism—who took the most notable lead in promoting vegetarianism and cow protectionism in the decades leading up to independence.[2] Hindu reform movements, such as the Arya Samaj, founded in 1875 by Swami Dayananda Saraswati, also played an important role in challenging what was seen as the spread of un-Indian practices (Copland 2014). By not eating meat, Gandhi had urged, Indians could positively distinguish themselves, and their nation, from their colonial oppressors.[3]

In addition, Gandhi helped to popularize veneration of the cow by describing it as *the* "central fact of Hinduism," and as the "gift of Hinduism to the world" (1999, 374). Cows were not just a "fundamental symbol" (Yang 1980, 585) but served as a kind of material synecdoche for the nation itself. Referencing Gandhi, then—and in particular his anticolonial, nationalist discourse—could be seen as a smart move on Modi's part, since the Mahatma's words appeal well beyond those on the Hindu militant wings of Indian politics. Such rhetoric served well contemporary claims not only that vegetarianism and cow protectionism were pan-Indian values but that they were among those under threat from invading Mughal and then British forces.

The Vedas themselves, however, seem to tell a rather different story, as explored in detail in chapter 1. Some commentators condemned as "blasphemous" a book by historian D. N. Jha (2002, xii) for its central claim that "the 'holiness' of the cow is a myth and its flesh was very much a part of the early Indian non-vegetarian food regimen and dietary traditions" (ix). But the balance of published historical research appears broadly supportive of Jha's view.[4] Brahmins (as well as other non-beef-eating castes), the ancient texts record, not only ate meat but also ate beef throughout the Vedic period, and continued to do so at least some of the time until the twelfth century CE, certainly in the context of sacrifices. Cattle were valuable because they provided meat as well as labor, dairy products, and dung. It had only been with the arrival of Buddhism and Jainism, around 500 BCE, and their promotion of *ahimsa*, the doctrine of nonviolence to all living things, that the notion of *protecting* cows started slowly to take wider hold across the region, and, even then, recorded attitudes were characterized more by ambivalence than by unquestioning veneration. While contemporary attitudes toward cattle clearly have historical roots, then, they look unlikely to be anchored in the specifically indigenous, Hindu history that much of the present discourse places them in.[5]

If the historical record does not quite match the rhetoric, then neither does the rhetoric accurately describe the current landscape in India. When I told people about my research, non-Indianist colleagues and acquaintances routinely expressed surprise that *anyone* in India ate beef. But according to a recent survey, not only is beef the most consumed meat after chicken, its consumption rose between 2005 and 2012 by 14 percent in urban areas and 35 percent in rural ones[6] and has continued to rise each year subsequently, with around 1.05 million metric tons of beef expected to be consumed in 2018.[7] Such claims come at a time when, despite portrayals of India as a vegetarian nation, meat eating more generally—especially of chicken—is on the rise. Upwards of 60 percent of Indians identify as nonvegetarian. At the same time, India's position as the world's largest exporter of beef also places the idea of India as an unquestioningly cattle-venerating nation under severe strain.[8] In 2018—in spite of Modi's stated desires to curb what he called a "pink revolution" in 2014—exports were again expected to increase over the previous year, with India accounting for a fifth of all the world's beef shipments, the majority of them to Southeast Asia and the Middle East.[9] Although it is true that as much as 40 percent of the population *do* follow a broadly vegetarian diet, that many Indian meat eaters also draw a line at beef, and that beef exports are, at least officially, of buffalo rather than cow meat, claims that India is, or ever was, an unequivocally cow-loving, predominantly vegetarian nation clearly demand further scrutiny. Empirical reality undermines the rhetoric.

SUSTAINING "SACRED COW" NARRATIVES IN THE PRESENT

Having discussed *how* cattle came to occupy the official status that they do, the second question is concerned with how that status is sustained—and reasserted with such authority in the present—when both the historical and empirical evidence appear so shaky. How, to put it another way, do we account for the disconnect between the rhetoric and the on-the-ground realities? Part of the answer, as this book demonstrates, is because the rhetoric, however unsubstantiated by the public record, appeals simultaneously to a number of groups of people and on a number of different fronts.

Globalization and Economic Liberalization

First, there is something about the wider contemporary context that helps to sustain the narratives of militant Hindu nationalism, cow veneration among them. This is an era in which, as many scholars have noted, "modernizing and globalizing forces unfolding throughout much of the contemporary world" (Froerer 2007, 4) have fed into and sustained new nationalisms. In India, the rapid changes of the past few decades, particularly the processes of economic liberalization that have gathered momentum since the 1990s, have had major effects on how people live. The opening up of markets and growth of private enterprise have meant that wide swathes of the growing middle classes, now less able to secure solid government jobs-for-life, feel less assured than at any time since independence, and thus more vulnerable to external threats. At the same time, economically poor Hindus, as squeezed as they always were, have sometimes found comfort in rhetoric about national strength and pride. Nationalism offers them something positive to identify with, or against. And sufficiently large numbers of both groups—as elsewhere across the world—seemed primed to be sold the idea that what threatens their livelihoods is not so much poor governance or corruption (as much as they might also blame those things) but, in the absence of other sufficiently compelling narratives, the "other" within (Hansen 1999). In such an environment, national symbols around which populations can coalesce—the holy cow being one of them—offer comfort and a sense of belonging.

Resisting "the Other"

The cow's *specific* symbolic value in this context springs, at least in part, from Gandhi's challenge to colonial muscularity through vegetarianism and, especially, respect for the cow as one of the central motifs of the freedom struggle in the early to mid-1900s. That it appeared to be successful in ushering in the postcolonial period offers a rationale for its reappropriation by supporters of *Hindutva* in the current era of globalization. If the British constituted the enemy to be fought off in the first half of the twentieth century, in the twenty-first century the implicit threat, from the perspective of the Hindu right, comes at least partly in the form of India's Muslim, Christian, and Dalit populations. But the genius of focusing on cow veneration in particular—as well as vegetarianism more generally—is that its promotion can achieve the same exclusionary effects without directly voicing the prejudices that underpin them. To criticize those who trade in or eat beef can successfully be framed as a justifiable response to an attack on Hindu cultural values, backed, however dubiously, by reference to the historical record. Direct attacks on non-Hindu others on the basis of religious—or in the case of Dalits, putatively *inherent* differences—are harder to defend publicly, particularly on an international stage. Vigilantes and activists might well openly equate the Indian nation with Hindu values—as the often rabidly anti-Islamic, anti-Christian, or anti-Dalit sentiments articulated on social media bear witness to—but official discourses are necessarily more circumspect.

To declare openly that non-Hindus are non-Indians would also pose a significant challenge to wooing the "vote banks" of Muslims, Christians, and those from the lowest castes that the BJP depends upon, in some areas, to maintain an electoral advantage. Framing the battle in terms of who eats and who does not eat beef, however, avoids such direct confrontation on the basis of identity, euphemistically rendering a push against cattle slaughter as a matter of cultural preference, rather than violence, structural and symbolic, inflicted against those who eat meat (Osella 2008, 4). Some Dalits, Christians, and even Muslims might be brought back into the fold by joining their fellow Indians in giving up beef.[10] The BJP has made particular efforts to claim Dalits as part of Hindu society (S. Gupta 2016).[11]

Liberal Silences and Converging Forces

At the same time, framing the arguments in terms of heritage or cultural preference—rather than expressing them in terms that explicitly discriminate against particular communities—also helps to evade liberal critique, especially from those outside India sensitive to charges of neocolonialism. Similarly, environmentalists—with their comparable appeal to liberal sentiment—have, albeit unwittingly, also lent support to the hegemony of vegetarianism and bovine inviolability.

The disconnect between rhetoric and reality, then, is sustained through the convergence of a number of forces that, collectively, give weight and appeal to a particular narrative. In short, these are the following: the wider backdrop of emerging nationalisms and, in the Indian context, the past colonial struggles from which contemporary nationalism drew strength; the successful framing of cattle veneration as cultural rather than also political; and the contemporary appeal of neotraditionalist environmentalism. Together, these (and quite possibly other) forces have successfully enabled a reimagining of history, one deployed to justify the sidelining of nonconforming Muslims, Dalits, and other non-Hindu Indians in the present. Such a reimagining also involves (and demands) a *simplifying* of that history. More complex historical accounts—including an exploration of *why* certain things were eaten or not eaten at particular times, rather than assuming a direct line of comparison with the present—are self-evidently harder to marshal a consensus around.

MEAT CONSUMPTION IN CONTEXT

Focusing the spotlight tightly on cattle—or slightly more broadly, on meat consumption—and what it might be taken to signify also strips out the wider historical and material contexts within which particular foods are eaten, in particular ways, at particular points in time. Chapter 2, however, discussed of the complex mesh of circumstances within which the most everyday, taken-for-granted foodstuffs are embedded. Something as apparently simple and noncontentious as drinking tea, for example—strong, sweet, milky, and served in tiny cups or glasses—had been made a possibility in the contemporary moment for some of my South Indian friends through a confluence of seemingly randomly connected circumstances. These include historical processes, such as the ways in which tea plantations had been set up and managed by colonial powers in the first place (Besky 2014). But they are also shaped by particular ecological conditions—soils that favored dark tannic varieties of tea rather than the green teas of China, and landscapes that facilitated dairy farming—as well as the economic need for tea growers to find markets for those leaves not fit for the lucrative export trade. Technological innovations, from the widening availability of fridges and packaged (and sometimes powdered) milk, sugar, and tea (in affordably small packets) to gas burners on which milk and water could easily be boiled together, have also made the regular serving of tea at home a possibility for my informants in ways that it might not otherwise have been. These factors, in turn, shape not only the range of culinary choices available to the families I knew but also the symbolic values that can be attached to such comestibles.

And while this might at first appear tangential to people's decisions over whether to eat or not eat beef, it is significant, because the scrutiny that might be applied to tea might also be applied to beef consumption. Doing so demonstrates that the circumstances in which food choices are made are not only, or even mostly, ideological. Food choices are embedded in a mesh of historical socioeconomic, political, and cultural circumstances, in particular in relation to intersecting stories of industrialization, ecological change, globalization, and technological advances. To eat or not eat beef, while it might suggest affiliation with one community or another, also depends on where one lives, cost, availability, and taste, all factors that themselves are affected by wider circumstances. To make religious offerings to cattle, on the other hand, requires easy physical access to the animals, as well as certain kinds of behavior—docile, slow-moving—on the part of those cows that render them amenable to veneration. The complex reasons for eating or not eating beef or for respecting cows in the present go well beyond a selective interpretation of the Vedic and subsequent texts, an insight that suggests we need to look past the rhetoric, important though that is, and instead at *how* people are engaged in the trading, slaughter, and consumption of beef (among other foods) in their everyday lives. This brings us to a further set of questions, those that consider what light a specifically ethnographic inquiry might throw on the current situation in relation to cattle slaughter and beef consumption in India.

THE CASE FOR ETHNOGRAPHY

This book has been about drawing a more complicated, fine-grained picture of how bovine animals are understood and experienced in contemporary South Asia than those generally captured, for instance, in media reports. This more intricate picture challenges the hegemonic view that the beef industry is necessarily confined to a non-Hindu "other" and that respect for cattle—often merged more generally into vegetarianism—is confined to upper-caste Hindus. It also enables us to see the *political* work that promotion of cow veneration does on the ground, how it enables persecution of the "other" without having to name it as such.

High-Caste Complicity in the Beef Business

First, my work with cattle traders, meat sellers, and others demonstrates very clearly that high-caste Hindus as well as Dalits, Christians, and Muslims are complicit in sustaining the domestic beef industry, even if they do not necessarily participate as customers of the end product. Indeed, without the sale of excess cattle by non-beef-eating, sometimes vegetarian caste Hindus to meat sellers—often through brokers who themselves do not eat beef—the trade could not operate at all. Nor, crucially, as many of my interlocutors pointed out, would the rearing of cattle for products so valued by high-caste Hindus—milk, ghee, curd, dung, and *panchagavya*—be tenable in many cases if cattle could not be sold once they were no longer productive. In areas of the northern "cow belt" where public opinion or regulation has rendered the resale of cattle extremely difficult, for example, dairy farmers were reported to be abandoning older animals and male calves, which in turn were encroaching on arable land—forcing at least one Brahmin farmer to resort to shooting an offending animal. Cattle shelters, too, had become so overcrowded in some places that the animals were reportedly starving

(Ghose 2017). As noted above, maintenance of the cow's symbolic status was also contingent on its ontological and material status: cows that threatened one's livelihood or became prohibitively expensive to maintain were harder to venerate.

High-caste engagement with the cattle trade, as my tracing of the bovine animal's journey from cattle shed to the beef market in chapter 3 demonstrates, was only possible through careful maintenance of "strategic ignorance" (Chua 2009). All parties had come to recognize the value of *not* knowing about the parts of the beef chain that did not directly concern them, ensuring there was no contradiction in decrying beef eating while simultaneously selling one's cattle, unknowingly, to meat traders. Not knowing also maintained the illusion of a radical distinction between high-caste, vegetarian, and/or non-beef-eating Hindus on the one hand and those who slaughter and consume cattle on the other.

Complexities of Human-Cattle Relations

Maintaining that dichotomy—necessary if the spotlight on a non-Hindu "other," as the enemy of Indian values, was to be sustained—also required a demonization of those on the wrong side of the equation. But my ethnographic data again offered nuance to the assumption that respect for cattle was something particular to high-caste Hindus. Not only did the Dalit, Christian, and Muslim cattle herders I knew draw on the same kinship idioms in relating to their animals as their Hindu counterparts—seeing them as mothers, sisters, brothers, and children—they were also equally (and in some cases I knew, more) circumspect about selling their nonproductive cows and buffaloes knowingly into the beef market.

They also drew much finer distinctions than the simplistic split relied on by cattle protectionists to embed their message in the public imagination. Many beef eaters I knew, for example—Dalits and Christians in particular—drew a distinction between the *slaughtering* of animals, something done by the (usually Muslim) "cutting man," and the actual *eating* of their flesh. Such a distinction has a long history, one used also by Brahmins and Buddhists, who once drew the line at being directly involved in animal sacrifice but not necessarily at eating the meat produced by it, and who have even argued that sacrifice is different from slaughter, or that the violence inherent in a sacrificial slaughter might actually be thought of as nonviolence (B. Smith 1990, 201).[12]

Other informants in the present also draw a distinction between the flesh of the cow and that of the buffalo. Some Muslims, for example, reject buffalo meat as inherently low-caste ("*Who* would eat buffalo!?" as one cow-beef-eating informant exclaimed), while some Dalits and Christians avoid cow meat because of its association with Muslims and, particularly in the case of Dalits, because they saw buffalo meat as especially well suited to their bodily constitutions. Bringing other kinds of meat into the equation—donkey meat, pork, or what my friends in Bhavanipur described as "jungle meats," for example—added further complexity. Decisions over what meat to eat and when, over the course of life, require innumerable further distinctions being drawn, few of which are captured by a straightforward beef-versus-non-beef division. This also challenges the notion that those following a nonvegetarian diet are any less discerning about what they do and do not eat than those who identify as vegetarian.

Distinctions between Vegetarianism and Nonvegetarianism

Not only is the distinction drawn between beef eaters and non–beef eaters an erroneous one but so too is that drawn more generally between vegetarianism and nonvegetarianism—a distinction used, again, to mirror the difference between the highest ritually ranking Hindu caste groups and their lower-caste and non-Hindu others. The problems of such an absolute distinction are multiple. First, documentation of what people actually eat on a day-to-day basis shows that very few people—with the exception of those directly involved in the selling of meat—eat it much more than once a week, when it plays a key role in distinguishing between the ordinary working day and time denoted as special. The nonvegetarian in coastal Andhra is, for the most part, in practice vegetarian (I knew one nonvegetarian woman in Hyderabad, for example, who ate considerably less meat over the course of the year than some of the men from vegetarian households I knew).

At the same time, what constitutes a vegetarian is also less straightforward or categorical than it at first appears. For one thing, vegetarian diets not only are delineated in terms of whether people eat meat and eggs or not but often placed other plant-based foods within the "non-veg" category. Onions, garlic, mushrooms, and alcohol, for example, are sometimes considered nonvegetarian, in that, like meat, they are considered heating, while mushrooms, because they grow into "the shape of a head" (Dubois 1906, 87), or tomatoes, "because their color resembles blood" (O'Malley 1932, 118) are likewise contentious (see also Staples 2016, 79–80). Anthropologist Sarah Lamb (2000) argued that the division between hot and cold foods was often more important in determining what her informants ate than a straight vegetarian/nonvegetarian split. The Brahmin widows who populate her monograph avoided meat and fish, to be sure, but also onions and gravy, betel nut, and even certain kinds of dal because they were all categorized as *garam* (hot) and were thus unsuitable for their bodies. To complicate the matter still further, such categorizations might also vary between groups: while some Dalits in Kerala saw onions as cooling, for example, Brahmins in the same region saw them as heating, and some drew further distinctions between red onions, which were hot, and white onions, which were cool (Osella and Osella 2008a, 180). The inclusion of nonmeat items within the nonvegetarian category, however, makes sense in contexts where "non-veg" is understood as an ontological category extending beyond what people do and do not eat and describing the non-normative more generally (Novetzke 2017). In this definition, pornography or swear words, for example, might also be considered "non-veg."

Even those who identify as vegetarian, however, do not necessarily eschew meat altogether. The discreetly darkened rooms and closed-off booths of many restaurants that sold nonvegetarian cuisine are, like the walled compounds of the meat market, in part a display of sensitivity to those who do not wish to encounter meat consumption, but they are also about enabling the transgressive consumption of meat by those—mostly men—who identify as vegetarian but sometimes eat it anyway (Ghassem-Fachandi 2012). A further important distinction, one that Lucia Michelutti (2008) draws out particularly well, is that between the vegetarian *household* and the individual members within it who might sometimes, in very specific contexts, eat meat. The Yadav households her interlocutors reside in consider themselves vegetarian, for example, but, as she shows, the men of those households eat meat in the context of sacrifices, when medical need demands it, to create secular democratic unity with their Muslim allies, and, especially, at monthly barbeques with other men to assert their masculinity. Henrike Donner (2008) and Pat Caplan (2008) each make a similar distinction between vegetarian women, who uphold the dietary values of the household, and others, namely children and men, for whom the rules might in certain circumstances be relaxed. My own data, used in chapter 4 especially, show comparable blurring of lines between vegetarian and nonvegetarian, especially because people also change their eating habits across the life cycle and according to context. If I have demonstrated nothing else by highlighting all these complexities, I hope at least to have shown that the ubiquitous oppositions of vegetarianism and nonvegetarianism, beef and non-beef—essential though they are to the maintenance of high-caste hegemony—are woefully inadequate for describing the much more complicated eating habits of actual people in the course of their everyday lives.

Beyond Nationalism

What is also highlighted by the ethnography is that, while it might be instructive to chart the ebbs and flows of cattle slaughter and beef consumption in relation to the ups and downs of Hindu nationalism (something I attempted, on a small scale; see Staples 2018), nationalist fervor is only one of the factors at play in determining people's choices of whether to eat or not to eat beef. And even if we were to restrict our analysis strictly to correlations between Hindu nationalism and beef consumption, the results would not be clear-cut. A surge in nationalist rhetoric led some of my lower-middle-class Christian informants in coastal Andhra in 2000 to celebrate their consumption of beef with renewed vigor, to be sure, but for others—particularly those living in close proximity to non-beef-eating households and without strong support networks—the state promotion of cow protectionism made them more likely to give up beef altogether, or at least to conceal it. Eating beef conveyed different messages to different audiences, some positive, some negative, and some more ambivalent.

However, attitudes and practices with respect to beef are also shaped in relation to changes in the price, taste, availability, and status of other kinds of food, as well as in relation to wider discourses about health and the environment. For most of my friends, who identified neither as Dalit activists nor as Hindu nationalists, the debates around cattle slaughter captured in the national and regional press were of only peripheral concern, ideological debates that figured only marginally in their food choices. Goat, for example, had virtually disappeared from the weekly menus of my informants in coastal Andhra and Hyderabad, both because fewer people were rearing them—due in part to pressures on land and the environmental threats to their health that made them harder to raise successfully—and because of associated upward surges in price.

The biggest impact, however, had come from the industrialization of chicken production. Not only was it now competitively priced compared to beef—which in the 1980s had been comparatively much cheaper—but broiler chicken was also available in different forms. It appeared, for example, as burgers in fast-food outlets and as chicken Manchurian on Chinese takeaway carts, as well as in traditional chicken *pulusu* or fry at home on Sundays, or at weddings and other feasts marking the course of life. The tender meat of broiler chickens could even make an appearance in a high-class sandwich, as a chicken seller I interviewed boasted, something that the tougher "country" birds would never have been suitable for. And although health concerns as well as benefits were expressed by my informants in respect to chicken, its price, respectability, and versatility—not to mention the successful marketing of it—had, for most families I spent time with in Anandapuram, Bhavanipur, and Hyderabad, made it the default nonvegetarian option.

Meat and Class Distinction

Finally, meat eating relates not only to caste and community but also and increasingly to class. For internationally oriented, upper-middle-class urban Indians, eating meat—even beef—was not transgressive but a marker of cosmopolitan sophistication. Those I worked with in coastal Andhra and Hyderabad were not, clearly, from those classes, but they nevertheless drew productively on those imaginaries as an alternative way of framing meat that went beyond the splits between Hindu fundamentalists and Dalit or Muslim activists that dominated media representations. Eating meat and, crucially, eating it in particular ways, from this perspective helped both to maintain a positive self-identity and to secure and improve one's status vis-à-vis one's peers.

In one sense, class-based kudos in relation to food was attained in complete opposition to food-related demonstrations of caste status. The very foods and styles of eating that communicated urbanity—beef and noodles eaten with chopsticks among colleagues in an international hotel restaurant, for example—would, read purely in caste or communal terms, indicate low status. The appeal of being identified through the idiom of class rather than caste or religion in contemporary India, for those "othered" by their culinary habits, is perhaps self-evident, and the examples in chapter 6 show the work some of my informants put in to raise their class status. However, at the same time, the very capacity to demonstrate sophistication through eating otherwise taboo foodstuffs also remained highly linked to caste position and the social and cultural capital that might by harnessed from that. It is easier and less socially risky, despite the apparent paradox, for members of a non-beef-eating caste to heighten their class status through strategic consumption of beef than it was for Dalits to do so. Food in India *always* needs to be seen through the lenses of caste and community politics, even if these are not in themselves sufficient to explain the contemporary foodscape.

BUSTING DICHOTOMIES

What then, in closing, does all this tell us in a more generalizable sense? These final sections draw out some wider theoretical contributions.

The Material and the Symbolic

First, the cases discussed in this book offer support to long-standing claims by anthropologists—dating back to Sidney Mintz and Jack Goody in the 1980s—that the material aspects of food cannot be divorced from its symbolic aspects. It is not just that the material preconfigures the symbolic but that the very materiality of our most potent symbols is what gives them their power and their capacity to be deployed in different ways at different times and in different contexts. The much-admired chewiness and distinctive flavors of meat, for example, stand in contrast to the softer textures of cooked legumes and vegetables, providing a visceral reminder of the specialness of meat versus the everydayness of other foods. Indeed, it is the very bland softness of industrially produced chicken that makes it such an inadequate substitute for the tougher, more flavorsome home-reared birds about which people reminisced. The corporeal presence of bovines, however, and their capacity to provide milk, fuel, and other products, also integrates them into families as kin and helped to sustain their spiritual status. Symbolic meanings can also change as material circumstances change, or change in relation to other things. The capacity for an offering of tea to be taken as a marker of respect, for example, had been lessened now that almost everyone in the places where I worked could access single-portion packets of tea and refrigerated milk from shops close by. At the same time, affordable plastic duplicates of otherwise high-status items—from china dinner plates to crystal glasses—enabled guests to enact shows of respect that they sometimes struggled to achieve in the past.

Likewise, the material presence of cattle can also challenge the symbolic meanings attributed to them—as the high-caste Hindus referred to above discovered when they encountered stray cows eating their crops, or when more cows than could be cared for were sent to cattle shelters. Veneration, in such cases, became a practical impossibility. Marvin Harris (1966) was, of course, too reductionist in making his case that, in order to survive, a religious doctrine also needed to make rational, economic sense. He failed to distinguish adequately between dominant bovine-related discourses and on-the-ground realities in relation to cattle in India, and drew too radical a distinction between the economic and the religious. But, as work by the so-called "new materialists" has posited, he was right to argue that ideological positions cannot be adequately understood outside the material contexts within which they are embedded.

On the opposite side of the ideological fence from the cow protectionists, faced with affordable, readily available chicken, even those for whom beef was an outward marker of their celebration of Christianity and a rejection of high-caste Hindu values had begun to shift from beef to chicken as their most widely eaten meat. Ideological struggles, in short, only ever provide part of the picture, and this book has suggested how we might begin to contextualize such struggles.

The Trouble with "Culture"

In trying to situate this book within anthropological and sociological studies of food, I noted in the introduction that, as an ethnographic study, it was located most obviously among those exploring cultural aspects of food and eating. In placing it there, however, I have also been critical of the very notion of "culture" as an implicitly apolitical category for describing representations of people's practices and beliefs. That is, of course, nothing new in itself. "Culture" has already been widely critiqued within anthropology over recent decades.[13] Nevertheless, the need to recognize the limits of cultural relativism, both intellectually and ethically, bears restating in the contexts described in this book, given the efforts of powerful brokers—the architects of *Hindutva* in particular—to deploy "culture" as a static, coherent, and uncontested set of values. It similarly challenges the idea that very different sets of practices among different groups of people might be understood in relation to alternative ontologies—a notion advanced by McKim Marriott (1976; 1990), who argued that we needed to understand Indians' experiences through their own categories. Marriott's ethical commitment to avoiding the ethnocentrism of explaining Indian society through theoretical models developed elsewhere—shared by those who later pushed for the "ontological turn" in anthropology (for example, Henare, Holbraad, and Wastell 2007)—was a worthwhile intervention (for example, Staples 2003). But assuming that there were distinctive Indian, or Hindu, ways of being in the world that could be compared to, say, Western European ones, was problematic in the same way that a coherent, bounded notion of Indian "culture" was problematic. The categories and values deployed in the creation and promotion of *Hindutva*, for example, while undeniably *Indian*, are no more or no less so than those brought to bear by Dalit activists to demand their culinary rights.

A critical ethnographic approach of the kind utilized here, by contrast, treats cultural or ontological claims as contested, shifting, and, as such, politically motivated and ripe for exploration. Neither culture nor ontology are neutral, existing somehow beyond or separate from those who live in the worlds created by them; they can be raised by human agents as potential weapons. We need to continue asking by whom, why, and how claims to alterity are invoked in any given context, and who stands to benefit from those claims. Fine-grained ethnography, as I hope this book makes plain, helps to answer those questions.

Complicating Binaries

Related to this intervention has been an attempt throughout the book to trouble the binary pairings through which the debates on cattle veneration and beef eating have traditionally been understood and through which they are often presented in everyday discourse. These pairings are, in particular, those drawn between the rabid Hindu right on the one hand and the subaltern, beef-devouring Dalit or Muslim activist on the other; between the vegetarian and the nonvegetarian; and between respectable and nonrespectable meats. Like popular readings of "culture," however, these pairings are not simply the structural apparatus of external social scientists—Western philosophical categories, as Marriott might have seen them—attempting to impose order on disorderly data, even as their heuristic value might appeal when we stumble across them. Nor, as anthropologists more drawn to demonstrating the universality of human cognitive categories do, am I claiming that we all think in binary oppositions.[14]

Rather, these dichotomies reflect the imaginaries of those who position themselves on either side of an ongoing debate, and thus demand critical analytical attention. But although framing the discussion in those terms has real constraining or enabling effects on how people in South India come to experience themselves and perceive others, they also exclude—and consequently silence—a great swathe of the population who position themselves neither on one side nor the other. This book, in attempting to bring in the voices of those currently excluded from the discussion—those who take far more ambivalent positions in relation to cattle slaughter and beef eating—also challenges us to consider whose voices are included and excluded in discussions about what social groups think, feel, and do more generally. Work toward a more comprehensive inclusion of perspectives also requires us, as my interrogation of class and caste has revealed, to shift away from linear high-to-low scales of social differentiation to think about other, different kinds of formulations.

LAST WORDS

For the most part, my beef-eating friends in India did not object, in the way that some activists did, to curbs on the public consumption of beef, nor were they overly bothered—so long as they could still access it at a reasonable price—whether the meat they ate was officially legal or not. Often affectively engaged with their own cattle, they also empathized with others who chose to venerate the cow, even professing to believe in the doctrine of *ahimsa*, while at the same time remaining comfortable about eating beef as they saw fit and when the situation allowed. Nor did they frame their culinary activities in terms of competing cultural claims or as a matter of rights; as several people put it, they simply did what they did, and would continue doing it as long as it made sense to them to do so, regardless of what others said. This was the way things were. And although some of them, particularly the butchers and meat sellers who had experienced the sharp end of cow-protectionist vigilantism, were visibly angry and/or afraid, the dominant emotion expressed was one of bemused resignation or of ambivalence. People adjusted.

"Why do they want to do this? Why do they want to stop people like us from eating beef?" Edwin, the brother-in-law of Miriam, my former Hyderabad cook, asked me when we gathered at his house one Sunday morning. He tutted and shook his head despondently, before leaning over to splash more whiskey into the glasses of the several other men who were assembled there, whiling away the time after church as the women of the family finished preparing lunch. Das, my fieldwork assistant, and I had joined them there after a couple of hours spent interviewing Aziz, the Muslim butcher who ran the beef shop on the next street. It was, I suspect, our presence that had provoked Edwin's apparently rhetorical questions. "They should let people do what they want to do. How can they stop it?" he added. "The only problem now is that *everyone* is eating it. Brahmins, Vaisyas, all of them. It is why goat mutton is now 500 rupees per kilo, and even beef is 250 rupees a kilo or more. It's too much." With a dismissive "what can we do?" gesture of his hands, he drained his glass, got up from the mat on the floor, and, his hunger suitably heightened from the alcohol, went to sit at the table in the adjoining room. His wife, Ruth, ladled beef curry for him onto a steel plate already piled high with boiled rice, and he began eating heartily.

The ways of the government, the vigilantes, and even the high-caste people who had apparently switched to eating meat were all irksome, to be sure, and had Das and I not bought the beef from Aziz's shop, my hosts would most likely have been eating chicken for lunch that Sunday. But although Edwin was well versed in the same newspaper stories of cattle-related vigilantism and beef festivals that I have discussed in this book—and could, as our conversations showed, engage with the dichotomies through which they were framed—like the other men in the family, and like my informants elsewhere, he did not position himself firmly on one side or the other. Nor was he always consistent in his opinions. Aziz's meat was costly not just because of the cow protectionists, he implied, but because demand, even for poorer-quality meat, enabled Aziz to push up his prices. He was someone with whom Edwin was friendly, but, as a Muslim, Aziz was also seen as someone who moved in different worlds. In other conversations, Edwin praised what he saw as the government's moves, however ineffectual he recognized them as being, to curb corruption. The ambivalence he and others expressed in relation both to cattle slaughter and beef consumption related, as he described it, to his perceived powerlessness to do anything, or the futility of outward protest. But, as the pleasure on his face as he tucked into the beef curry his wife had just prepared demonstrated, neither did apparently dominant narratives decrying the consumption of cattle deter him from eating and enjoying it.

GLOSSARY

ABBREVIATIONS

H   Hindi
S   Sanskrit
Ta   Tamil
Te   Telugu
U   Urdu

Adivasi (H)   indigenous people, synonymous with "Scheduled Tribes" in official nomenclature
ahimsa (S)   the injunction not to take life
arrack   a locally distilled liquor, often produced from coconut sap or sugarcane
attu kallu (Ta)   a traditional wet grinding stone

Banganapalle   Andhra Pradesh town from which the region's most common type of mango takes its name
belam (Te)   also called jaggery, a concentrated, golden-colored, syrupy flavored cane sugar, usually sold in solid blocks or tennis-ball sized spheres
bonda (Te)   a deep-fried ball of potato encased in a crispy gram flour batter

carom (Te)   hot (as in spicy); also chili powder
chakralu (Te)   a deep-fried, crispy, and spiral-shaped savory snack made with rice and gram flours
chapati (H)   a simple flatbread of whole-wheat flour, water, and salt, usually dry fried

chappels (Te)   simple sandals, flip-flops, or slippers, as contrasted with shoes

coolie (H/T)   a casual, daily-paid laborer, or—as in "coolie work"—used to show that the work itself is casual

dal (H)   a dish made from pulses, rendered *pappu* in Telugu

Dalit (H)   literally "broken" or "scattered," the self-adopted term to describe those formally known as "Untouchables" or, in the government's official terminology, "Scheduled Castes" (SCs)

dandora (Te)   a proclamation by a village announcer, often accompanied by a drum to draw attention as he (and in my experience it was always a man) marches through the lanes of the community

dhoti (H)   a traditional men's garment, often white, tied around the waist and covering the legs

dondakaya fry (Te)   a dry, fried vegetable accompaniment to rice or chapatis, the main ingredient of which—*dondakaya*—translates in English as "ivy gourd"

doragaru (Te)   the Telugu term *dora* (from the Turanian root *tur*, meaning swift or powerful) means, according to C. P. Brown's dictionary (1903, 612), a chief, a baron, a lord, master, owner, ruler, or king. Susan Bayly (1999, 327) described the *dora*s as a class of "fortress-dwelling land-controllers"—or "little kings"—from what is now the state of Telangana. In Anandapuram, the term—as a prefix to the honorific *garu* (comparable to the Hindi suffix—*ji*)—was used almost exclusively in relation to foreign men, rather than the term *ayya garu*, or "sir," which was a more common honorific for local men.

dosa (Ta)   a savory pancake made of fermented ground rice and *urad dal* (black gram), usually served with coconut chutney, *sambar*, and/or chili powder, and sometimes stuffed with potatoes

dosakaya (Te)   round yellow cucumber

gangi (Te)   a thin rice porridge, sometimes eaten for breakfast

gari (Te) (pl. garelu)   a deep-fried doughnut-shaped snack made from ground *urad dal* (black gram), usually served with chutney

ghee (S)   clarified butter

ginne (Te)   a bowl, often favored—particularly by older people—over a plate as a receptacle for rice-based meals

idli (Te)   a steamed, circular-shaped, spongy-textured cake of fermented ground rice and *urad dal* (black gram), commonly served with chutney, *sambar*, and/or chili powder

jonnalu (Te)   sorghum, used as an ingredient in *sangati*—a thick, filling porridge, used instead of rice, or sometimes mixed with it

Kapu (Te)   also called Naidu, one of the politically and economically dominant Sudra subcastes of Andhra Pradesh

keema (U)   a minced beef-based dish, eaten mostly by Muslims

kirana shop (Te)   a small convenience shop

kozhavi (Ta)   a stick, or pestle, used in conjunction with an *attu kallu* (see above) or wet grinding stone

kūra (Te)   often translated to me as "curry," the word signifies any dish eaten as an accompaniment to rice or chapatis

kurta (H)   a long, usually collarless Indian men's shirt, usually worn untucked

lakh (S)   one hundred thousand

lungi (Te)   a long-skirt, sarong-like garment worn by men, particularly in villages and at home

Lutyens' ecosystem   taking its name from the colonial era architect Edwin Lutyens, who planned the central administrative area in Delhi, the phrase is increasingly used in (mostly) right-wing media to refer to what they describe as a cosmopolitan, elite group of journalists, (mostly) left-leaning politicians, and others operating within the so-called echo chamber of Lutyens' Delhi

Madiga (Te)   one of Andhra Pradesh's two main Dalit (see above) castes, formerly Untouchables or Scheduled Castes. Their traditional occupations are as leatherworkers, including work tanning hides and as cobblers.

Mala (Te)   the other of the two main Andhra Pradesh Dalit (see above) castes, formerly Untouchables or Scheduled Castes

masala (H)   a mixture of ground spices or other flavorings (a mixture of garlic, fresh ginger, and other herbs might, for instance, be referred to as a "wet masala")

mixie   everyday term for an electric food processor or grinder

Naidu (see Kapu)

panchayat (H)   the most basic administrative unit, a village council or committee

pappu charu (Te)   a thin, soup-like lentil accompaniment to rice

perugu (Te)   curds or yogurt, generally eaten with rice at the end of a meal

perugu charu (Te)   a thin, savory dish made from combining curds with fried mustard seeds, curry leaves, onions, green chilies, salt, and turmeric

pulusu (Te)   a wet or stew-like accompaniment to rice

puri (Te)   a deep-fried flatbread, made from wholemeal flour, usually served either with chutney or a simple potato curry

rasam (Te)   tamarind water, usually flavored with ground black peppercorns and chili powder, either served with rice toward the end of the meal or occasionally drunk on its own

rava upma (Te)   semolina-based savory porridge, often cooked with mustard seeds, green chilies, curry leaves, and either peanuts or cashews

Reddi (Te)   a Sudra subcaste—roughly on par with Kapus—locally considered to be a high-ranking, traditionally landowning farming caste

saddi annam (Te)   leftover cooked rice soaked in cool water overnight and eaten for breakfast the next morning

sambar (Te)   a thin lentil and mixed vegetable–based stew, made sour with tamarind. At festival meals, it is often served after the main meat dishes or dry vegetarian accompaniments, and before the *rasam* (see above) and *perugu* (see above). It also serves as a classic accompaniment to *idli*s and *dosa*s.

sangati (Te)   a heavy porridge made from *ragi* (finger millet) or *jonnalu* (sorghum), along with hand-pounded rice, which in many parts of Andhra served as the staple before industrially processed rice became ubiquitous

semiya (Te)   vermicelli, often served in the form of *semiya payasam*, a sweet vermicelli and milk pudding, mixed with cashews, dried fruit, and pieces of coconut

shandy   an agricultural market at which cattle are traded

talimpu (Te)   an oil-fried spice mixture added to season the *kūra* at the end of its preparation

tiffin   a snack, as opposed to a meal, although often used to refer to breakfast

urad dal (H)   black gram

varna (S)   a category, originally defined in the Vedic texts, that categorizes people as Brahmins, Kshatriyas, Vaisyas, or Sudras. Castes or *jatis* further subdivide each *varna*.

the Vedas (S) a body of religious texts, written around 3,500 years ago, that are seen as the source of Hindu scripture (also called "the Vedic texts")

Zebu a species of humped cow associated with South Asia, where it originated

NOTES

INTRODUCTION

1. See, for example, Copland (2014).
2. I have written about this extensively elsewhere. See Staples (2008; 2016; 2018, 63).
3. *Doragaru* is an honorific, usually reserved, in Anandapuram, for foreign men (*ayyagaru*, the alternative, was the term most likely deployed to address respected men from outside the village).
4. The only time I recall ever being served beef was during an NGO-run training course on appropriate technologies in the mid-1980s, held in a tribal community in Andhra Pradesh.
5. See, for example, Special correspondent, "Australia-born missionary, children, burnt alive in Orissa," *Rediff On the Net*, January 23, 1999, www.rediff.com/news/1999/jan/23oris.htm.
6. See Froerer (2007, 8–13) for a pithy overview of Hindu nationalist moves to encompass Christianity as well as Islam within its targets during the 1990s.
7. In addition to the BJP, the umbrella of the Sangh Parivar included the Rashtriya Swayamsevak Sangh (RSS), a paramilitary "cultural" and voluntary-service organization, and the Vishva Hindu Parishad (VHP), or World Hindu Council. Mawdsley (2006, 381–82) provides a useful overview of the main organizations that constitute the Sangh Parivar and some of the key analysts, up to the mid-2000s, who have documented and theorized its expanding influence in India.
8. See, for example, Murcott (1988).
9. For examples of press coverage of the event, see BBC News, "Violence Breaks Out at Indian Beef-Eating Festival," April 16, 2012; *Dalit Nation*, "Beef Food Festival Makes the Grass-Eating Manuvadis Shiver," May 2, 2012, http://dalitnation.wordpress.com/2012/05/02/beef-food-festival-makes-the-grass-eating-brahmins-and-banias-shiver/; and S. Rama

Krishna, "The Beef Eaters of Osmania," *Sunday Guardian*, April 22, 2012.

10 See, for example, *Times of India*, "Saffron Extremists Desecrated Temple to Trigger Riots: Cops," April 14, 2012; and *Ummid.com*, "Hyderabad Riots: Hindu Youths Held for Desecrating Temple," April 29, 2012, www.ummid.com/news/2012/April/29.04.2012/4_held_in_hyderabad_case.htm.

11 Abhinav Bhatt, "Government's 'Pink Revolution' Destroying Cattle, Says Narendra Modi," *NDTV*, April 2, 2014, www.ndtv.com/elections/article/election-2014/government-s-pink-revolution-destroying-cattle-says-narendra-modi-503604.

12 The full text of the legal change was published in *The Gazette of India* on May 23, 2017, and can be accessed at www.hindustantimes.com/india-news/centre-bans-cow-slaughter-across-india-cows-can-be-sold-only-to-farmers/story-8sFXJxiNmZ8eD6NXDgbvnL.html.

13 See, for example, Amnesty International India's June 28, 2017, call on the government to condemn vigilante attacks in far stronger terms, at www.amnesty.org/en/press-releases/2017/06/india-hate-crimes-against-muslims-and-rising-islamophobia-must-be-condemned/.

14 For examples of this, see P. Caplan (2008) and Donner (2008).

15 I enclose the word "chose" here in quotation marks as a reminder of the political dimensions of the often-naturalized term "choice"—which, as Anne Murcott has helpfully pointed out (personal communication, 2019), implies a free market in which everyone has comparable freedom of choice. As this book makes clear, this is far from always the case.

16 Van der Geest, Whyte, and Hardon (1996, 155), for example, document these transformations in relation to pharmaceuticals.

17 For examples of work on class in India, see Dickey (2016), Fernandes (2009), Donner (2008), and Säävälä (2003).

18 In her thesis, Xu draws extensively on the wider corpus of sensory ethnography to define "participant sensation," especially the insights of Stoller (1989), Howes (2006), and Pink (2009).

19 I quote here from the back-cover blurb of Beatty's (2019) *Emotional Worlds*, in which he sets out a narrative approach to understanding emotion.

20 See, for example, Stewart's (2007) *Ordinary Affects*, which, as Beatty (2019, 211) notes, attempts to be performative and evocative rather than analytical or discursive, as it seeks to express as much as to explain emotional response.

21 For examples of village studies, see Srinivas (1952; 1955), Dube (1955), and Béteille ([1965] 1996).

22 For examples, see Bouglé (1971), Dubois (1906), Senart (1930), and O'Malley (1932).

23 For a summary of Dumont's arguments, see Quigley (1994, 35) and Staples (2007, 137).
24 For a more detailed discussion of these debates, see Berger (2012).
25 Critiques of Harris's analysis include Freed and Freed (1972), Simoons (1979), Korom (2000), and Lodrick (2005).
26 In addition to Coole and Frost's large set of mostly theoretical papers—emerging out of political science and the humanities rather than the social sciences—see, for example, Shapiro (2005).
27 See also Jalais's (2010) comparable work on animal-human relations—in her case between fishermen and tigers—in the Sundarbans.
28 See also Van der Veer (1994) on the connection between the materiality of the cow and her ritual significance.
29 See, for example, Janeja (2010) on eating practices in Kolkata; Roncaglia (2013) on Mumbai's lunch delivery system; Anjaria (2016) on street food, also in Mumbai; or Solomon (2016), yet again in Mumbai, with a focus on obesity and diabetes.
30 See, for example, Ray (2004), on Bengali migrants to the United States.
31 Bhushi 2018, 12. For the interview with Shatrugna cited by Bhushi, see Abhirup Dam, "Vegetarianism and the Politics of Food in Modern India," *Sunday Guardian*, November 30, 2013.
32 See, for example, Mines and Yargi's (2010) attempt at reintroducing the village as a unit of ethnographic analysis in India, and Tilche and Simpson's (2016) return to past village studies.
33 See, for example, Gewertz and Errington (2010) and Staples and Klein (2017a).
34 Tommy Wilkes and Roli Srivastava, "Protests Held across India after Attacks against Muslims," *Reuters*, June 28, 2017.
35 See also Hurn (2013) and Sutton (1997) for comparable discussions of being vegan and vegetarian, respectively, in field sites dominated by meat eaters.
36 See, for example, the report by Dean Nelson, "Drinking Milk from Non-Indian Cows 'Could Make Children Turn to Crime,'" *Telegraph*, April 24, 2015.
37 Quote sourced from a report in *First Post*, "RSS Reveals Secret to Reducing Crime and Reforming Convicts, and Yes, It's to Do with Cows," April 24, 2015, www.firstpost.com/business/rss-reveals-secret-reducing-crime-reforming-convicts-yes-cows-2211406.html.
38 The Muslims I worked with in Hyderabad identified either as Sunni and Shia Muslims or, within the latter category, Imami Ismaili Muslims, led by the Aga Khan. Although I subsequently learned that butchers are often *pasmanda* Muslims—a low caste within the Muslim community, as the historian Mohammad Sajjad (2014) discusses—none of those I interviewed during my fieldwork, perhaps unsurprisingly, identified themselves as such.

39 Indeed, when I checked with my Hindi/Urdu-speaking informants what the words were for beef, their first responses were *"gosht."*
40 Harish Damodaran, "Sharp Spike in Buffalo Meat Export via South Ports Raises Beef Question," *Indian Express*, October 1, 2017, http://indianexpress.com/article/india/sharp-spike-in-buffalo-meat-export-via-south-ports-raises-beef-question-4869096/.

CHAPTER ONE: DIFFERENTIAL HISTORIES OF MEAT EATING IN INDIA

1 A phenomenon explored in ethnographic detail by Jeffrey (2010).
2 "Habitus" is the term French sociologist Pierre Bourdieu used to describe the ways in which action is constituted through a mixture of individually and collectively embodied constraints and freedom, within these constraints, to act (Bourdieu 1990, 52ff.). In short, "habitus" is the embodiment of history.
3 See, for example, Anthony (2007), Bryant and Patton (2005), Bryant (2001), and Patton (2005). Bryant and Patton's (2005) collection of essays from archaeologists and historians of the Harrapan and Vedic periods presents in detail the debates about the continuities and discontinuities between what have been designated by historians as two distinct historical epochs.
4 Griffith's translation of the Rigveda is downloadable from www.sanskritweb.net/rigveda/griffith-p.pdf (accessed February 6, 2018). The relevant passage is verse 12 or hymn XC.
5 See, for example, Deliège (1993).
6 Although see Patton (2005) for a more critical discussion of the relationship between the Harappans and the Aryans.
7 See, for example, Korom (2000) and Lodrick (2005).
8 Even though the distinctions between the sacred and the profane, or between the "religious" and the "economic," have been shown to be facets of Western rather than universal classifications. See Adcock (2010; 2018) for a detailed explication of this argument.
9 See also Achaya (1994, 53) and Lodrick (2005, 61).
10 See, for example, Achaya (1994, 55) and Staples (2018, 62).
11 See Achaya (1994, 56) and Legge (1972) on early evidence of vegetarianism, and Sachua (2005, 152–53) on beef taboos among Brahmins.
12 See, for example, Srinivas (1952), Dube (1955), and Béteille ([1965] 1996).
13 See, for example, Daniel (1987, 186), Cantlie (1981), and Khare (1976a; 1976b; 1992).
14 For evidence of this, see Yang (1980, 586) and Robb (1986, 303).
15 See Robb (1986, 296, 300) for a detailed analysis of these disorders.

16 Laws on cattle slaughter vary from state to state. Some impose a ban on the slaughter of "agricultural cattle" or "bovines," which might include buffaloes; others allow the slaughter of buffaloes over a certain age (over eight in Andhra Pradesh, above twelve or thirteen in Maharashtra, over fourteen in West Bengal). In Andhra, cattle slaughter is covered by the Andhra Pradesh Prohibition of Cow Slaughter and Animal Preservation Act of 1977.

17 The ABVP translates into English as the All-India Student Council and is the student wing of the nationalist Rashtriya Swayamsevak Sangh (RSS). Although there are no explicit links between the ABVP and the BJP, Narendra Modi, the BJP leader, is also a member of the RSS.

18 S. Rama Krishna, "The Beef Eaters of Osmania," *Sunday Guardian*, April 22, 2012.

19 See *Times of India*, "Saffron Extremists Desecrated Temple to Trigger Riots: Cops," April 14, 2012; and *Ummid.com*, "Hyderabad Riots: Hindu Youths Held for Desecrating Temple," April 29, 2012, www.ummid.com/news/2012/April/29.04.2012/4_held_in_hyderabad_case.htm.

20 Ankita Dwivedi Jori, "Bull for Buffaloes: A Day in the Life of Trucks Carrying Cattle through Delhi," *Indian Express*, September 13, 2015. http://indianexpress.com/article/india/india-others/bull-for-buffaloes-a-day-in-the-life-of-trucks-carrying-cattle-through-delhi/#sthash.uIQsY251.dpuf.

21 Syed Firdaus Asraf, "The Man Who Inspired the Meat Ban in Mumbai." *Rediff.com*, September 8, 2015, www.rediff.com/news/interview/the-man-who-inspired-the-meat-ban-in-mumbai/20150908.htm.

22 Kamlesh Damodar Sutar, "Politics Heats Up in Mumbai over Meat Ban during Jain Festival," *India Today*, August 29, 2016, www.indiatoday.in/india/story/meat-ban-mumbai-shiv-sena-mns-congress-bjp-paryushan-337924-2016-08-29. For a critique of the Shiv Sena's stance, see *Indian Express*, "One Man's Meat," September 14, 2015, http://indianexpress.com/article/opinion/editorials/one-mans-meat/#sthash.oDd2tPaM.dpuf.

23 See, for example, *Hindustan Times*, "Digvijaya Supports Ban on Cow Slaughter as a 'Good Hindu,'" June 26, 2014, www.hindustantimes.com/india/digvijaya-supports-ban-on-cow-slaughter-as-a-good-hindu/story-uyfwMkMtWJD2UvmOzaIhyJ.html.

24 Shaju Philip, "Kerala: College Teacher under Fire for Facebook Comments Defending Beef Fest," *Indian Express*, October 7, 2015, http://indianexpress.com/article/india/india-news-india/kerala-college-teacher-under-fire-for-facebook-comments-defending-beef-fest/.

25 Samanwaya, Rautray, "Supreme Court Allows Sale and Consumption of Beef in Jammu and Kashmir," *Economic Times*, September 14, 2015, https://economictimes.indiatimes.com/news/politics-and-nation

/supreme-court-allows-sale-consumption-of-beef-in-jammu-and-kashmir/articleshow/49234964.cms.

26 Anand Mishra, "PM Modi Speaks: Gau Rakshaks Anti-Social, So Angry to See Shops in Cow's Name," *Indian Express*, August 7, 2016, http://indianexpress.com/article/india/india-news-india/narendra-modi-mygov-townhall-gau-rakshaks-anti-social-so-angry-to-see-shops-in-cows-name-2958803/.

27 See, for example, *Livemint*, "Cow Slaughter: Supreme Court Rejects Plea Seeking Nationwide Ban," January 27, 2017, www.livemint.com/Politics/AanCh6hoY5qncH8iCMxUoJ/Cow-slaughter-Supreme-Court-rejects-plea-seeking-nationwide.html; and Bhadra Sinha, "Cattle Trade for Slaughter: Supreme Court Suspends Ban across India," *Hindustan Times*, July 12, 2017, www.hindustantimes.com/india-news/supreme-court-puts-on-hold-ban-on-cattle-trade-for-slaughter-govt-says-new-rules-by-august-end/story-WypElt9CMgFZP1wxPsLdgJ.html.

28 For a critique of the new regulations, see Anup Surendranath, "A Constitutional Misadventure," *Indian Express*, May 30, 2017, http://indianexpress.com/article/opinion/columns/a-constitutional-misadventure-cow-slaughter-gau-rakshak-beef-ban-4679912/.

29 Sowmiya Asok, "Govt to Roll Back Move to Ban Sale of Cattle for Slaughter," *Indian Express*, November 30, 2017, http://indianexpress.com/article/india/govt-to-roll-back-move-to-ban-sale-of-cattle-for-slaughter-4961219/. See also *Hindustan Times*, "Madras HC Extends Stay on Ban on Cattle for Sale for Slaughter by 4 More Weeks," June 28, 2017, www.hindustantimes.com/india-news/madras-hc-extends-stay-on-ban-on-cattle-sale-for-slaughter-by-4-more-weeks/story-vCqvUA3jgZ4XvzLJZ8pBWP.html.

30 For statistics, see, for example, Delna Abraham and Ojaswi Rao, "86% Killed in Cow-Related Violence Since 2010 Are Muslim, 97% Attacks after Modi Govt Came to Power," *Hindustan Times*, July 16, 2017, www.hindustantimes.com/india-news/86-killed-in-cow-related-violence-since-2010-are-muslims-97-attacks-after-modi-govt-came-to-power/story-w9CYOksvgk9joGSSaXgpLO.html.

31 Special correspondent, "Buffalo Meat Exports Fall 4.35% in April-May," *The Hindu*, July 20, 2017, www.thehindu.com/business/Industry/buffalo-meat-exports-fall-435-in-april-may/article19310477.ece.

32 T. V. Jayan, "'Cow Slaughter Ban Can Cost India Dearly,'" *The Hindu*, January 11, 2018, www.thehindubusinessline.com/economy/agri-business/cow-slaughter-ban-can-cost-india-dearly/article9756523.ece.

33 Dipankar Ghose, "Held after Cows Starve to Death in His Own Gaushala, BJP Leader Blames Own Government," *Indian Express*, August 19,

2017, http://indianexpress.com/article/india/chhattisgarhs-durg-district-held-after-cows-starve-to-death-in-his-gaushala-bjp-leader-blames-own-govt-4803289/.

34 See, for example, Matt Wade and Cassandra O'Connor, "Holy Cow, No Beef in Delhi for Commonwealth Games," *Sydney Morning Herald*, July 24, 2010.

35 Bhushi (2018, 12) takes her 88 percent statistic from the Anthropological Survey of India (ASI), an eight-year study completed in 1993, although see also Achaya (1994, 57), Mehta et al. (2002), and Novetzke (2017, 367) for alternative statistics, the lowest estimate of which is 60 percent.

CHAPTER TWO: EVERYDAY SOUTH INDIAN FOODWAYS

1 Online OECD data accessed from https://data.oecd.org/agroutput/meat-consumption.htm.

2 See, for example, Barthes ([1961] 1997) or Douglas (1972).

3 In taking this journey through my ethnographic material, I have been inspired by the holistic, historically informed approaches to the study of food pioneered by Goody (1982) and Mintz (1985), both of whom did a great deal to successfully bring together the symbolic and the material. The material necessarily precedes the symbolic in producing the circumstances for the latter to arise, examples of which will follow later in the chapter. But I have also been aided by a reengagement with the work of scholars usually set in opposition to one another: cultural materialists, like Marvin Harris on the one hand and those drawn to more symbolic explanations (Douglas 1972; Geertz 1973; Barthes [1961] 1997) on the other. Entrenched debate between the two sides has long since become stale, one of the reasons, perhaps, that explicit reference to either has become sidelined in contemporary analyses. Why, after all, should we refight the battles of the 1970s? As "the new materialists" have argued more recently, however, there is still something to be gained from recognizing the entanglements of the symbolic and the material. Food may well serve as a signifier, a meal or an item of food both summarizing and transmitting a situation. The capacity of such signifiers to convey meaning, however, is intricately intertwined with history and their own contingent, material qualities. In focusing on the economic value of the cow, its products, and its labor, Harris took a somewhat reductionist view of what constituted the material, but if we expand our attention to the material to encompass, for example, phenomenological approaches, or those that take embodiment seriously (Bourdieu 1990; Coole and Frost 2010; Csordas 1994; Haraway 1991; Leder 1990; Merleau-Ponty 1962; Scheper-Hughes and Lock 1987; and Staples 2007, 100–105), a whole new

set of possibilities through which to engage anthropologically with foodways is opened up. It is this capacity for what food signifies to change in relation to material conditions in the broadest sense that enables us to rethink the dichotomy drawn by symbolism and materiality.

4 For more on tea's place in the Indian food system see Besky's (2014) ethnographic analysis of tea plantations in India.

5 See, for example, Bergeaud-Blacker, Fischer, and Lever (2016); and Kjaernes, Harvey, and Warde (2007).

6 For a summary of the Deepam BPL connection scheme launched in Andhra Pradesh in 1999 and 2000 see, for example, *Times of India*, "Andhra Pradesh Government Sanctions 3 Lakh LPG Connections to BPL Women as Dussehra Offer," October 2, 2014.

7 Britannia cookies, according to the company's website (http://britannia.co.in/about-us/overview, accessed March 26, 2018), are available in five million outlets across India and reach more than 50 percent of Indian homes. Parle-G, according to its manufacturer, is "the world's largest selling biscuit" as well as one of the country's oldest, having been sold since 1929 (www.parleproducts.com/about, accessed March 26, 2018).

8 Religious fasting, in Anandapuram—followed by the most devout churchgoers on Tuesday, Thursday, and Saturday evenings—equated to not eating rice (as well as meat and, usually, vegetarian curries); chapatis with chutney, sweetmeats, or fruit, for example, might be consumed as alternatives to "food" during a fast.

9 Curd—the English term used to gloss the Telugu *perugu*—is what in the UK would likely be referred to as yogurt. When prepared at home, milk is boiled and cooled to a temperature at which one could immerse a finger for at least a few seconds, and then a little curd, from an existing batch, is added to enable the transformation to take place overnight. In the warmer months in coastal Andhra, room temperature is sufficient for the milk to curdle; in cooler climes it might be necessary to keep the curd pot in a warmer place.

10 For details on the Green Revolution, see Frankel (1971) and Chaudhuri (2005).

11 This, again, is wholly consistent with cross-cultural accounts dating back at least as far as Audrey Richards's descriptions of the Bemba's consumption of sorghum gruel, made palatable with relish (1939, 46) and Mintz and Schlettwein-Gell's (2001) discussion of the "core-fringe-legume hypothesis."

12 See also Kantor's evocative description of winnowing grain in rural Bihar, an activity that "entails attuning the body to the surrounding environment and materiality of the moment" (2019, 248).

CHAPTER THREE: FROM CATTLE SHED
TO DINNER PLATE

1. A comparable sense of risk accompanied a number of my fieldwork encounters—including some at butcher shops as well as at the locations of cattle slaughter—and, it should be noted, it was not a risk equally shared between all participants. I, as a white, male foreign observer, was clearly exposing myself to less danger than those who were partaking in the activities I was documenting. And although the stakes were already high for those involved in cattle slaughter, whether I was there or not, my presence nevertheless had the potential to bring unwanted attention to them.
2. For evidence of this from various sources, see Achaya (1994, 57), Bhushi (2018, 12), Mehta et al. (2002), and Novetzke (2017, 367).
3. Based on claims by Chigateri (2008, 17) and Palash Ghosh, "Where's the Beef? In India, Believe It or Not," *International Business Times*, May 14, 2013, www.ibtimes.com/wheres-beef-india-believe-it-or-not-1258469.
4. For reference to the recent European food scandals, see Staples and Klein (2017b) and Felicity Lawrence, "Horsemeat Scandal: Timeline. Ten Key Moments of Revelation in the Investigation," *The Guardian*, May 10, 2013.
5. For a description of what distinguishes halal from haram (prohibited), see Bergeaud-Blackler, Fischer, and Lever (2016, 3).
6. See, for example, Staples (2017, 242) and Campbell (2009, 162).
7. See, for example, Harish Damodaran, "Sharp Spike in Buffalo Meat Export via South Ports Raises Beef Question," *Indian Express*, October 1, 2017, http://indianexpress.com/article/india/sharp-spike-in-buffalo-meat-export-via-south-ports-raises-beef-question-4869096.
8. For an example of press coverage of the event, see Aditi Vatsa, "Dadri Lynching: Delhi CM Arvind Kejriwal Claims He Was Initially Stopped from Entering Bisara," October 4, 2015, http://indianexpress.com/article/india/india-news-india/kejriwal-stopped-from-entering-dadri-village-asks-why-me.
9. On the anthropology of ignorance more generally and its relation to power, see also Mair, Kelly, and High (2012, 14).

CHAPTER FOUR: CATTLE SLAUGHTER, BEEF EATING,
AND AMBIVALENCE

1. Malas are one of two major Dalit (Scheduled Caste) groups in coastal Andhra.
2. On the subaltern politics of disgust—as separate from Brahminical disgust—see Tayob (2019).

3 Naidu—or Kapu, an alternative name for the same subcaste—is known as one of Andhra Pradesh's economically and politically dominant Sudra *varna* castes, along with the Reddis and the Kammas. Chief ministers, for example, have mostly come from those castes.
4 The Erukala (or Yerukala) community is a Scheduled Tribe or indigenous group, originally known as forest-dwelling hunters.
5 For a more detailed analysis of disgust, see Ghassem-Fachandi (2010; 2012, 150–51).
6 There had been recent media reports about the state's high court calling on civic bodies to clamp down on the sale of donkey, which was apparently being made available in some city shops in larger towns and cities. See, for example, Amrutha Vasireddy, "Andhra High Court Fumes over Rampant Slaughter of Donkeys for Meat," *Times of India*, November 9, 2017, which reports on a street restaurant allegedly selling the meat. Other reports express concern that working donkeys were being stolen and sold across state borders to satisfy people's demands for their meat. See, for example, B. Chandrashekhar, "Donkeys Being Sold for Meat from Kurnool," *The Hindu*, November 5, 2012, www.thehindu.com/todays-paper/tp-national/tp-andhrapradesh/donkeys-being-stolen-for-meat-from-kurnool/article4065857.ece.
7 Under the current reservations system, a certain percentage of college places and government jobs are reserved for members of Scheduled Castes and Tribes (i.e., Dalits and Adivasis), as well as members of what are designated Backward Castes.

CHAPTER FIVE: HEALTH, THE ENVIRONMENT, AND THE RISE OF THE CHICKEN

1 For such interpretations, see Dube (1955), Béteille ([1965] 1996), Khare (1976b; 1992), Marriott (1990), and Srinivas (1952).
2 In what is perhaps his most famous essay, "Deep Play: Notes on a Balinese Cockfight," Geertz moots the idea, for example, of "culture as an assemblage of texts" (1975, 448), explaining that "cultural forms can be treated as texts, as imaginative works built out of social materials" (449).
3 Statistics sourced from www.indianmirror.com/indian-industries/poultry.html.
4 One lakh is 100,000.
5 Sourced from Godrej's website: www.godrejagrovet.com/godrej-tyson-foods.aspx.
6 For examples of Ayurvedic and humoral medicine, and emic understandings of them, see Nichter (2008), Horden and Hsu (2013), Langford (2002), and Zimmermann (2013).

7   For ethnographic examples of these variations, see Staples (2008) and Kantor (2019).
8   See, for example, *Dalit Nation*, "Beef Food Festival Makes the Grass Eating Manuvadis Shiver," May 2, 2012, http://dalitnation.wordpress.com/2012/05/02/beef-food-festival-makes-the-grass-eating-brahmins-and-banias-shiver.
9   A term developed by McKim Marriott (1976, 110) to denote that, because Hindu thought does not separate actors from their actions in the way that Western philosophical traditions do, neither can code and substance be assumed to be separable.
10 For additional examples of the documented capacities of heating foods, see Carstairs (1957, 84, 188), Mayer (1960, 44–45), and Beck (1969).
11 For examples, see Cantlie (1981), Donner (2008), and P. Caplan (2008).
12 See also Zimmermann (1999, 187).
13 On the risks of antibiotics fed to chickens, see, for instance, B. Balasubramanian, "Antibiotics in the Chicken We Eat," *The Hindu*, April 20, 2016, www.thehindu.com/sci-tech/health/policy-and-issues/antibiotics-in-the-chicken-we-eat/article6376564.ece; or, on the potential dangers of growth hormones, Kaniza Garari, "Poultry Injected with Growth Hormone Despite Ban Imposed by Centre," *Deccan Chronicle*, June 15, 2016, www.deccanchronicle.com/nation/current-affairs/150616/poultry-injected-with-growth-hormone.html.
14 For the organization's website, see www.downtoearth.org.in.
15 On goat production, see Shrivastava 2018, and on waste disposal by abattoirs, see Nidhi and Dua 2015.
16 I have also begun to make this contention elsewhere (Staples 2017; 2018, 69).
17 For examples, see Grove, Damodaran, and Sangwan (1998), Jha (2002), Kelkar and Nathan (1991), and Lutgendorf (2000).
18 www.peopleforanimalsindia.org. For more from anthropologists on the PFA, see Dave (2014) and Govindrajan (2018).
19 For the organization's website, see www.peopleforanimalsindia.org/gaudaan.php.
20 For a link to the film, see www.MeatKills.in. For news coverage of the film and its launch, see *Hindustan Times*, "First You Eat Meat, Then Meat Eats You: Maneka Gandhi," September 18, 2017, www.hindustantimes.com/india-news/first-you-eat-meat-then-meat-eats-you-maneka-gandhi/story-N5Rj4ZQpwEG0yJ51hVITQK.html.

CHAPTER SIX: FROM CASTE TO CLASS IN FOOD

1   As meat eaters wishing to dine in the newspaper *The Hindu*'s staff canteen discovered when they were politely requested to refrain (Gorringe and Karthikeyan 2014).

2 See, for example, *Indian Express*, "Pilibhit Cops Look for Man Who Supplied 40 Kg Beef for Wedding," May 17, 2018, http://indianexpress.com/article/india/pilibhit-cops-look-for-man-who-supplied-40-kg-beef-for-wedding-5179810.
3 Although, as Favero (2005) sets out in relation to the young, cosmopolitan men he worked with in New Delhi, this should not be taken to mean that such places were imagined necessarily as "Western."
4 For examples of this, see Dumont (1980), Dirks (2001), and Quigley (1999).
5 See also Inden (1990) and Bayly (1999).
6 For proponents of this view, see Barnett (1977) and Mencher (1974).
7 Examples of this can be found in Fuller and Narasimhan (2007, 122) and Dickey (2016, 5). Goody (1982, 97, 175, 183) makes a similar point. On the embodiment of these capacities, see especially McGuire (2011).
8 Although not exclusively. According to Fuller and Narasimhan (2007, 135), the IT professionals they worked with in Chennai did not exhibit the anxiety commonly attributed to those of their social strata.
9 For examples of this work, see Conlon (1995), Dewey (2012), Nandy (2004), Liechty (2005), Ray and Srinivas (2012a), and Siegel (2010). P. Caplan (2008) and Donner (2008) are also useful on comparable changes in domestic environments.
10 For examples of these trends elsewhere in small-town India in the immediate aftermath of economic liberalization, see Pankaj Mishra's (1995) travelogue *Butter Chicken in Ludhiana*, which critically documents a journey to small towns across the subcontinent. Upamanyu Chatterjee's novel *English, August* ([1988] 1998) is another evocative account of provincial India in broadly the same era.
11 See also my description of a vegetarian feast, which achieves the same kind of impact (Staples 2014).
12 On the notion of the "big man" on India, see Staples (2018), M. Mines (1994), and L. Caplan (1999).

CONCLUSION

1 See, for example, Gethin Chamberlain, "Delhi Divided over Beef Ban on Athletes' Menu at Commonwealth Games," *The Guardian*, January 17, 2010.
2 See, for example, Ghassem-Fachandi (2012, 153–54).
3 See Premanand Mishra (2015, 85) and, on British colonial meat eating, also Sengupta (2010).
4 For examples of this, see Achaya (1994), Korom (2000), Lodrick (2005), Harris (1985), and B. Smith (1990).
5 This popular discourse is often reflected in, and perpetuated by, school textbooks. See, for example, Hasan (2002, 196), who documents how

references to beef consumption in ancient India were being deleted from school history books by the National Council of Educational Research Training (NCERT).
6. Statistics drawn from National Sample Survey Organisation (NSSO) data and analyzed by IndiaSpend. See Chaitanya Mallapur, "Indian Beef-Eating Up, Chicken Tops Meat Surge," *IndiaSpend*, April 8, 2015, www.indiaspend.com/cover-story/indian-beef-eating-up-chicken-tops-meat-surge-71788.
7. Figures taken from www.statista.com/statistics/826722/india-beef-and-veal-consumption.
8. Figures taken from Meat and Livestock Australia (MLA) 2017, www.mla.com.au/globalassets/mla-corporate/prices--markets/documents/os-markets/red-meat-market-snapshots/mla-ms_india_-snapshot-2017.pdf.
9. Abhinav Bhatt, "Government's 'Pink Revolution' Destroying Cattle, Says Narendra Modi," NDTV, April 2, 2014, www.ndtv.com/elections/article/election-2014/government-s-pink-revolution-destroying-cattle-says-narendra-modi-503604. "Pink revolution" was the term used by Narendra Modi in a pre-election rally to criticize the expansion of slaughterhouses before the 2014 general election.
10. Note, for example, the claims at www.peopleforanimalsindia.org/gaudaan.php, on the website of leading animal welfare organization, People for Animals, that the Mughals, as well as Hindus, also venerated the cow as a "uniquely *Indian* symbol" (my emphasis).
11. See Harper (2000, 278) on Madigas giving up beef in the 1920s or Mosse (1999) on similar moves taken by Paraiyar Catholics in Tamil Nadu. See also Smita Gupta's more recent comment piece, "The Dalit-Hindutva Paradox," *The Hindu*, February 9, 2016, www.thehindu.com/opinion/op-ed/The-Dalit-Hindutva-paradox/article14068231.ece; and Hardtmann's (2008) claim of a consensus among Dalits—or at least Dalit activists—that they are *not* Hindus.
12. See also V. Das (2013) for alternative interpretations of what sacrificial slaughter might have meant.
13. For examples of some of the debates about "culture," see Abu-Lughod (2008), Hobart (2000), Kuper (1999), Merry (2003), and Mol (2002).
14. For the case in support of binary thinking being part of the human condition, see, for example, Astuti (2001) and Carey, Solomon, and Bloch (2001).

REFERENCES

Abu-Lughod, Lila. 2008. "Writing Against Culture." In *The Cultural Geography Reader*, edited by Timothy S. Oakes and Patricia L. Price, 50–59. London: Routledge.

Achaya, K. T. 1994. *Indian Food: A Historical Companion*. Oxford: Oxford University Press.

Adcock, C. S. 2010. "Sacred Cows and Secular History: Cow Protection Debates in Colonial North India." *Comparative Studies of South Asia, Africa and the Middle East* 30, no. 2 (August): 297–311.

———. 2018. "Cow Protection and Minority Rights in India: Reassessing Religious Freedom." *Asian Affairs* 49, no. 2 (June): 340–54.

Ambedkar, Bheemrao. 1948. *The Untouchables*. New Delhi: Siddharth Books.

Ammer, Christine. 2013. *The American Heritage Dictionary of Idioms*. 2nd ed. Boston: Houghton Mifflin Harcourt.

Anjaria, J. S. 2016. *The Slow Boil: Street Food, Rights, and Public Space in Mumbai*. Palo Alto: Stanford University Press.

Anthony, David W. 2007. *The Horse, the Wheel, and Language*. Princeton, NJ: Princeton University Press.

Appadurai, Arjun. 1981. "Gastro-Politics in Hindu South Asia." *American Ethnologist* 8, no. 3 (August): 494–511.

———, ed. 1986. *The Social Life of Things: Commodities in Cultural Perspective*. Cambridge: Cambridge University Press.

———. 1988. "How to Make a National Cuisine: Cookbooks in Contemporary India." *Comparative Studies in Society and History* 30, no. 1 (January): 3–24.

Arun, C. J. 2004. "From Outcaste to Caste: The Use of Symbols and Myths in the Construction of Identity: A Study of Conflict between the Paraiyars and the Vanniyars in Tamil Nadu, South India." PhD diss., University of Oxford.

Astuti, R. 2001. "Are We All Natural Dualists? A Cognitive Developmental Approach." *Journal of the Royal Anthropological Institute*, n.s., 7, no. 3 (September): 429–47.

Baehr, Peter. Forthcoming. "Unmasking, or Theoretical Exposure." In *The Cambridge Handbook of Social Theory*, edited by Peter Kivisto. 2 vols. New York: Cambridge University Press.

Bargi, Drishadwati. 2014. "Beef, Babasaheb and Bhadralok." *Kindle*, May 2, 2014. http://kindlemag.in/beef-babasaheb-bhadrolok/.

Barnett, Steve. 1977. "Identity, Choice and Caste Ideology in Contemporary South India." In *The New Wind: Changing Identities in South Asia*, edited by Kenneth David, 393–414. The Hague/Paris: Moulton.

Barthes, Roland. (1961) 1997. "Toward a Psychosociology of Contemporary Food Consumption." In *Food and Culture: A Reader*, edited by Carole Counihan and Penn Van Esterik, 20–27. New York: Routledge.

Basu, Amrita, and Atul Kohli. 1998. "Introduction." In *Community Conflicts and the State in India*, edited by Amrita Basu and Atul Kohli, 1–6. New Delhi: Oxford University Press.

Bayly, Susan. 1999. *Caste, Society, and Politics in India from the Eighteenth Century to the Modern Age*. Cambridge: Cambridge University Press.

Beatty, Andrew. 2019. *Emotional Worlds: Beyond an Anthropology of Emotion*. Cambridge: Cambridge University Press.

Beck, B. E. F. 1969. "Colour and Heat in South Indian Ritual." *Man*, n.s., 4 no. 4 (December): 553–72.

Bergeaud-Blackler, Florence, Johan Fischer, and John Lever, eds. 2016. *Halal Matters: Islam, Politics and Markets in Global Perspective*. Abingdon, UK: Routledge.

Berger, Peter. 1963. *Invitation to Sociology: A Humanist Perspective*. New York: Anchor Books.

———. 2012. "Theory and Ethnography in the Modern Anthropology of India." *HAU: Journal of Ethnographic Theory* 2, no. 2 (Fall): 325–57.

Besky, Sarah. 2014. *The Darjeeling Distinction: Labor and Justice on Fair-Trade Tea Plantations in India*. Berkeley: University of California Press.

Béteille, André. (1965) 1996. *Caste, Class, and Power: Changing Patterns of Stratification in a Tanjore Village*. Oxford: Oxford University Press.

———. 1991. *Society and Politics in India: Essays in Comparative Perspective*. London: Athlone Press.

———. 1997. "Caste in Contemporary India." In *Caste Today*, edited by Christopher J. Fuller, 150–79. New Delhi: Oxford University Press.

Bhushi, Kiranmayi, ed. 2018. *Farm to Fingers: The Culture and Politics of Food in Contemporary India*. Cambridge: Cambridge University Press.

Bouglé, C. 1971. *Essays on the Caste System*. Translated by David Pocock. Cambridge: Cambridge University Press.

Bourdieu, Pierre. 1984. *Distinction: A Social Critique of the Judgement of Taste*. London: Routledge.

———. 1986. "The Forms of Capital." In *Handbook of Theory and Research for the Sociology of Education*, edited by John G. Richardson, 241–58. Westport, CT: Greenwood.

———. 1990. *The Logic of Practice*. Translated by Richard Nice. Cambridge: Polity Press.

Broomfield, John. 1968. *Elite Conflict in a Plural Society: Twentieth-Century Bengal*. Berkeley: University of California Press.

———. 2016. "The Frustration of the *Bhadralok*: Pre-Independence Politics in Bengal." *South Asia: Journal of South Asian Studies* 39, no. 1 (April): 217–21.

Brown, C. P. 1903. *A Telugu-English Dictionary*. 2nd ed. Madras: Asian Educational Series.

Bryant, Edwin F. 2001. *In Quest of the Origins of Vedic Culture: The Indo-Aryan Invasion Debate*. New York: Oxford University Press.

Bryant, Edwin F., and Laurie L. Patton, eds. 2005. *The Indo-Aryan Controversy: Evidence and Inference in Indian History*. Abingdon, UK: Routledge.

Campbell, Ben. 2009. "Fields of Post-Human Kinship." In *European Kinship in the Age of Biotechnology*, edited by Jeanette Edwards and Salazar Carles, 162–78. Oxford: Berghahn.

Cantlie, Audrey. 1981. "The Moral Significance of Food Among Assamese Hindus." In *Culture and Morality: Essays in Honour of Christoph von Fürer-Haimendorf*, edited by Adrian C. Mayer, 42–64. Delhi: Oxford University Press.

Caplan, Lionel. 1999. "Gifting and Receiving: Anglo-Indian Charity and Its Beneficiaries in Madras." In *Tradition, Pluralism and Identity: In Honour of T. N. Madan*, edited by V. Das, D. Gupta, and P. Uberoi, 283–305. New Delhi: Sage Publications.

Caplan, Patricia. 2008. "Crossing the Veg/Non-Veg Divide: Commensality and Sociality among the Middle Classes in Madras/Chennai." In Osella and Osella 2008b, 118–42.

Carey, Susan, Gregg Solomon, and Maurice Bloch. 2001. "Zafimaniry: An Understanding of What is Passed on from Parents to Children: A Cross-Cultural Investigation." *Journal of Cognition and Culture* 1, no. 1 (January): 43–68.

Carstairs, G. M. 1957. *The Twice Born: A Study of a Community of High-Caste Hindus*. London: Hogarth Press.

Chakravarti, A. K. 1974. "Regional Preference for Food: Some Aspects of Food Habit Patterns in India," *Canadian Geographer*, 18, no. 4: 395–410.

Chatterjee, Upamanyu. (1988) 1998. *English, August: An Indian Story*. New Delhi: Penguin.

Chaudhuri, Sabuj Kumar. 2005. "Genetic Erosion of Agrobiodiversity in India and Intellectual Property Rights: Interplay and Some Key Issues." *Patentmatics* 5, no. 6 (June), http://eprints.rclis.org/7902/1/Patentmatics_June_2005.pdf.

Chigateri, Shraddha. 2008. "'Glory to the Cow': Cultural Difference and Social Justice in the Food Hierarchy in India." In Osella and Osella 2008b, 10–35.

Chua, Liana. 2009. "To Know or Not to Know? Practices of Knowledge and Ignorance among Bidayuhs in an 'Impurely' Christian World." *Journal of the Royal Anthropological Institute* 15, no. 2 (June): 332–48.

Conlon, Frank. 1995. "Dining Out in Bombay." In *Consuming Modernity: Public Culture in a South Asian World*, edited by Carol A. Breckenridge, 90–128. Minneapolis and London: University of Minnesota Press.

Coole, Diana, and Samantha Frost. 2010. *New Materialisms: Ontology, Agency, and Politics*. Durham, NC: Duke University Press.

Copland, Ian. 2014. "History in Flux: Indira Gandhi and the 'Great All-Party Campaign' for the Protection of the Cow, 1966–68." *Journal of Contemporary History* 49, no. 2 (April): 410–39.

Corbridge, Stuart, and John Harriss. 2000. *Reinventing India: Liberalization, Hindu Nationalism and Popular Democracy*. Cambridge: Polity Press.

Csordas, Thomas J. 1994. "Introduction: The Body as Representation and Being-in-the-World." In *Embodiment and Experience*, edited by Thomas J. Csordas, 1–26. Cambridge: Cambridge University Press.

Daniel, E. Valentine. 1987. *Fluid Signs: Being a Person the Tamil Way*. Berkeley: University of California Press.

Das, Kalyan. 2015. "To Eat or Not to Eat Beef: Spectres of Food on Bengal's Politics of Identity." *Economic and Political Weekly* 50, no. 44 (October 31): 105–14.

Das, Veena. 2013. "Being Together with Animals: Death, Violence and Noncruelty in Hindu Imagination." In *Living Beings: Perspectives on Interspecies Engagements*, edited by Penelope Dransart, 17–31. London: Bloomsbury Academic.

Dave, Naisargi N. 2014. "Witness: Humans, Animals, and the Politics of Becoming." *Cultural Anthropology* 29, no. 3 (August): 433–56.

Deliège, Robert. 1993. "The Myths of Origin of the Indian Untouchables." *Man*, n.s., 28, no. 3 (September): 533–49.

Desai, Amit. 2008. "Subaltern Vegetarianism: Witchcraft, Embodiment and Sociality in Central India." In Osella and Osella 2008b, 96–117.

Dewey, Susan. 2012. "'Teaching Modern India How to Eat': 'Authentic' Foodways and Regimes of Exclusion in Affluent Mumbai." In Ray and Srinivas 2012a, 126–42.

Dickey, Sara. 2016. *Living Class in Urban India*. New Brunswick: Rutgers University Press.

Dirks, Nicholas B. 1997. "The Policing of Tradition: Colonialism and Anthropology in Southern India." *Comparative Studies in Society and History* 39, no. 1 (January): 182–212.

———. 2001. *Castes of Mind: Colonialism and the Making of Modern India*. Princeton, NJ: Princeton University Press.

Dittrich, Christoph. 2009. "The Changing Food Scenario and the Middle Classes in the Emerging Megacity of Hyderabad, India." In *The New Middle Classes: Globalizing Lifestyles, Consumerism and Environmental Concern*, edited by Hellmuth Lange and Lars Meier, 269–80. Netherlands: Springer.

Dixon, Jane. 2002. *The Changing Chicken: Chooks, Cooks, and Culinary Cuisine*. Sydney: University of New South Wales Press Ltd.

Doniger, Wendy, and Martha C. Nussbaum, eds. 2015. *Pluralism and Democracy in India: Debating the Hindu Right*. Oxford: Oxford University Press.

Donner, Henrike. 2008. "New Vegetarianism: Food, Gender and Neo-Liberal Regimes in Bengali Middle-Class Families." In Osella and Osella 2008b, 143–69.

Douglas, Mary. (1970) 1996. *Natural Symbols: Explorations in Cosmology*. London: Routledge.

———. 1972. "Deciphering a Meal." *Daedalus* 101, no. 1 (Winter; Myth, Symbol, and Culture): 61–81.

Dube, S. C. 1955. *Hindu Village*. London: Routledge and Kegan Paul.

Dubois, J. A. 1906. *Hindu Manners, Customs and Ceremonies*. Translated by Henry K. Beauchamp. 3rd ed. Oxford: Clarendon Press.

Dumont, Louis. 1980. *Homo Hierarchicus: The Caste System and Its Implications*. Chicago: University of Chicago Press.

Dwivedi, O. P. 1990. "Satyagraha for Conservation: Awakening the Spirit of Hinduism." In *Ethics of Environment and Development: Global Challenge, International Response*, edited by J. Ronald Engel and Joan Gibb Engel, 201–12. Tucson: University of Arizona Press.

———. 1997. "Vedic Heritage for Environmental Stewardship." *Worldviews* 1, no. 1: 25–36.

Favero, Paolo. 2005. *India Dreams: Cultural Identity Among Young Middle-Class Men in New Delhi*. Stockholm Studies in Social Anthropology 56. Stockholm: Almquist and Wiksell International.

Fernandes, Leela. 2009. "The Political Economy of Lifestyle: Consumption, Indian New Middle Class and State-Led Development." In *The New Middle Classes: Globalizing Lifestyles, Consumerism and Environmental Concern*, edited by Hellmuth Lange and Lars Meier, 219–36. Heidelberg: Springer.

Fischer, Johan. 2017. "Veg or Non-veg? On Fieldwork and Food in India." FocaalBlog, October 24, 2017. www.focaalblog.com/2017/10/24/johan-fischer-veg-or-non-veg.

Frankel, Francine R. 1971. *India's Green Revolution: Economic Gains and Political Costs*. Princeton, NJ: Princeton University Press.

Freed, Stanley A., and R. S. Freed. 1972. "Cattle in a North Indian Village." *Ethnology* 11, no. 4 (October): 399–408.

Froerer, Peggy. 2007. *Religious Division and Social Conflict: The Emergence of Hindu Nationalism in Rural India*. New Delhi: Social Science Press.

Fuller, C. J., and Haripriya Narasimhan. 2007. "Information Technology Professionals and the New-Rich Middle Class in Chennai (Madras)." *Modern Asian Studies* 41, no. 1 (January): 121–50.

Gandhi, Mohandas. 1954. *How to Serve the Cow*. Ahmadabad: Navajivan Publishing House.

———. 1999. *The Collected Works of Mahatma Gandhi* (New Delhi: Publications Division Government of India), www.gandhiashramsevagram.org/gandhi-literature/collected-works-of-mahatma-gandhi-volume-to-98.php.

Geertz, Clifford. 1973. *The Interpretation of Cultures: Selected Essays*. New York: Basic Books.

———. 1975. "Deep Play: Notes on the Balinese Cockfight." In *The Interpretation of Cultures: Selected Essays*, by Clifford Geertz, 412–53. London: Hutchinson.

———. 1978. "The Bazaar Economy: Information and Search in Peasant Marketing." *American Economic Review* 68, no. 2 (May): 28–32.

———. 1998. "Deep Hanging Out." *New York Review of Books* 45, no. 16 (October 22): 69–72.

Gewertz, Deborah, and Frederick Errington. 2010. *Cheap Meat: Flap Food Nations in the Pacific Islands*. Berkeley: University of California Press.

Ghassem-Fachandi, Parvis. 2010. "On the Political Use of Disgust in Gujarat." *South Asian History and Culture* 1, no. 4 (October): 557–76.

———. 2012. *Pogrom in Gujarat: Hindu Nationalism and Anti-Muslim Violence in India*. Princeton, NJ: Princeton University Press.

Ghose, Dipankar. 2018. "Chhattisgarh Horror: In Two More Gaushalas Dozens of Carcasses, Starving Cows." *Indian Express*, August 20, 2017. https://indianexpress.com/article/india/chhattisgarh-durg-district-horror-in-2-more-gaushalas-dozens-of-carcasses-starving-cows-bjp-harish-verma-4804717/.

Ghosh, Palash. 2013. "Where's the Beef? In India, Believe It or Not." *International Business Times*, May 14, 2013. www.ibtimes.com/wheres-beef-india-believe-it-or-not-1258469.

Gold, Ann. 2015. "Food Values Beyond Nutrition." In *The Oxford Handbook of Food, Politics, and Society*, edited by Ronald J. Herring, 545–67. Oxford: Oxford University Press.

Goody, Jack, 1982. *Cooking, Cuisine and Class: A Study in Comparative Sociology*. Cambridge: Cambridge University Press.

Gopal, Lallanji. 1980. *Aspects of the History of Agriculture in Ancient India*. Varanasi: Bharati Prakashan.

Gopal, Sarvepalli, ed. 1997. *Selected Works of Jawaharlal Nehru*. Vol. 20. New Delhi: Oxford University Press.

Gorringe, Hugo, and D. Karthikeyan. 2014. "The Hidden Politics of Vegetarianism: Caste and the Hindu Canteen." *Economic and Political Weekly* 49, no. 20 (May 17): 20–22.

Gould, William. 2004. *Hindu Nationalism and the Language of Politics in Late Colonial India*. Cambridge: Cambridge University Press.

Govindrajan, Radhika. 2018. *Animal Intimacies: Interspecies Relatedness in India's Central Himalayas*. Chicago: University of Chicago Press.

Graf, Katharina. 2016. "Beldi Matters: Negotiating Proper Food in Urban Moroccan Food Consumption and Preparation." In *Halal Matters: Islam, Politics, and Markets in Global Perspective*, edited by Florence Bergeaud-Blacker, Johan Fischer, and John Lever, 72–90. London: Routledge.

Griffith, R. T. H. 1896. *The Hymns of the Rigveda*. Translation, 2nd ed. www.sanskritweb.net/rigveda/griffith-p.pdf, accessed February 4, 2018.

Grove, Richard, Vinita Damodaran, and Satpal Sangwan, eds. 1998. *Nature and the Orient: The Environmental History of South and Southeast Asia*. New Delhi: Oxford University Press.

Guha, Ramachandra. 2006. *How Much Should a Person Consume? Environmentalism in India and the United States*. Berkeley: University of California Press.

Gundimeda, Sambaiah. 2009. "Democratization of the Public Sphere: The Beef Stall Case in Hyderabad's Sukoon Festival." *South Asia Research* 29, no. 2 (July): 127–49.

Gundimeda, Sambaiah, and V. S. Ashwin, 2018. "Cow Protection in India: From Secularizing to Legitimating Debates." *South Asia Research* 38, no. 2 (July): 156–76.

Gundimeda, Sambaiah, V. B. Tharakeshwar, and Uma Bhrugubanda. 2012. "Editorial: What's the Menu? Food Politics and Hegemony." *Anveshi* 1, no. 4 (September): 2–3.

Gupta, Dipankar. 2000. *Mistaken Modernity: India Between Worlds*. New Delhi: Harper Collins Publishers.

Gupta, Smita. 2016. "Comment: The Dalit-Hindutva Paradox." *The Hindu*, February 9, 2016. www.thehindu.com/opinion/op-ed/The-Dalit-Hindutva-paradox/article14068231.ece.

Hacking, Ian. 1998. *Mad Travelers: Reflections on the Reality of Transient Mental Illnesses*. Cambridge, MA: Harvard University Press.

Hansen, Thomas Blom. 1999. *The Saffron Wave: Democracy and Hindu Nationalism in Modern India*. Princeton, NJ: Princeton University Press.

Haraway, Donna J. 1991. *Simians, Cyborgs, and Women: The Reinvention of Nature*. New York: Routledge.

———. 2008. *When Species Meet*. Minneapolis: University of Minnesota Press.

Hardtmann, Eva-Maria. 2008. *The Dalit Movement in India: Local Practices, Global Connections*. Oxford: Oxford University Press.

Harper, S. B. 2000. *In the Shadow of the Mahatma: Bishop V. S. Azariah and the Travails of Christianity in British India*. Richmond, UK: Curzon Press.

Harris, Marvin. 1966. "The Cultural Ecology of India's Sacred Cattle." *Current Anthropology* 7, no. 1 (February): 51–66.

———. 1985. *Good to Eat: Riddles of Food and Culture*. Long Grove, IL: Waveland Press, Inc.

———. 1989. *Cows, Pigs, Wars, and Witches: The Riddles of Culture*. New York: Vintage Books.

Hasan, Mushirul. 2002. "The BJP's Intellectual Agenda: Textbooks and Imagined History." *South Asia* 25, no. 3: 187–209.

Henare, A., M. Holbraad, and S. Wastell, eds. 2007. *Thinking Through Things: Theorising Artefacts in Ethnographic Perspective*. Abingdon, UK: Routledge.

Hobart, Mark. 2000. *After Culture: Anthropology as Radical Metaphysical Critique*. Yogyakarta: Duta Wacana Press.

Holwitt, Pablo. 2017. "Strange Food, Strange Smells: Vegetarianism and Sensorial Citizenship in Mumbai's Redeveloped Enclaves." *Contemporary South Asia* 25, no. 4: 333–46.

Horden, Peregrine, and Elisabeth Hsu, eds. 2013. *The Body in Balance: Humoral Medicines in Practice*. New York: Berghahn Books.

Howes, David. 2006. "Charting the Sensorial Revolution." *Senses and Society* 1, no. 1: 113–28.

Hurn, Samantha. 2013. "Confessions of a Vegan Anthropologist: Exploring the Trans-Biopolitics of Eating in the Field." In *Why We Eat, How We Eat: Contemporary Encounters Between Foods and Bodies*, edited by Anna Lavis and Emma-Jane Abbots, 219–36. London: Ashgate Publishing.

Inden, Ron. 1990. *Imagining India*. Oxford: Basil Blackwell.

Jaffrelot, Christophe. 1996. *The Hindu Nationalist Movement and Indian Politics: 1925 to the 1990s*. London: Hurst & Company.

———. 1998. "The Politics of Processions and Hindu-Muslim Riots." In *Community Conflicts and the State in India*, edited by Amrita Basu and Atul Kohli, 58–92. New Delhi: Oxford University Press.

———. 2018. "Hindu Rashtra, De Facto: It Is at Once a Society, Civilisation, Nation—and State." *Indian Express*, August 12, 2018. https://indianexpress.com/article/opinion/columns/hindu-rashtra-de-facto-bjp-rss-gau-rakshak-mob-lynching-5301083/.

Jalais, Annu. 2010. *Forest of Tigers: People, Politics and Environment in the Sundarbans*. London: Routledge.

Jamwal, Nidhi, and Neha Dua. 2015. "The Meat You Eat." *Down to Earth*, June 7, 2015. www.downtoearth.org.in/indepth/the-meat-you-eat-13283.

Janeja, Manpreet K. 2010. *Transactions in Taste: The Collaborative Lives of Everyday Bengali Food*. New Delhi: Routledge.

Jeffrey, Craig. 2010. "Timepass: Youth, Class, and Time among Unemployed Young Men in India." *American Ethnologist* 7 no. 3 (August): 465–81.

Jha, D. N. 2002. *The Myth of the Holy Cow*. London: Verso.

Jung, Y. 2014. "Ambivalent Consumers and the Limits of Certification: Organic Foods in Post-Socialist Bulgaria." In *Ethical Eating in the Post-Socialist and Socialist World*, edited by Y. Jung, J. A. Klein, and M. Caldwell, 93–115. Berkeley: University of California Press.

Kantor, Hayden. 2019. "A Body Set Between Hot and Cold: Everyday Sensory Labor and Attunement in an Indian Village." *Food, Culture and Society* 22, no. 2: 237–52.

Kapur, Akash. 2011. "The Shandy: The Cost of Being a Cow Broker in Rural India." *New Yorker*, October 10, 2011.

Kelkar, Govind, and Dev Nathan. 1991. *Gender and Tribe: Women, Land and Forests in Jharkhand*. London: Sage Publications.

Khare, R. S. 1976a. *Culture and Reality: Essays on the Hindu System of Managing Foods*. Simla, India: Indian Institute of Advanced Study.

———. 1976b. *The Hindu Hearth and Home*. New Delhi: Vikas.

———. 1992. *The Eternal Food: Gastronomic Ideas and Experiences of Hindus and Buddhists*. Albany: State University of New York Press.

———. 1994. *On and About Postmodernism: Writing/Rewriting*. Baltimore: University of America Press.

———. 2006. *Caste, Hierarchy, and Individualism: Indian Critiques of Louis Dumont's Contributions*. Oxford: Oxford University Press.

———. 2012. "Globalizing South Asian Food Cultures: Earlier Stops to New Horizons." In Ray and Srinivas 2012a, 237–54.

Kjaernes, Unni, Mark Harvey, and Alan Warde. 2007. *Trust in Food: A Comparative and Institutional Analysis*. Basingstoke, UK: Palgrave Macmillan.

Klein, Jakob A. 2017. "Buddhist Vegetarian Restaurants and the Changing Meanings of Meat in Urban China." In Staples and Klein 2017a, 252–76.

Klein, Jakob A., and James L. Watson, eds. 2016. *The Handbook of Food and Anthropology*. London: Bloomsbury Academic.

Korom, Frank J. 2000. "Holy Cow! The Apotheosis of Zebu, or Why the Cow is Sacred in Hinduism." *Asian Folklore Studies* 59, no. 2: 181–203.

Kosambi, D. D. 1975. *An Introduction to the Study of Indian History*. Bombay: Popular Prakashan.

Koster, Martjin, and Yves van Leynseele. 2018. "Brokers as Assemblers: Studying Development Through the Lens of Brokerage." *Ethnos* 83, no. 5: 803–13, https://doi.org/10.1080/00141844.2017.1362451.

Kuper Adam. 1999. *Culture: The Anthropologist's Account*. Cambridge, MA: Harvard University Press.

Lahariya, Chandrakant, and S. K. Pradhan. 2006. "Emergence of Chikungunya Virus in Indian Subcontinent After 32 Years: A Review." *Journal of Vector Borne Diseases* 43, no. 4 (December): 151–60.

Lamb, Sarah. 2000. *White Saris and Sweet Mangoes: Aging, Gender, and Body in North India*. Berkeley: University of California Press.

Langford, Jean M. 2002. *Fluent Bodies: Ayurvedic Remedies for Postcolonial Imbalance*. Durham, NC: Duke University Press.

Latour, Bruno. 2005. *Reassembling the Social: An Introduction to Actor-Network-Theory*. Oxford: Oxford University Press.

———. 2010. "An Attempt at a 'Compositionist Manifesto'." *New Literary History* 41, no. 1: 465–72.

Leder, Drew. 1990. *The Absent Body*. Chicago: University of Chicago Press.

Legge, J. 1972. *The Travels of Fa-Hsien*. New Delhi: Oriental Publishers.

Lévi-Strauss, Claude. 1963. *Structural Anthropology*. New York: Basic Books.

———. 1966. "The Culinary Triangle." *Partisan Review* 33, no. 4 (Fall): 586–95.

Liechty, Mark. 2005. "Carnal Economies: The Commodification of Food and Sex in Kathmandu." *Cultural Anthropology* 20, no. 1 (February): 1–38.

Lodrick, Deryck. 2005. "Symbol and Sustenance: Cattle in South Asian Culture." *Dialectical Anthropology*, 29, no. 1 (March): 61–84.

Lutgendorf, Philip. 2000. "City, Forest, and Cosmos: Ecological Perspectives from the Sanskrit Epics." In *Hinduism and Ecology: The Intersection of Earth, Sky, and Water*, edited by Christopher K. Chapple and Mary Tucker, 245–68. New Delhi: Oxford University Press.

Mair, Jonathan, Ann H. Kelly, and Casey High. 2012. "Introduction: Making Ignorance an Ethnographic Object." In *The Anthropology of Ignorance: An Ethnographic Approach*, edited by Casey High, Ann H. Kelly, and Jonathan Mair, 1–32. New York: Palgrave Macmillan.

Malinowski, Bronisław. 1935. *Coral Gardens and Their Magic*. 2 vols. London: George Allen and Unwin Ltd.

Mankekar, Purnima. 1999. *Screening Culture, Viewing Politics: An Ethnography of Television, Womanhood, and Nation in Postcolonial India*. Durham, NC: Duke University Press.

Marriott, McKim. 1968. "Caste Ranking and Food Transactions: A Matrix Analysis." In *Structure and Change in Indian Society*, edited by Milton Singer and Bernard S. Cohen, 133–71. Chicago: Aldine.

——. 1976. "Hindu Transactions: Diversity without Dualism." In *Transactions and Meaning: Directions in the Anthropology of Exchange and Symbolic Behavior*, edited by Bruce Kapferer, 109–42. Philadelphia: Institute for the Study of Human Issues.

——. 1990. "Introduction." In *India through Hindu Categories*, edited by McKim Marriott, xi–xvi. New Delhi: Sage.

Mathews, Andrew S. 2005. "Power/Knowledge, Power/Ignorance: Forest Fires and the State in Mexico." *Human Ecology* 33, no. 6 (December): 795–820.

Mauss, Marcel. (1925) 1990. *The Gift*. London: Routledge.

Mawdsley, Emma. 2006. "Hindu Nationalism, Neo-traditionalism and Environmental Discourses in India." *Geoform* 37, no. 3 (May): 380–90.

Mayer, Adrian C. 1960. *Caste and Kinship in Central India*. London: Routledge and Kegan Paul.

Mazzarella, William. 2003. *Shoveling Smoke: Advertising and Globalization in Contemporary India*. Durham, NC: Duke University Press.

McGuire, M. L. 2011. "'How to Sit, How to Stand': Bodily Praxis and the New Urban Middle Class." In *A Companion to the Anthropology of India*, edited by I. Clark-Decès, 117–36. Oxford: Wiley-Blackwell.

Mehta, R., R. G. Nambiar, S. K. Singh, S. Subrahmanyam, and C. Ravi. 2002. *Livestock Industrialization, Trade and Social-Health-Environmental Issues for the Indian Poultry Sector*. Rome: Food and Agriculture Organization.

Mencher, Joan. 1974. "The Caste System Upside Down, or the Not-So-Mysterious East." *Current Anthropology* 15, no. 4 (December): 469–93.

Menon, Rashmi. 2014. "Real Good Vegetable." *Afaqs!*, January 23, 2014. www.afaqs.com/news/story/39762_Real-Good-Vegetable.

Merleau-Ponty, Maurice. 1962. *Phenomenology of Perception*. Translated by C. Smith. London: Routledge and Kegan Paul.

Merry, Sally Engle. 2003. "Human Rights Law and the Demonization of Culture (And Anthropology Along the Way)." *Political and Legal Anthropology Review* 26, no. 1 (May): 55–76.

Michelutti, Lucia. 2004. "'We (Yadavs) Are a Caste of Politicians': Caste and Modern Politics in a North Indian Town." *Contributions to Indian Sociology*, n.s., 38, no. 1–2 (February): 43–71.

———. 2008. "'We Are Kshatriyas but We Behave like Vaishyas': Diet and Muscular Politics Among a Community of Yadavs in North India." In Osella and Osella 2008b, 76–95.

Mines, Diane P., and Nicolas Yargi, eds. 2010. *Do Villages Matter? Relocating Villages in the Contemporary Anthropology of India*. Delhi: Oxford University Press.

Mines, Mattison. 1994. *Public Faces, Private Voices: Community and Individuality in South India*. Berkeley: University of California Press.

Mintz, Sidney. 1979. "Time, Sugar and Sweetness." *Marxist Perspectives* 2, no. 4 (Winter 1979–80): 56–73.

———. 1985. *Sweetness and Power*. New York: Viking.

———. 1996. *Tasting Food, Tasting Freedom: Excursions into Eating, Culture, and the Past*. Boston: Beacon Press.

Mintz, Sidney, and Daniela Schlettwein-Gsell. 2001. "Food Patterns in Agrarian Societies: The 'Core-Fringe-Legume Hypothesis.' A Dialogue." *Gastronomica: The Journal of Food and Culture* 1, no. 3 (Summer): 40–52.

Mishra, Pankaj. 1995. *Butter Chicken in Ludhiana: Travels in Small Town India*. New Delhi: Penguin India.

Mishra, Premanand. 2015. "Colonialism and Its Gastro-Politics: Re-visiting Gandhi's Vegetarianism." *Gandhi Marg Quarterly* 37, no. 1: 79–102.

Mol, Annemarie. 2002. *The Body Multiple: Ontology in Medical Practice*. Durham, NC: Duke University Press.

Mosse, David. 1999. "Responding to Subordination: The Politics of Identity Change Among South Indian Untouchable Castes." In *Identity and Affect: Experiences of Identity in a Globalising World*, edited by John R. Campbell and Alan Rew, 64–104. London: Pluto Press.

———. 2010. "The Catholic Church and Dalit Christian Activism in Contemporary Tamil Nadu." In *Margins of Faith: Dalit and Tribal Christianity in India*, edited by Rowena Robinson and Joseph Marianus Kujur, 235–62. New Delhi: Sage.

Murcott, Anne. 1988. "Sociological and Social Anthropological Approaches to Food and Eating." In *Sociological and Medical Aspects of Nutrition*, edited by G. H. Bourne, 1–40. Basel: Karger.

Nanda, Meera. 2002. *Breaking the Spell of Dharma and Other Essays*. Delhi: Three Essays Collective.

Nandy, Ashis. 2004. "The Changing Popular Culture of Indian Food: Preliminary Notes." *South Asia Research* 24, no. 1 (May): 9–19.

Narayanan, Yamini. 2018. "Cow Protection as 'Casteised Speciesism': Sacralisation, Commercialisation and Politicisation." *South Asia: Journal of South Asian Studies* 41, no. 2: 331–51, https://doi.org/10.1080/00856401.2018.1419794.

Natrajan, Balmurli, and Suraj Jacob. 2018. "'Provincialising' Vegetarianism: Putting Indian Food Habits in Their Place." *Economic and Political Weekly* 53, no. 9 (March 3): 54–64.

Nichter, Mark. 2008. "Coming to Our Senses: Appreciating the Sensorial in Medical Anthropology." *Transcultural Psychiatry* 45, no. 2 (June): 163–97.

Novetzke, Christian Lee. 2017. "Non-Veg." *South Asia: Journal of South Asian Studies* 40, no. 2 (June): 366–69.

O'Malley, L. S. S. 1932. *Indian Caste Customs*. Cambridge: Cambridge University Press.

Ortner, Sherry. 2003. *New Jersey Dreaming*. Durham, NC: Duke University Press.

Osella, Caroline. 2008. "Introduction." In Osella and Osella 2008b, 1–9.

Osella, Caroline, and Filippo Osella. 2008a. "Food, Memory, Community: Kerala as Both 'Indian Ocean' Zone and as Agricultural Homeland." In Osella and Osella 2008b, 170–98.

———, eds. 2008b. *Food: Memory, Pleasure and Politics*. Special issue, *South Asia: Journal of South Asian Studies* 31, no. 1 (April).

Palshikar, Suhas, Sanjay Kumar, and Sanjay Lodha. 2017. *Electoral Politics in India: The Resurgence of the Bharatiya Janata Party*. New Delhi: Routledge India.

Pandey, Gyanendra, 1983. "Rallying Round the Cow: Sectarian Strife in the Bhojpuri Region, 1888–1917." In *Subaltern Studies*, vol. 2, edited by Ranajit Guha, 60–129. Delhi: Oxford University Press.

Parry, Jonathan P. 1999. "Two Cheers for Reservation: The Satnamis and the Steel Plant." In *Institutions and Inequalities: Essays in Honour of André Béteille*, edited by Ramachandra Guha and Jonathan P. Parry, 128–69. New Delhi: Oxford University Press.

Patton, Laurie L. 2005. "Introduction." In *The Indo-Aryan Controversy: Evidence and Inference in Indian History*, edited by Edwin F. Bryant and Laurie L. Patton, 1–18. Abingdon, UK: Routledge.

Petryna, Adriana, Andrew Lakoff, and Arthur Kleinman. 2006. *Global Pharmaceuticals: Ethics, Markets, Practices*. Cambridge: Cambridge University Press.

Pink, Sarah. 2009. *Doing Sensory Ethnography*. London: Sage Publications.

Pinney, Christopher. 1995. "Moral Topophilia: The Significations of Landscape in Indian Oleographs." In *The Anthropology of Landscape: Perspectives on Place and Space*, edited by Eric Hirsch and Michael O'Hanlon, 78–113. Oxford: Oxford University Press.

———. 2004. *Photos of the Gods: The Printed Image and Political Struggle in India*. London: Reaktion.

Prahalad, C. K. 2009. *The Fortune at the Bottom of the Pyramid: Eradicating Poverty through Profits*. Upper Saddle River, NJ: Pearson Education, Inc.

Prakash, Om. 1961. *Foods and Drinks in Ancient India*. Delhi: Munshi Ram Manohar Lal.

Quigley, Declan. 1994. "Is a Theory of Caste Still Possible?" In *Contextualising Caste*, edited by Mary Searle-Chatterjee and Ursula Sharma, 25–48. Oxford: Blackwell.

———. 1999. *The Interpretation of Caste*. New Delhi: Oxford University Press.

Rabobank International. 1993. *The World Poultry Market*. Utrecht: Rabobank.

Ramakrishnan, Sriram. 2018. "Dalit vs Brahmin, Hindu vs Muslim: The Failed Anti-Modi Narrative." *Economic Times*, March 6, 2018. https://economictimes.indiatimes.com/news/politics-and-nation/dalit-vs-brahmin-hindu-vs-muslim-the-failed-anti-modi-narrative/articleshow/63180476.cms.

Ranal, Uday. 2015. "Fast Moving Cattle-Goats Is New FMCG on Online Sites." *Times of India*, September 14, 2015.

Ray, Krishnendu. 2004. *The Migrant's Table: Meals and Memories in Bengali-American Households*. Philadelphia: Temple University Press.

Ray, Krishnendu, and Tulasi Srinivas, eds., 2012a. *Curried Cultures: Globalization, Food, and South Asia*. Berkeley: University of California Press.

———. 2012b. "Introduction." In Ray and Srinivas 2012a, 3–28.

Reddy, Gayatri. 2005. *With Respect to Sex: Negotiating Hijra Identity in South India*. Chicago: University of Chicago Press.

Richards, Audrey. 1932. *Hunger and Work in a Savage Tribe: A Functional Study of Nutrition Among the Southern Bantu*. London: Routledge.

———. 1939. *Land, Labour and Diet in Northern Rhodesia*. Oxford: Oxford University Press.

Robb, Peter. 1986. "The Challenge of Gau Mata: British Policy and Religious Change in India, 1880–1916." *Modern Asian Studies* 20, no. 2: 285–319.

Robbins, Paul. 1999. "Meat Matters: Cultural Politics along the Commodity Chain in India." *Cultural Geographies* 6, no. 4 (October): 399–423.

Roncaglia, Sara. 2013. *Feeding the City: Work and Food Culture of the Mumbai Dabbawalas*. Cambridge: Open Book Publishers.

Roy, Parama. 2002. "Meat-Eating, Masculinity, and Renunciation in India: A Gandhian Grammar of Diet." *Gender and History* 14, no. 1 (April): 62–91.

Säävälä, Minna. 2003. "Auspicious Hindu Houses: The New Middle Classes in Hyderabad, India." *Social Anthropology* 11 no. 2 (June): 231–247.

Sachua, E. C. 2005. *Alberuni's India*. Vol. 2. Marston Gate, UK: Elibron Classics.

Sajjad, Mohammad. 2014. *Muslim Politics in Bihar: Changing Contours*. Delhi: Routledge.

Scheper-Hughes, Nancy, and Margaret Lock. 1987. "The Mindful Body: A Prolegomenon to Future Work in Medical Anthropology." *Medical Anthropology Quarterly* 1, no. 1 (March): 6–41.

Schwartz, Marvin. 1991. *Tyson: From Farm to Market*. Fayetteville: University of Arkansas Press.

Sébastia, Brigitte. 2017. "'Beef is Our Secret of Life': Controversial Consumption of Beef in Andhra Pradesh, India." In *Eating Traditional Food: Politics, Identity and Practices*, edited by Brigitte Sébastia, 104–28. Abingdon, UK: Routledge.

Sen, Atreyee. 2007. *Shiv Sena Women: Violence and Communalism in a Bombay Slum*. London: C. Hurst and Co. and Indianapolis: Indiana University Press.

——. 2012. "'Exist, Endure, Erase the City' (Sheher mein jiye, is ko sahe, ya ise mitaye?): Child Vigilantes and Micro-cultures of Urban Violence in a Riot-Affected Hyderabad Slum." *Ethnography* 13, no. 1 (March): 71–86.

Senart, É. 1930. *Caste in India: The Facts and the System*. Translated by Sir Denison Ross. London: Methuen.

Sengupta, Jayanta. 2010. "Nation on a Platter: The Culture and Politics of Food and Cuisine in Colonial Bengal." *Modern Asian Studies* 44, no. 1 (January): 81–98.

Shapiro, Ian. 2005. *The Flight from Reality in the Human Sciences*. Princeton, NJ: Princeton University Press.

Shiva, Vandana. 1999. "Ecological Balance in an Era of Globalization." In *Global Ethics and Environment*, edited by Nicholas Low, 47–69. London: Routledge.

Shrivastava, Kumar Sambhav. 2018. "The Goat Gamble." *Down to Earth*, August 16, 2018. www.downtoearth.org.in/coverage/the-goat-gamble-2329.

Siegel, B. 2010. "Learning to Eat in a Capital City: Constructing Public Eating Culture in Delhi." *Food, Culture and Society: An International Journal of Multidisciplinary Research* 13, no. 1(March): 71–90.

Simoons, Frederick J. 1979. "Questions in the Sacred Cow Controversy." *Current Anthropology* 20, no. 3 (September): 467–93.

Sinha, Subir, Shubhra Gururani, and Brian Greenberg. 1997. "The 'New Traditionalist' Discourse of Indian Environmentalism." *Journal of Peasant Studies* 24, no. 3 (April): 65–99.

Smith, Brian. K. 1990. "Eaters, Food, and Social Hierarchy in Ancient India: A Dietary Guide to a Revolution of Values." *Journal of the American Academy of Religion* 58, no. 2 (Summer): 177–205.

Smith, Monica. 2006. "The Archaeology of Food Preference." *American Anthropologist* 108, no. 3 (September): 480–93.

Solomon, Harris. 2016. *Metabolic Living: Food, Fat, and the Absorption of Illness in India*. Durham, NC: Duke University Press.

Srinivas, M. N. 1952. *Religion and Society among the Coorgs of South India*. Oxford: Oxford University Press.

———, ed. 1955. *India's Villages*. Bombay: Asia Publishing House.

———. 1966. *Social Change in Modern India*. Berkeley: University of California Press.

Srinivasan, Doris. 1979. *Concept of Cow in the Rigveda*. Delhi: Motilal Banarsidass.

Staples, James. 2003. "Disguise, Revelation and Copyright: Disassembling the South Indian Leper." *Journal of the Royal Anthropological Institute*, n.s., 9, no. 2 (May): 295–315.

———. 2007. *Peculiar People, Amazing Lives: Leprosy, Social Exclusion and Community-Making in South India*. Delhi: Orient Longman.

———. 2008. "'Go On, Just Try Some!': Meat and Meaning-Making among South Indian Christians." In Osella and Osella 2008b, 36–55.

———. 2012a. "Suicide in South Asia: Ethnographic Perspectives." *Contributions to Indian Sociology* 46, no. 1–2 (February and June): 1–28.

———. 2012b. "The Suicide Niche: Accounting for Self-Harm in a South Indian Leprosy Colony." *Contributions to Indian Sociology* 46, no. 1–2 (February and June): 117–44.

———. 2014. "Civilizing Tastes: From Caste to Class in South Indian Foodways." In *Food Consumption in Global Perspective: Essays in the Anthropology of Food in Honour of Jack Goody*, edited by Jakob A. Klein and Anne Murcott, 65–86. New York: Palgrave Macmillan.

———. 2015. "Personhood, Agency and Suicide in a Neo-liberalising South India." In *Suicide and Agency: Anthropological Perspectives on Self-Destruction, Personhood, and Power*, edited by Ludek Broz and Daniel Muenster, 27–46. Farnham, UK: Ashgate.

———. 2016. "Food, Commensality and Caste in South Asia." In *The Handbook of Food and Anthropology*, edited by Jakob A. Klein and James L. Watson, 74–93. London: Bloomsbury Academic.

———. 2017. "Beef and Beyond: Exploring the Meat Consumption Practices of Christians in India." In Staples and Klein 2017a, 232–51.

———. 2018. "Appropriating the Cow: Beef and Identity Politics in Contemporary India." In *Farm to Fingers: The Culture and Politics of Food in Contemporary India*, edited by Kiranmayi Bhushi, 58–79. Cambridge: Cambridge University Press.

Staples, James, and Jakob Klein, eds. 2017a. *Consumer and Consumed*. Special issue, *Ethnos* 82, no. 2.

———. 2017b. "Introduction: Consumer and Consumed." In Staples and Klein 2017a, 193–212.

Stewart, Kathleen. 2007. *Ordinary Affects*. Durham, NC: Duke University Press.

Stoller, Paul. 1989. *The Taste of Ethnographic Things: The Senses in Anthropology*. Philadelphia: University of Pennsylvania Press.

Striffler, Steve. 2005. *Chicken: The Dangerous Transformation of America's Favorite Food*. New Haven, CT: Yale University Press.

Sundar, Nandini. 2010. "Vigilantism, Culpability and Moral Dilemmas." *Critique of Anthropology* 30, no. 1 (March): 113–21.

Sutton, David. 1997. "The Vegetarian Anthropologist." *Anthropology Today* 13, no. 1 (February): 5–8.

———. 2001. *Remembrance of Repasts: An Anthropology of Food and Memory*. Oxford: Berg.

Tayob, Shaheed. 2019. "Disgust as an Embodied Critique: Being Middle Class and Muslim in Mumbai." *South Asia: Journal of South Asian Studies* 42, no. 6 (December): 1192–1209, https://doi.org/10.1080/00856401.2019.1663654.

Tilche, Alice, and Edward Simpson. 2016. "Village Restudies: Trials and Tribulations." *Economic and Political Weekly* 51, no. 26–27 (June 25): 32–42.

Vailles, Noëlie. 1994. *Animal to Edible*. Cambridge: Cambridge University Press.

Van der Geest, Sjaak. 2006. "Anthropology and the Pharmaceutical Nexus." *Anthropological Quarterly* 79, no. 2 (Spring): 303–14.

Van der Geest, Sjaak, Susan Reynolds Whyte, and Anita Hardon. 1996. "The Anthropology of Pharmaceuticals: A Biographical Approach." *Annual Review of Anthropology* 25 (October): 153–78.

Van der Veer, Peter. 1994. *Religious Nationalism: Hindus and Muslims in India*. Berkeley: University of California Press.

Wallace, Paul. 2015. *India's 2014 Elections: A Modi-Led BJP Sweep*. New Delhi: Sage.

Watson, James L., and Jakob A. Klein. 2016. "Introduction: Anthropology, Food and Modern Life." In *The Handbook of Food and Anthropology*, edited by Jakob A. Klein and James L. Watson, 1–27. London: Bloomsbury Academic.

Whyte, Susan, Sjaak van der Geest, and Anita Hardon. 2002. *Social Lives of Medicines*. Cambridge: Cambridge University Press.

Wiley, Andrea S. 2011. "Milk for 'Growth': Global and Local Meanings of Milk Consumption in China, India, and the United States." *Food and Foodways* 19, no. 1–2: 11–33.

Wilk, Richard. 2017. "The Ambiguous (but Important) Materiality of Food." In *Exploring the Materiality of Food "Stuffs": Transformation, Symbolic Consumption and Embodiment*, edited by Louise Steel and Katharina Zinn, 271–82. Abingdon, UK: Routledge.

Wood-Gush, D. G. M. 1959. "A History of the Domestic Chicken from Antiquity to the 19th Century." *Poultry Science* 38, no. 2 (March): 321–26.

Xu, Chenjia. 2019. "Eating Things: Foodies, Bodies and Lives in Contemporary Urban Beijing." PhD thesis, SOAS, University of London.

Yang, Anand A. 1980. "Sacred Symbol and Sacred Space in Rural India: Community Mobilization in the 'Anti-Cow Killing' Riot of 1893." *Society for Comparative Studies in Society and History*, 22, no. 4 (October): 576–96.

Zimmermann, Francis. 1999. *The Jungle and the Aroma of Meats: An Ecological Theme in Hindu Medicine*. Delhi: Motilal Banarsidass.

———. 2013. "Aiming for Congruence: The Golden Rule of Ayurveda." In *The Body in Balance: Humoral Medicines in Practice*, edited by Peregrine Horden and Elisabeth Hsu, 218–34. New York: Berghahn Books.

INDEX

Page numbers in *italic* refer to illustrations.

A

Adivasis, 82, 107, 108. *See also* Saoras
Advani, L. K., 44
agriculture, 14, 72, 122, 137–38, 146, 169
ahimsa, 24, 40, 163, 164, 178
Akhlaq, Mohammad, 12, 46, 98
Al-Biruni, 40
alcohol, 39, 67–68, 103, 110, 143, 156, 178; fried foods and, 109–10, 139; as "heating," 131
Al-Kabeer, 82
Ambedkar, Bhimrao, 40, 159
animal rights organizations, 136
animal sacrifice. *See* sacrifice of animals
antibiotics and hormones ("medicines"), meat industry use of, 72, 133, 137
anti-Muslim violence. *See* Muslims: vigilantism against
Appadurai, Arjun, 16–17, 25, 93, 100, 120
Arya Samaj, 41, 42, 164
Atla Taddi, 57

attacks, vigilante. *See* vigilantism
Australia, 129
avoidance of knowledge. *See* compartmentalization of knowledge
āvu mānsam. *See* cow meat (*āvu mānsam*)
Ayurvedic diet, 106, 130, 131, 133, 171–72

B

babies: buffalo milk for, 55; first feeding of rice, 36, 38
Baehr, Peter, 49
Bajrang Dal, 90
Bargi, Drishadwati, 159
barley, 38
Basantpur riot, 1893, 42
beef (buffalo meat). *See* buffalo meat (*eddu mānsam*)
beef (cow meat). *See* cow meat (*āvu mānsam*)
"beef" (word), 33

219

beef exports, 32, 45, 48, 81, 88, 97, 112, 165
beef festivals, 45, 46, 51, 104, 111, 114, 157, 159
beef trade, 67, 77–101; customer travel, 62, 77; government regulation, 13, 47, 114; prices, 91, 92, 110, 111, 113, 138, 173, 177–78, 179; sellers, 17, 42, 47–48, 86–91, 87, 95–97
belam. *See* jaggery
Béteille, André, 145
beverages. *See* alcohol; coffee; milk; soft drinks; tea
bhadralok status group, 142, 146, 159–60
Bharatiya Jana Sangh, 44
Bharatiya Janata Party (BJP), 6, 10, 12, 44–46, 50, 114, 117, 140; Dalit vote, 167; Maneka Gandhi, 136
Bhave, Vinobha, 44
Bhushi, Kiranmayi, 22
Bijlani, Ramesh, 137
binary views, 82–83, 101, 139, 144, 177; pro-beef/anti-beef, 7–8, 105; vegetarian/nonvegetarian, 53, 105, 117–18, 171–72
biriyanis, 61, 62, 69, 123, 155, 157; food stands, 91, 98; meat, 63, 77, 98, 156
Biruni, Muhammad ibn Ahmad. *See* Al-Biruni
biscuits (cookies). *See* cookies
BJP. *See* Bharatiya Janata Party (BJP)
black gram (*urad dal*), 38, 56, 66, 75
blood pressure, high. *See* hypertension
Bourdieu, Pierre, 80, 148, 190n2
bowls, 60, 76, 152, 153, 154
Brahmins, 31, 41, 114, 142, 145, 146; *ahimsa*, 40; beef eating, 38, 39, 40, 50, 92, 164; as "cool caste," 131; cow

killing, 48, 49; Dharmaśāstras, 39; Rigveda, 37; Saora relations, 81; widows, 171–72
brains, consumption of, 66–67, 92
bread. *See* flatbreads
breakfast, 54–57
British in India, 41–43, 50–51, 71, 135–36, 145, 163–64
brokers. *See* cattle brokers
Broomfield, John, 146
Buddhism, 40, 50, 164
buffaloes. *See* water buffaloes
buffalo meat, 6, 31–32, 91, 98, 132, 170–71; exports, 97
buffalo milk, 55, 62, 72, 83
butchers, 32, 47, 79, 86–93, 96, 111–12, 120, 178–79, 189n38; on customers, 91, 110; distinguished from meat eaters, 94; suppliers, 84, 88, 95; uncertainty on what to feed vegetarians, 30; views of government, 111–12; violence against, 13
butter, 39. *See also* ghee
buttermilk, 6, 36, 63, 152, 156

C

calves, 43, 84, 87, 169
Campbell, Ben, 94
Caplan, Pat, 172
caste, 14, 27, 39–41, 105, 115, 141–61, 174; dietary proscription and, 51; in food studies, 23, 26; "high-caste complicity" in beef trade, 169–70; "hot" and "cool," 131; in Vedic texts, 37–38, 39. *See also* Brahmins; Dalits; Reddis; Yadavs
Catholics, 18, 32, 68–69, 81
cattle, stray. *See* stray cattle

cattle, unproductive and excess, 48, 84, 85, 95, 169, 170
cattle as kin, 93, 94–95, 170, 175
cattle brokers, 84, 85, 86, 88, 95–96, 169
cattle markets (shandies), 47, 84, 85, 87–88, 93–94, 96–99; online sales, 84; supplied by vigilantes, 110
cattle shelters, 48, 110, 169–70, 175
cattle slaughter, 77–80, 82, 86, 89; early history, 40; regulation and bans, 10, 13, 34, 44, 46, 47, 50, 112–14, 116–17, 163, 191n16; untouchability and, 38
chapatis, 57, 60, 63, 69
cheese, 21. *See also* paneer
chemical fertilizers, 72–73, 137
chicken eggs. *See* eggs
chickens and chicken meat, 66–67, 81, 92, 104, 122–29, 133–34, 139, 175–76; broilers, 13, 124, 125–26, 127, 134, 138, 175; chicken farms and industrialization of production, 13, 137, 138, 173; chicken raising, 124–25; chicken slaughter, 113, 125, 128; "country chickens," 36, 84, 124, 125, 134, 173, 175; health and, 133–34; McDonald's, 129, 139; price, 91, 126, 173; rationale for eating, 112; respectability, 106, 118. *See also* processed chicken
chicken shops, 112, 123
chicken soup, 21
children: chicken purchasing by, 128; diet, 36, 131, 132, 172; government-funded lunch program, 26, 63, 163. *See also* babies
chilies, 57, 58, 62, 65, 109; in raita, 61–62, 151
chili powder, 21, 56, 57, 73–74, 109, 154

Chinese food, 63, 123, 127, 142, 157, 173
Christianity, 9, 10, 35, 115
Christians, 8–11, 15, 79, 114, 115, 140–41; "bovine symbolism" and, 12; cattle slaughter and, 86, 113; environment and, 135; meat eating, 9, 18, 32, 68, 111, 158; meat purchases, 91; view of pork, 107. *See also* Catholics
chutneys, 56, 57, 58. *See also gongura patchidi*
class, 115, 141–61, 174; performance of, 146, 148, 155, 156–57, 159
coffee, 55, 88, 153
college student activism. *See* student activism
colonial era, 41–43, 50–51, 71, 135–36, 145, 163–64; tea, 71, 168
commodities, subsidized. *See* subsidized commodities
Commonwealth Games, Delhi, 2010, 51, 163
Communist Party, 35
compartmentalization of knowledge, 93–101, 170
Congress Party, 12, 13, 46
convenience foods, 59, 60, 65, 68–70, *70*, 73, 74, 75; compartmentalization of knowledge and, 93; health and, 130. *See also* fast food; food stalls and stands; processed chicken
convenience stores (tiffin shops), 54, 56, 59, *60*, 63
cookies, 59
cooking oil, 69, 109, 131, 154; flatbreads and, 69; *pucca* food and, 40; as subsidized commodity, 63; *talimpu* and, 59
"cooling foods" and "heating foods." *See* Ayurvedic diet
Copland, Ian, 41–42, 50

courts. *See* Madras High Court; Supreme Court of India
cow meat (*āvu mānsam*), 77, 80–81, 87, 91, 102, 109; buffalo meat distinguished from, 31–32, 132, 170–71; preference for, 32, 91; price, 80
Cow Preservation League, 42
cow protection and veneration, x, 12, 13, 34, 43–52, 163, 165–66; colonial era, 41–43; direct action, 41–42, 88; Mohandas Gandhi, 42–43, 164; PFA, 136; shelters, 48–49, 175; state promotion of, 173. *See also* cattle slaughter: regulation and bans; vigilantism
"cow riots" (1890s), 42
cows, 24, 121, 163, 168–69; "bovine symbolism," 12; motherhood link, 35; in Rigveda, 39; sale and purchase, 88, 100. *See also* cow meat; cow protection and veneration; zebu cows
crabmeat, 108, 157
cultural capital, 80, 148–49, 152, 154–55, 156, 158, 174
cups, plates, drinking glasses, etc., 28, 76, 153, 154, 175; leaf plates, 16, 119. *See also* bowls
curd, 5–6, 36, 61–62, 63, 65, 68–69, 152
curry (*kūra*), 54, 58–59, 63, 69, 73, 109
"curry points," 54, 63, 65

D

dairy products and dairy industry, 29, 68, 83–84, 169. *See also* butter; cheese; curd; ice cream; milk
dal, 5, 62, 65, 151, *151*, 152, 171–72; first feeding to babies, 36. *See also* black gram (*urad dal*)

Dalits, 16, 31–32, 38, 111, 114–16; beef eating, 36, 45, 51, 68, 111, 121, 132; beef festivals, 157; BJP and, 167; dietary stereotypes, 130; dominant assumptions, 82; electorate, 51, 167; as "hot caste," 130–31; lunch hosts, 150–53; meat purchasing, 91, 92; Modi and, 47; student activism, 114, 135; violence against, 47; wealthy, 156–57. *See* Madigas; Malas
Daniel, E. Valentine, 131
Das, Kalyan, 142, 159–60
Dayananda Saraswati, Swami, 41, 42, 164
denial of knowledge. *See* compartmentalization of knowledge
dessert, 151–52, 153, 154
Dewey, Susan, 144
Dharmaśāstras, 39, 114
dharna. *See* hunger strikes
diabetes, 14, 63, 130, 133
Dickey, Sara, 148, 149
diet and health. *See* health
dinner (evening meal), 62–66, 153–54
Dirks, Nicholas, 145
disease. *See* diabetes; health; hypertension
dishes. *See* cups, plates, drinking glasses, etc.
division of labor. *See* gendered division of labor
Dixon, Jane, 122, 129
donkeys and donkey meat, 108, 171, 196n6
Donner, Henrike, 127, 172
"don't ask, don't tell." *See* compartmentalization of knowledge

dosas, 56, 57, 69, 88, 124
Douglas, Mary, 74, 93
draft animals, 3, 34, 83, 94, 96
dried meat, 109, 110
drinking. *See* alcohol
drinking glasses. *See* cups, plates, drinking glasses, etc.
drug industry. *See* "pharmaceutical nexus"
Dumont, Louis, 23, 25, 26; *Homo Hierarchus*, 144–45
dung, 4–5, 31, 34; as fertilizer, 39, 72. See also *panchagavya*
Dwivedi, O. P., 135–36, 139

E

eating out. *See* fast food; food stalls and stands; restaurants
ecology. *See* environment
eddu mānsam. *See* buffalo meat (*eddu mānsam*)
eggs, 62, 123, 124
Eid al-Adha, 12, 42, 46, 113
either/or thinking. *See* binary views
elections and electoral politics, 10, 44, 51, 114, 167; Modi, 12, 45, 47, 163
entertaining (feeding others), 8–9, 30, 74, 92, 150–54, 161. *See also* feasts
environment, xi, 13–14, 24, 41, 134–38; tea and, 71
environmentalists and environmentalism, 135, 136, 139, 140, 167
ethics and morality, 22, 40–41, 50; of cattle slaughter, 11, 79–80, 112–13
evening meal. *See* dinner (evening meal)
The Evidence: Meat Kills (Jain), 136–37
exports. *See* meat exports; tea: exports

F

farming. *See* agriculture
fast food, 64, *64*, 69, 123, 127, 128–29, 142. *See also* McDonald's
fasting, protest. *See* hunger strikes
fasting, religious, 63, 194n8
Favero, Paolo, 144, 147, 149
feasts, 119, 141, 156–57, 173
fertilizers, chemical. *See* chemical fertilizers
fish eating, 8, 36, 66, 67, 69, 104, 118, 150–51, 152
flatbreads, 56, 57, 64, 88. *See also* chapatis
food stalls and stands, 56, 63, 68, 73, 88, 91, 123, 124, 173
food studies: bibliography, 22–26
fridges. *See* refrigerators and refrigeration
fried foods, 40, 66, *66*, 88, 109–10, 123, 127, 129; flatbreads, 57, 88. See also *pakoras*
Froerer, Peggy, 166
frozen meat, 88, 97, 123, 127
fruit: dried, 152; fresh, 58, 59

G

Gandhi, Indira, 44, 47, 50, 136
Gandhi, Maneka, 136, 137
Gandhi, Mohandas, 37, 42–43, 50, 140, 164, 166
garam ("hot") foods, 106, 131, 172
gas ranges, 58, 69, 75, 168
gau rakshaks (cow protectors), 47, 48, 105
Gaurakshini Sabha, 41
Geertz, Clifford, 19, 83, 120

INDEX 223

gendered division of labor: men as shoppers, 14, 62, 92, 102, 106–7; women as cooks and servers, 60–61, 74, 153
Ghassem-Fachandi, Parvis, 110
ghee, 5, 34, 38, 40, 56, 57, 69, 169. See also *panchagavya*
goats and goat meat, 36, 66–67, 92, 98, 121–22, 123, 131, 173; price, 138, 178
Godrej Group, 126–27, 129
gongura patchidi, 30, 119, 151, *151*, 156, 157
Goody, Jack, 11, 24–25, 81
government, village. See panchayats (village councils)
government bans on cattle slaughter. See cattle slaughter: bans and attempted bans
government collusion and complicity, 80, 99
government-subsidized commodities. See subsidized commodities
government-subsidized lunch program, 63
Govindrajan, Radhika, 20, 25
Graf, Katharina, 128
green chilies. See chilies
Green Revolution, 14, 72, 75, 124, 138
grinding stones (*attu kallu*), 56, 73, 75
Gundimeda, Sambaiah, 45

H

halal meat, 86
Hansen, Thomas, 10
Harrapans, 37, 38
Harris, Marvin, 24, 25, 35, 175

health, 14, 130–34, 137–38; rationale for meat eating, 106, 141; rationale for not eating beef, 109, 127, 141
"heating foods" and "cooling foods." See Ayurvedic diet
high blood pressure. See hypertension
The Hindu Hearth and Home (Khare), 24
Hinduism, 34, 135; Mohandas Gandhi view, 43, 50, 164. See also *Hindutva*; Vedic texts
Hindus, 6, 81; "bovine symbolism" and, 12, 51; butchers and beef sellers, 86, 111, 117; cattle slaughter and, 86, 113–14; Christian relations, 141; colonial era, 41; deference to feelings of, 102–3, 141; dominant assumptions, 82; environment and, 136; festivals, 57; Indira Gandhi and, 44; lynching by, 12, 46, 98; poor, 166. See also nationalism, Indian/Hindu; non-Hindu other; Rashtriya Swayamesevak Sangh (RSS)
Hindutva, 10, 127, 136, 166, 176
Homo Hierarchus (Dumont), 144–45
hormones and antibiotics, meat industry use of. See antibiotics and hormones, meat industry use of
hotel restaurants, 82, 100, 142–43, 157, 174
hunger strikes, 44, 45
hypertension, 130, 132

I

ice cream, 65
idlis, 56, 57, 63, 69, 75, 88, 124
infants. See babies
Islam, 10, 49. See also Eid al-Adha; Muslims

J

jaggery, 38, 55, 72
Jain, Dinesh, 46, 51
Jain, Mayank: *Evidence*, 136–37
Jains and Jainism, 12, 40, 46, 50, 164
Jha, D. N.: *Myth of the Holy Cow*, 49, 164
"jungle meats." *See* wild game ("jungle meats")
"junk foods." *See* convenience foods; fast foods

K

kaccha foods and *pucca* foods, 40
Kammas, 158
Kapus (Naidus), 106, 146
keema (minced beef), 69, 90
Khare, R. S., 24, 26
kinship with cattle. *See* cattle as kin
kirana shops. *See* convenience stores
Klein, Jakob, 23, 24
knowledge, compartmentalization of. *See* compartmentalization of knowledge
Korom, Frank, 43
kūra. *See* curry (*kūra*)

L

Lal, Shankar, 31
lamb, 67, 71
Lamb, Sarah, 106, 171
Laws of Manu. *See* Manu Smriti
leftovers, 57, 60, 69, 92
lentils, 36, 63, 68, 74; *pappu charu*, 62. *See also sambar*
Lévi-Strauss, Claude, 27
Liechty, Mark, 148

livestock markets. *See* cattle markets (shandies)
lunch, 57–62, 150–53, *151*; government program, 26, 63, 163
lynching, 12, 46, 98, 101

M

Madigas, 9, 16, 31–32, 54–67, 79, 105, 107, 115; beef eating, 31–32, 68, 81, 121, 132; butchers, 86
Madras High Court, 13, 47
Malas, 55, 67, 68, 102–3, 107, 115, 121, 132, 159
mangoes, 58, 59
Manu Smriti, 39
Marriott, McKim, 23, 25, 176
Marxism, 24, 25, 35, 145, 148
masalas (spice mixtures), 61, 73, 109, 131
Mathews, Andrew, 99
Mawdsley, Emma, 135–36
McDonald's, 97, 128–29, 139, 142, 143
meat consumption statistics, 53, 116, 165
meat exports, 82, 112; New Zealand, 71. *See also* beef exports
meat sellers. *See* beef sellers; chicken shops
medicine, beef as, 132–33
Michelutti, Lucia, 172
milk, 31, 34, 35–36, 39, 55–56, 74, 76; in Rigveda, 39; use in tea, 5, 54, 55, 72, 168. *See also* buffalo milk
millet, 17, 72
minced beef. *See keema* (minced beef)
Mintz, Sidney, 23, 24–25
Modi, Narendra, 12, 43, 45, 47, 163, 164, 165
Muslims, 6, 69, 120, 160; beef eating, 32, 36, 69; beef festivals, 114, 157;

Muslims (*continued*)
biriyani stands, 63; "bovine symbolism" and, 12; butchers, 89–90, 93–94, 96–97, 98, 111–12, 120, 179, 189n38; cattle slaughter and, 86; colonial era, 41, 42; communal dining, 60; dietary stereotypes, 130; dominant assumptions, 82; environment and, 135; meat eating, 6, 68, 92, 104, 113; meat purchasing, 86, 91; Modi and, 47; pork-eating abstention, 107; vigilantism against, 12, 32, 41–42, 46, 98
mutton, 118, 156
mutton, goat. *See* goats and goat meat
The Myth of the Holy Cow (Jha), 49

N

Naidus. *See* Kapus (Naidus)
Nandy, Ashis, 11
nationalism, Indian/Hindu, 10, 41, 114, 130, 135, 139, 143, 165–66, 173; Mohandas Gandhi, 50, 164. *See also* Bharatiya Janata Party (BJP)
Nehru, Jawaharlal, 43–44
New Zealand, 71
non-Hindu other, 83, 101, 120, 156, 166–67
noodles, 63, 64, 65, 66, 74, 139, 174; instant, 69, 70

O

offal. *See* organ meat
oil, cooking. *See* cooking oil
onions, 109, 154; Ayurvedic views on, 131, 171, 172; in lentil dishes, 62; as "non-veg," 171; in omelets, 62; in *perugu charu*, 65; in raitas, 61, 151; as subsidized commodity, 63
organ meat, 66–67, 79, 86–87, 92, 109
Ortner, Sherry, 148
Osmania University, 12, 45
other, non-Hindu. *See* non-Hindu other

P

pakoras, 63, 66, 123, 127, 139
panchagavya, 39, 169
panchayats (village councils), 86, 99
paneer, 64, 69
pappu. See dal
Paryurshan Parva, 46, 51
pastries, 65
People for Animals (PFA), 136
performance of class. *See* class: performance of
pesticides, 122, 137–38
"pharmaceutical nexus," 100
pickles, 57–58, *58*
plates. *See* cups, plates, drinking glasses, etc.
pork, 21, 67, 107–8, 121, 157, 171
porridge, 57, 72
poverty rations. *See* ration cards and ration shops
Prahalad, C. V., 71
prawns, 62, 104, 108, 122
pressure cookers, 69
Prevention of Cruelty to Animals Act, 47
processed chicken, 123, 127–28, 173
processed foods. *See* convenience foods
protests and protestors, 6; anti–beef eater and anti–cattle slaughter, 12, 32, 45, 47, 104, 145; student, 46, 104
pucca foods and *kaccha* foods. *See kaccha* foods and *pucca* foods

pulusu, 63, 74, 104, 109, 127, 129, 156, 173
puris, 57, 88

R

raitas, 61–62, 151, 152
Raju, Solomon, 156, 157
Rana, Sanjay, 46
rasam, 57, 62, 65, 156
Rashtriya Swayamesevak Sangh (RSS), 31, 135, 187n7
ration cards and ration shops, 63
Rawal, Vikas, 48
Ray, Krishnendu, 22, 26
Reddis, 84, 92, 146
refrigerators and refrigeration, 56, 59, 62, 75, 87, 89, 92; chicken sales and, 125; fast-food restaurants, 123
restaurants and restaurateurs, 13, 56, 64, 110, 144, 148, 157, 159; meat purchases, 77, 91, 98. *See also* fast food; hotel restaurants
rice, 36, 38, 58–59, 61, 62–63, 68, 72, 73; bazaar purchases, 63; in "core-fringe-legume" pattern, 71; in *idlis*, 56; as metonym for "food," 73; as subsidized commodity, 63
Rigveda, 37, 39
riots and rioting, 42, 50
Rock Starz, 64, 123, 127
Roman Catholics. *See* Catholics
Roy, Parama, 42
RSS. *See* Rashtriya Swayamesevak Sangh (RSS)

S

"sacred cow" (idiom), 163
sacrifice of animals, 39, 40, 170; cattle, 42, 50, 164

sambar, 56, 65, 119, 156
Sangh Parivar, 10, 187n7
Sanskritization, 23
Saoras, 81
Sarvadaliya Goraksha Maha-Abiyan Samiti (SGMS), 44
Scheduled Castes. *See* Dalits
seating arrangements, 60–61, *61*
Sen, Atreyee, 111
shandies (livestock markets and auctions). *See* cattle markets (shandies)
Shatrugna, Veena, 26
sheep, 67. *See also* lamb; mutton
Shiva, Vandana, 135, 139, 140
Shiv Sena, 44, 46, 111
shrimp hatcheries, 122
Singh, Digvijaya, 46
slaughter of cattle. *See* cattle slaughter
Smith, Brian, 39
snacks, 57–62, 67–68. *See also* convenience stores (tiffin shops)
social class. *See* class
Society for Environmental Communications, 135
soft drinks, 59, 74
soups, 21, 62, 156
spices, 28, 36, 56, 73–74; masalas, 61, 73, 109, 131; sale and purchase, 63, 69, 73, 74; use in tea, 55. *See also* chili powder; *garam* foods
Srinivas, M. N., 23
Srinivas, Tulasi, 22, 26
states' rights and state legislation, 10, 43, 46, 47, 81
stray cattle, 3, 5, 48
street food. *See* food stalls and stands
student activism, 45, 51, 111, 135

Student Federation of India, 51
subsidized commodities, 63
Sudras, 105, 121, 146, 158. *See also* Kapus (Naidus); Reddis
sugar, 54–55, 71–72; as subsidized commodity, 63
supper. *See* dinner (evening meal)
Supreme Court of India, 46, 47
surreptitious beef eating, 103, 110–11, 143, 172
swine flu, 137

T

tableware. *See* cups, plates, drinking glasses, etc.
takeout food, 13, 54, 56, 173. *See also* fast food; food stalls and stands
tamarind water. *See rasam*
Tayob, Shaheed, 79–80
tea, 5, 54–55, 71–72, 76, 168; exports, 71, 168
tea shops, 54, 55, 76
technology, 13, 41, 69, 72, 75, 168. *See also* refrigerators and refrigeration
tiffin stalls and shops, 56, 63, 88, 124
Tiwari, Mohan, 48
Tyson Foods, 126–27

U

United States: chicken, 126, 127; meat-eating statistics, 53
university beef festivals. *See* beef festivals
unproductive cattle. *See* cattle, unproductive and excess
urad dal. *See* black gram (*urad dal*)

V

Vaisyas, 37, 105, 132, 178
varnas, 37–38, 39. *See also* Brahmins; caste; Sudras; Vaisyas
Vedic texts, 37–40, 45, 49, 163, 164
vegan diet, 29, 136
vegetables, 38, 57, 62, 68, 72, 109, 153; "non-veg," 171; sale and purchase, 107. *See also* dal; onions
vegetarian cattle owners, 95, 100
vegetarianism, 8–9, 10, 29–30, 51–52, 53, 105, 163; early historic references, 40; household-individual distinction, 172; McDonald's and, 128–29; men-women distinction, 172; Mohandas Gandhi, 42–43, 140, 166; percent of population identifying with, 165; upscale restaurants and, 143; virtual, 74, 106. *See also* vegan diet
Verma, Harish, 48–49
vigilantism, 12–13, 41–42, 45–48, 50, 88, 90, 163, 167, 178; cattle seizure, 110; effect on business, 91; intended "othering" effect, 101; meat identification and, 97, 98; PFA, 136; police protection of, 99; state and, 116, 117. *See also* lynching
Vishva Hindu Parishad, 44, 90, 187n7
Vivekananda, Swami, 42
Vyāsasmṛti, 38

W

water buffaloes, 31, 43, 83, 84, 97; accidental deaths, 84; as draft

animals, 94; sale and purchase, 86, 88, 100. *See also* buffalo meat; buffalo milk
Watson, James, 23, 24
wedding feasts, 119, 141, 156–57
wheat, 38, 57
widows, 102, 106, 131, 171–72
wild game ("jungle meats"), 108, 121, 171
willful ignorance. *See* compartmentalization of knowledge
Wilk, Richard, 21

X

Xu, Chenjia, 20

Y

Yadavs, 53, 85, 172
Yāgnavalkya, 39–40
Yang, Anand, 42
yogurt. *See* curd

Z

zebu cows, 3, *4*, 31, 77, 78, 97

CULTURE, PLACE, AND NATURE
Studies in Anthropology and Environment

Sacred Cows and Chicken Manchurian: The Everyday Politics of Eating Meat in India, by James Staples

Gardens of Gold: Place-Making in Papua New Guinea, by Jamon Alex Halvaksz

Shifting Livelihoods: Gold Mining and Subsistence in the Chocó, Colombia, by Daniel G. L. Tubb

Disturbed Forests, Fragmented Memories: Jarai and Other Lives in the Cambodian Highlands, by Jonathan Padwe

The Snow Leopard and the Goat: Politics of Conservation in the Western Himalayas, by Shafqat Hussain

Roses from Kenya: Labor, Environment, and the Global Trade in Cut Flowers, by Megan A. Styles

Working with the Ancestors: Mana *and Place in the Marquesas Islands,* by Emily C. Donaldson

Living with Oil and Coal: Resource Politics and Militarization in Northeast India, by Dolly Kikon

Caring for Glaciers: Land, Animals, and Humanity in the Himalayas, by Karine Gagné

Organic Sovereignties: Struggles over Farming in an Age of Free Trade, by Guntra A. Aistara

The Nature of Whiteness: Race, Animals, and Nation in Zimbabwe, by Yuka Suzuki

Forests Are Gold: Trees, People, and Environmental Rule in Vietnam, by Pamela D. McElwee

Conjuring Property: Speculation and Environmental Futures in the Brazilian Amazon, by Jeremy M. Campbell

Andean Waterways: Resource Politics in Highland Peru, by Mattias Borg Rasmussen

Puer Tea: Ancient Caravans and Urban Chic, by Jinghong Zhang

Enclosed: Conservation, Cattle, and Commerce among the Q'eqchi' Maya Lowlanders, by Liza Grandia

Forests of Identity: Society, Ethnicity, and Stereotypes in the Congo River Basin, by Stephanie Rupp

Tahiti Beyond the Postcard: Power, Place, and Everyday Life, by Miriam Kahn

Wild Sardinia: Indigeneity and the Global Dreamtimes of Environmentalism, by Tracey Heatherington

Nature Protests: The End of Ecology in Slovakia, by Edward Snajdr

Forest Guardians, Forest Destroyers: The Politics of Environmental Knowledge in Northern Thailand, by Tim Forsyth and Andrew Walker

Being and Place among the Tlingit, by Thomas F. Thornton

Tropics and the Traveling Gaze: India, Landscape, and Science, 1800–1856, by David Arnold

Ecological Nationalisms: Nature, Livelihood, and Identities in South Asia, edited by Gunnel Cederlöf and K. Sivaramakrishnan

From Enslavement to Environmentalism: Politics on a Southern African Frontier, by David McDermott Hughes

Border Landscapes: The Politics of Akha Land Use in China and Thailand, by Janet C. Sturgeon

Property and Politics in Sabah, Malaysia: Native Struggles over Land Rights, by Amity A. Doolittle

The Earth's Blanket: Traditional Teachings for Sustainable Living, by Nancy Turner

The Kuhls of Kangra: Community-Managed Irrigation in the Western Himalaya, by Mark Baker

Lightning Source UK Ltd.
Milton Keynes UK
UKHW010736191020
371617UK00012B/361

9 780295 747880